Praise for 10 Seconds (

'A riveting book jam-packed with Nadine's mindset secrets. An inspiring story delivered with her signature amount of humour. I highly recommend it.'

Turia Pitt
Ultramarathon runner and catastrophic burns survivor
Author of *Everything to Live For*

'It is how Nadine shares her stories so others realise they are not alone that makes this so powerful, to show that courage is not just for the strong—it is for those who feel exactly the opposite. Nadine makes a contribution as a role model, teacher and guide—whilst remaining one of us . . . humble and real. Sometimes life presents us with rare gems, people who are put in our path, who with a few quiet words speak so loudly to what you need to hear in that moment—Nadine was this for me.'

Naomi Simson
Star of TV's *Shark Tank* and founder of Red Balloon
Author of *Ready to Soar*

'I often ponder, what is the greater path for life, one that is unchallenged or one that glides on the bliss of simply not knowing any pain or any adversity. Nadine offers a powerful insight, through her lived experience, of something we can all use, something so simple and yet takes complete dedication to do . . . to take a deep breath, it's just 10 seconds of courage between you and what you fear, between where you are and where you want to be!'

(Dr) Gill Hicks AM MBE
London bombing survivor
Author of *One Unknown*

10
SECONDS OF
COURAGE

10 SECONDS OF COURAGE

HOW TO RECOGNISE AND EMBRACE THOSE LIFE-CHANGING MOMENTS

NADINE CHAMPION

ALLEN&UNWIN

SYDNEY · MELBOURNE · AUCKLAND · LONDON

First published in 2017

Allen & Unwin
83 Alexander Street
Crows Nest NSW 2065
Australia
Phone: (61 2) 8425 0100
Email: info@allenandunwin.com
Web: www.allenandunwin.com

Cataloguing-in-Publication details are available
from the National Library of Australia
www.trove.nla.gov.au

ISBN 978 1 76029 360 4

Set in 12/18 pt Sabon by Midland Typesetters, Australia
Printed and bound in Australia by Griffin Press

10 9 8 7 6 5 4 3 2 1

Contents

For my Sensei.

For the one in my corner.

For those in the fight of their lives.

For anyone who has ever been scared to try (just like me).

Courage is not the absence of fear, but rather the judgement
that something else is more important than one's fear.

—Ambrose Redmoon
(James Neil Hollingsworth)

INTRODUCTION

This is the exact moment, more than any other in my whole life, that has the power to create a spectacular outcome or utterly devastate me. My whole future rests on the next few minutes, *I think to myself as I peer around the heavy velvet curtain of the Sydney Opera House stage. My hands are shaking slightly. Not a single one of the thousands of people who will soon be staring right at me knows what is privately at stake for me. My heart pounds so forcefully I can hear it rhythmically booming inside my head. I push the air hard out of my lungs as the next pump-up song begins through my headphones.*

The Madonna-style microphone they have taped to my skin pulls at me awkwardly, as I start to sweat nervously. I wipe my palms and take a sip of water, desperately hoping my mouth doesn't go dry. Now I know why so many people are afraid to do this crazy thing I am about to face. It is wildly scary and blisteringly exposing. The adrenaline rushing through my blood-stream demands that I move. Past the stage crew in the darkness and to the back of the room. I distance myself down a small corridor away from the cameras and musicians. I'm still only metres from the curtain. Wishing I could get further away from the fear it holds, only makes me more aware of its gravitational pull. I can hear the surging cheers of the crowd, with only a thin barrier separating us. I turn the volume up and take the last few minutes for myself before everything changes forever.

Who will I be after this is over? This is the gamble of a lifetime, taken when I have already lost so many of my chips. Can I pull it off? I'm prepared to risk it all and perhaps fail, but what if I succeed? Or what if I find out I am now just a shell of who I used to be? What if I find out exactly who I have become now as I emerge from the greatest of storms?

I listen to the chorus of my best song and force a tense smile as I'm hurriedly moved back towards the point of no return. It's almost go time. My adrenalised heartbeat quickens and my body charges. This is it. I am both powerfully terrified and excited. I look around the edge of the curtain again at the centre of the stage. Soon under those lights I will find out my unequivocal truth. I fear it. I crave it. I have nothing left to lose . . .

◆

This is a story about finding the resilience to get back up when life knocks you down. It's not a tale of perfect shiny courage and getting everything right in the face of adversity. Instead, it's about face planting on life's concrete footpath, then lying there deciding whether to stay flat and bleeding, or to slowly find a way to stand upright again. I learnt how to pull myself back up from a once-in-a-lifetime teacher. You don't have to be interested in martial arts to relate to what he taught me. In fact, you don't have to be the least bit sporty at all. Look deeper than the physical pursuit this package was delivered in and you will find that the contents comes straight from the heart.

In our own way, we all have something worth fighting for in life—our families, love, health, success, to create a better place in the world or to make our mark on it. None of these deserve to be a battle, but it's unavoidable at times. Luckily, overcoming the hardest obstacles can mean we discover some of the most valuable treasures.

Many people face daily challenges that make mine look like a carnival ride, complete with fairy floss and a balloon to take home. Yet in sharing our own personal struggles both subtle and significant, we can also share our victories. I literally got an education in what happens if you give up on yourself or strive to win. My battles came in many forms both personally and as a competitive athlete, yet what I learnt in one arena always mirrored the other. That's why I have symbolically structured this book into five rounds, just like in a title bout. When the pressure builds to a pivotal point, we find out the truth of who we are. I was taught the most when forced to genuinely fight for survival, but perhaps not in the way you might assume.

It's in these life-changing moments where our hearts are truly tested and our fates decided. Only *you* have the power to determine who you will become. When the chips are down, the odds stacked against you and the next high pressure move has the potential to make or break.

Will you fold your cards or find the courage to go all in?

BE YOUR TRUE SELF

ROUND 1

KARATE KID IN A FLORAL DRESS

This photo was in the local paper at Christmas when
I wrote to Santa asking for a set of dumbbells.

1

Girl Versus Dress

My childhood was filled with riding bikes, building cubby houses and climbing trees—while occasionally getting so stuck in them that my dad had to stand on the roof of the car to get me down. I was not your standard little girl, in that the Barbie dolls I invariably received for Christmas lay mostly unused and mildly despised. Occasionally I would bring them out for an obligatory faux play session where I half-heartedly flung them around to the delight of whomever had blessed me with the Barbie Dream Car that festive season. The Ken doll was a lucky guy, keeping company with a harem of mint-conditioned blonde plastic ladies. From time to time he did some form of horizontal gymnastics with them in the cheeky positions little kids daringly think of as rude. These dolls were the gift you give to a little girl, but it was common knowledge this little girl would rather have a Tonka truck.

Yet the Barbies kept coming every year without fail, a well-intended suggestion that I might want to join the little lady team sometime soon. My mum would joke with me that she should put a pink ribbon in my hair so people would stop mistaking me for my brother David. Naturally I ran away looking horrified, as if she'd just suggested we eat worms for dinner. No way, Jose.

I spent many a recess with the other girls in primary school but for some pesky reason it looked like the boys got to have way more fun. Why play hopscotch when you could play football? I gave the game of elastics a whirl plenty of times, but I was always drawn away by the intense lure of Red Rover and dodgeball. I had an urge to run, to climb, to jump over things and crawl under them. I wasn't afraid to get dirty or skin my knee. I *was* afraid of always having to sit with the other girls and miss out on the best games.

There was a certain pride and playground street cred that came from being picked early for the teams. It didn't matter that I was a girl if I was a fast runner and good at catching. The boys wanted me on their team because I had an aptitude for sport and liked winning. The usual eight-year-old boy's refrain of 'Ew gross, I don't like girls' went out the window when the time came to choose sides. I was no longer relegated to the perceived lesser role of *girl* but instead was treated equally and vigorously included as one of the boys because I could play like one of the boys. It was an unusual position that I felt oddly comfortable in—traversing the line between the two groups, accepted by both and happily so. It's a place I still inhabit, great friends with the girls but sharing a lot in common with the boys.

My unexplained love for all the things that were traditionally boys' stuff was perplexing for my family. I just popped out a little tomboy, all long white-blonde hair and tanned skin, running around in my brother's old board shorts, while my mum endlessly attempted to convince me to wear a girl's one-piece swimsuit instead. Suffice to say it was a losing battle for many years, if only because she couldn't get me to stand still for long enough to force me to put it on. We negotiated small expeditions into girl-type things but there was usually a catch. I would offer up one concession if I got to keep another firmly in place.

This all came to a head when as a five-year-old I was asked to be a flower girl at my brother John's wedding. I received the news with a combination response. I was excited to be included, but was a bit hesitant about what the whole flower-girl thing might entail. Something in my gut was telling me this might involve frills or some type of flouncing around being ladylike, that I would neither be good at nor enjoy.

My half-brother John was the eldest child of my dad's first marriage. John and our sister Julie had both been born about twenty years before me, so were full-grown proper adults when I was a little kid. John was marrying a woman who had won Miss Universe, so naturally the wedding was to centre around the elegance of female beauty, from the bride right down to flower girls. This was going to be a toughie for little tomboy me.

As is customary, it had already been decided by the governing body of all things matrimonial that I would wear a flower girl dress (of course). Not just any dress, but one that came complete with lace and ribbons—every feminine frill of my worst night-mare. It was to be a floral pattern, which did not match with my usual fluoro beach wear aesthetic. Now this wouldn't be big news to most little ladies, but to me it was a wildly unwelcome revelation. My mum did her best to present the idea to me in a palatable way. She told me I would look pretty in a frock (not my highest priority), then she attempted to sell it to me as fun (I seriously doubted it) and she even went so far as to suggest that I might like it (fat chance).

I asked some initial fact-finding questions in the hopes that this compulsory dress wouldn't be too bad. I was wrong. The further I inquired, the more my inner tomboy heard fingernails down an imaginary couture chalkboard. My dress-wearing fate had been decided and Miss Universe's selection was more dire than I had initially feared. Yes, you got it, a white floral dress with lace and ribbons, featuring hand-rolled French seams and puffy little sleevelets. To top it all off, the outfit would be complemented by a lovely woven headpiece of flowers. But wait, there's more . . . I would be teaming my ensemble with some gorgeous strappy white leather sandals.

You've never seen a kid run so fast in the other direction.

For the sake of my family, I tried to play along. I didn't know why I wasn't enthusiastic like the other little girls who all seemed excited to get prettied up and wear dresses. I just simply didn't feel that way. It all seemed very impractical and like a lot of unnecessary, uncomfortably itchy fuss. I had never been to a wedding before, so couldn't quite grasp why it wasn't acceptable to wear something more casual. When we did the dress fitting, I was mortified at first sight then had to be coaxed/bribed to even try it on. Imagine you went to work one day and they presented you with a giant plastic lobster costume, with human resources announcing this would be the new company branded uniform. The whole dress thing just didn't feel right to me because I didn't understand why anyone would choose an outfit to make themselves deliberately less comfortable.

Once the fitting was over, the war began. Sides were drawn and the battle started—one faction (my family) with clear demands (wear the girly dress) and the other (me) in rampant retreat, wanting only for things to be how they used to be (no dress in sight). There were many tears along the way, with rousingly spirited speeches to the troops about duty and obligation. Some ground was gained, but then quickly lost again. After an exhausting last stand, peace talks were eventually convened and final treaties negotiated. There would be a frilly dress worn but only on one condition . . . I could wear my shorts underneath.

Miss Universe wasn't originally onboard with the idea and when I say she wasn't onboard I mean she was abjectly horrified. A woman who had experienced the highest echelons of being judged on her beauty and femininity wasn't really about to start driving the 'tomboys can wear shorts under their flower girl dress at my wedding' train. It was more like she was in the caboose crying as the train left the station and she was seriously unhappy about the impending trip. Well, at least that made two of us. Choo choo.

So the wedding day came, and the dress was worn. Many a photo was taken of me looking daintily pretty in my lacy white dress, sandals and flower headpiece. The only hint that something was amiss was the uncomfortable scowl on my face which I made whenever nobody was looking, as I pulled at the itchy lace and longed to run free from this gendered torture device. The wedding couldn't be over fast enough. I was a reluctant feminine angel, with a secret. My one saving grace on that little lady day had been the knowledge that at least I was wearing my shorts.

◆

Growing up, things were often a combination of the good and the not-so-good. Until the age of ten we lived in a motel that my parents owned and operated. This meant my young life was different from my friends in wonderful and uncommon ways. One of the best parts was the giant swimming pool that curved through the middle of the property. I thought of it as *my* swimming pool at *my* house. I just happened to share it with lots of random people.

Every week was a series of comings and goings with families travelling through. I quickly got used to making the best of new friends every school holidays, only to have to say goodbye to them abruptly after a week or two of fun in the sun (yes, I even let them swim in my pool). Sometimes the same family would bring their kids back each year and we would pick up our friendship where we had left off the year before.

We spent countless hours playing on the big yellow trampoline out the front until the bigger kids bounced one of us too high and the tears started flowing out of fear. One time I was bounced so high that my descent felt like it happened in slow motion. I went way up then watched in frightened anticipation as I came down face first towards the metal rail around the trampoline edge. I was lucky to narrowly miss smacking into it but that didn't mean I was out of danger. Unfortunately, as I landed my small head fitted right between the inch-thick solid metal springs and became lodged there. It jammed straight through the gap so fast that I could have sworn I heard a sound like a bubble popping as it went in.

'Stop jumping, stop jumping, her head is stuck!' the other kids frantically screamed. But my head stayed firmly wedged while the rest of my body continued to unwillingly bounce away until the other kids had come to a complete halt.

That trampoline also taught me the value of listening to your parents when they tell you not to go down a ladder facing the wrong way. After a solid jumping session the day before my fifth birthday, I slipped as I was climbing down backwards (facing away from the ladder, not upside down). I fell and fractured my arm. I put on a brave face, or as brave a face as you can when you're only four and your arm really hurts. I wanted the birthday festivities to go on as planned. When my nan saw that I couldn't rest my arm on the table at Pizza Hut for my birthday treat meal, she suggested to my mum that it might be broken. Val, my nan, had worked for many years at St Vincent's Hospital in Sydney so she had seen a fracture or two in her time. Turned out she was right. The next day a birthday photo was taken of me sitting beside the pool, all brown skin and orange board shorts, with my arm in a brand new white plaster cast. I was meant to be having a pool party for my birthday. The look of devastation on my face was worthy of the tragedy that had befallen me. Damn that dangerous big yellow trampoline.

It was weird living in a motel and not just because my friends were always disappearing, sometimes without even saying goodbye. The strangeness came from the difference between my life and other kids' lives, although I had no real concept of it at the time. Forgive me, as I'm mortified to say this, but I thought everybody had a housekeeper to change their sheets, and that their dinner arrived from the motel restaurant on a tray. Didn't all little kids get to choose anything they wanted off the menu when it was their birthday? At a young age my favourite special restaurant meal was lobster mornay. I had no idea that was unusual or not something you'd usually give to a small child. Because my parents were busy every night working and looking after my brother David and me, we didn't go to people's houses for dinner like other families might. That meant I had no frame of reference to compare my life with anyone else's. It was all I knew. Sounds fairly spoiled, right? Maybe, but it came at a price.

The flipside of the pool, housemaids and lobster eating was that my parents lived and worked in their business, twenty-four hours a day, seven days a week. I respected that they worked very hard and didn't get much downtime. There were strict rules about where I could go and with whom. I knew it was import- ant that my mum always knew where I was playing but I was too young to know why it mattered so much in a motel. There was a vague feeling of pressure in the air there and, looking back, I can only imagine how hard it must have been to work every single day for years without a break, while trying to raise two kids. The tension showed, mostly with Dad spending extra hours downstairs running the restaurant and having a few too many drinks.

There were times when I would be woken up in the middle of the night to the sound of my parents arguing. I always knew it was because Dad had been drinking again. I make no excuses for his behaviour, but experience has taught me it's not wise to judge anyone harshly. Instead I look at him with understanding and compassion. My dad was a good, intelligent man who'd had a challenging life, which led him to have an explosive temper at times when he drank. He would get out of control, apolo- gise the next day and work to fix things with my mum. That would usually be followed by a period of time when his drinking would be under control and my parents enjoyed a tender com- panionship. I both loved him dearly and was afraid of him at times. I learned to be wary of him after one frightening night when I was locked behind a bedroom door with Mum, while he kicked it in. There were times when we moved to a different house for a while without him or secretly got on a plane after a particularly bad night. Alcohol made him into a person who was nothing like the Dad I saw during the day.

On school holidays, my dad would take me to run errands with him. I loved those times so much. I knew when we had finished waiting in the Westpac Bank queue, holding Dad's white cloth money bag filled with coins and notes, we would go to the coffee shop together. We would sit against the wall in a big maroon leather booth. Dad would let me order pikelets or scones with jam and cream, plus a lime spider. He would have coffee and read the paper while I munched away happily, feeling special the whole time. I knew that this man, the one spending time with me as I chatted away to him over my treats, was the father I loved so dearly. Drinking made him someone I didn't recognise, but I saw my dad sitting in the booth as a person I knew well and adored.

Be your true self, even if other people don't get it.

2

Karate Kid Junior

When you're only six years old, you don't understand how things are 'supposed to be'. All you know is how things are. Sometimes they don't make much sense or are contradictory, both in the world around you and also within yourself. You are too young to be fully subject to the pressures of conformity and instead reside more in the place of just being, whether things make sense or not. I was still too young to comprehend that other kids' home lives were very different to mine. Heck, I didn't even know it was unusual to not be excited about wearing a flower-girl dress. There are always little girls who feel this way, but we are not the majority. We are just how we are. Not quite fitting into what we 'should' be, but also not that aware of the implications of being different. I was just exactly me.

Apparently *me* meant being a total tomboy. I loved my tiny blue hat that accidentally bore a striking resemblance to those traditionally worn by locomotive drivers. I ran around in my brother David's hand-me-down clothes, that I would endlessly beg my mum to let me wear. I knew what made me comfortable and despite wishing she could dress me in more appropriate miniature lady attire, Mum generally let me be who I was. I knew she wished on some level I was the standard issue daughter, but my mum also instilled in me a solid sense of self. She taught me that women are strong capable humans whose value is not dictated by the clothes and make-up they wear.

The most profound message I absorbed as a kid came in the form of a sticker my mum gave to me. In bold red and blue, the sticker said, 'Girls can do ANYTHING'. From the first time I saw it, I took it as gospel. My mum actively told me it was the truth, which served to make it more so (because she was a grown-up and she would know for sure). She wanted to make me strong and proud of who I was. She wanted me to know the message on that big white sticker was important and just for me. I stuck it to my bedroom mirror and spent every day looking at it, which meant it sank deep into my junior consciousness.

I wholeheartedly believed the words on that sticker and lived my young life that way. If the boys jumped into the creek and got muddy, well, I could do it, too. And if they kicked the ball far, I could kick it that far, too. I wasn't party to the 'throwing like a girl' phenomena I witnessed on the playground. The truth I saw was girls pretending not to be able to do what the boys could do, even though they were often physically capable. I found it baffling and this continued as we grew older and I watched teenage girls feign helplessness to get boys' attention. I trusted my little girl body to do all the things I wanted it to do. I felt strong and able to do everything I chose. While the sticker declared that girls can do anything, I had never thought to question why we couldn't. It did seem like other people had some strong ideas about what girls should do with their lives. I just knew I didn't feel like there was any limit on me, simply because I was a girl. At such a young age I was just perplexed as to why there was meant to be this big dividing difference there anyway.

When I say girls can do anything, I mean I wanted to do *every-thing*. I needed an outlet for my energy. I was always running around and being generally athletic in one way or another. I wasn't the kind of kid to sit and read a book all day. I wanted to be where the action was. It was all about swimming, jumping, climbing, riding, running and generally just never sitting still. On a summer morning I would go downstairs and have my breakfast in the back of the office while Mum looked after the motel reception. Those cornflakes barely touched my lips before I was begging to run back upstairs and put my togs on. Luckily the pool was directly beside the office, so Mum could keep an eye on me. Then it would be a full day of swimming, diving to the bottom for imagined treasure and playing non-stop games of Marco Polo (surely the number-one most annoying game for any adults within earshot).

My brother David is two years older than me, and though we are close in age, we didn't play together that much. We were just very different types of kids and being siblings didn't seem to give us that much in common. He was more an indoors kid and I was always outside. We had opposite natures and clashed regularly, much to my parents' chagrin. If there was a fight that could be had in the back of the car on a road trip, it was guaranteed we would have it. We had such different reactions to situations, that led us to fairly disparate lives. He was the kind of gentle kid whose nature meant he was a target for schoolyard bullies. They made things very difficult for him and I wished there was something I could do to stop it.

The bullying started when David was in primary school, with mean kids sensing he might not fight back if they picked on him. By the time he was in his first year of high school, things had gotten much worse. It was right around the time of the film *The Karate Kid*, which featured a lone teenage boy being victimised by a group of high school jerks. Looking for a possible solution, my parents decided to send David to martial arts classes. He was enrolled in a Tae Kwon Do school for lessons. I wanted to go along, too, but had to sit and watch. It was the first time I had ever seen martial arts in real life and I was instantly transfixed.

As I watched everyone line up in perfect formation to start the class, my heart started beating faster. All the crisp white uniforms and different coloured belts were magical to me. I wanted to jump up and join in. I dreamed of being at the front with the most senior students, doing the best moves and the highest kicks. The class was mostly adult men, but there were also some women and children. I couldn't seem to take my eyes off the teacher and his black belt. His uniform was made of a heavier canvas than the others and his belt was a deep black with gold bars along one side and embroidered writing along the other. I felt like a pirate seeing treasure for the first time. I was in awe, I was beaming, I was completely captivated by these newfound wonders and I would do anything to be a part of it. So the begging began . . .

◆

Watching that first martial arts class, I tried to learn as much as I could while squirming away sitting on the sidelines. I begged to join in, ping-ponging between asking Mum and trying not to miss anything. It was torturous being so close but only seeing instead of doing. I negotiated desperately until she finally asked if I could get in on the action. Towards the middle of the class the instructor agreed and I leapt into action in the back row. From that initial session it was like finding my true identity and it was a perfect fit.

I demonstrated my moves afterwards at home, as if doing some type of job interview for a Karate company. I was actively petitioning to make this my new sport/full-time life persona. In order to offset any possible tomboy-increasing effects that martial arts might have on me, I may have even offered to take up ballet as well. I had seen real live martial arts up close and I wanted to go back there as soon as possible.

My parents succumbed and the day finally came for my first full Tae Kwon Do lesson. I was so excited it felt even better than Christmas. There was a chance I might explode with nervous joy as I lined up with everyone else, enthusiastic to feel a part of something so special. As we started I was having so much fun, but was also very earnest for a ten-year-old. I wanted to be good at this. Actually, if I'm truly honest, I wanted to be great at it. There was no logical reason apart from the inexplicable happiness it gave me. I tried my best and loved every minute of it. I felt sad when the class ended as I could have kept going all night.

Afterwards, the chief instructor Glenn Puckeridge came over to my mum and asked her how long I had been doing martial arts. She was somewhat confused but told him that this was my first full class. He smiled at her and said, 'Well, your daughter is a natural.' We were both surprised and somewhat proud to hear his unexpected compliment. My heart swelled and I knew deep down that this was what I was always meant to do. I had found my passion, my place in the world. Little did I know that thirty years later I would still feel the same way about the movements and magic of martial arts.

Martial arts developed my self-confidence and gave me an avenue to foster some self-belief. It was an outlet, a lifeline and the foundation of a moral code. It gave me a discipline that has served me throughout my life—knowing how to line up straight and when to be quiet always comes in handy. Even as a ten-year-old my character was being deeply programmed without me realising it. The traits I saw being practised by the adults were so appealing to me even though I didn't fully understand what I was seeing. The more focused they were and the harder they tried, the more I wanted to be like them. Except for the guy who sounded like a stuck pig each time he did the necessary yell to finish a technique. No, probably not like him if I could help it.

Training became my whole world. I would spend countless hours in the backyard practising my patterns and fighting invisible opponents. My dad would proudly write articles about my martial arts in the Rotary Club newsletter, especially when I broke my first wooden board with a flying side kick. I may have bounced off it about five times before it finally broke, but it felt like a big achievement for a little person. I could hardly ever be coaxed to take off my white training suit and coloured belt. I wanted to be Daniel-san from *The Karate Kid* and have my very own Mr Miyagi. I wanted to do all of the waxing on and waxing off. I'd have been thrilled for my Sensei to have me 'paint the fence' as a way to teach me martial arts lessons like in the film.

I watched the scene at the end of *The Karate Kid* over and over again, where Daniel-san has to fight all of the Cobra Kai bad guys in the All Valley Tournament. He goes through hard challenges but eventually wins it all through self-belief and a special technique that Mr Miyagi taught him. While other kids wanted to be the Little Mermaid or Luke Skywalker, I dreamed of being the female version of Daniel-san. I wanted to wear a black belt, win a big tournament and have a profoundly memorable moment with my Sensei like in the final scene of the film. What I didn't know when I was ten years old was that one day I would put everything on the line in pursuit of that dream.

In the meantime I spent hours doing flying side kicks across the backyard while singing the *Karate Kid* theme song. I became adept at winning fights with the trees in the garden and snapping out kicks trying to touch only the tip of a leaf. Tae Kwon Do was 70 per cent kicking and a touch-contact sport. This meant the accuracy to hit while just barely touching your target was highly prized. It took quite a bit of skill and self-control but I was determined to practice until I could do it perfectly.

I soon had the chance to test it out in real life. I was playing down near a creek one day when two slightly older boys started teasing me. They had seen me practising my martial arts and were making fun of me. The more they teased, the more upset I became. Eventually one of the boys came threateningly close to me and before I knew it my little leg flew up and zipped past his face, almost touching the end of his nose. He looked totally startled. I told them to leave me alone and I don't know who was more scared at that point, them or me, but they sure left quickly. Apparently all that time I'd spent firing kicks at the backyard flora was paying off after all.

I was no pushover even when I was young, always the kind of kid who would try to stick up for myself or anyone else. I had a keen sense of fairness and would regularly find myself retrieving a ball from some meanie who'd taken it from the littler kids. Throughout my childhood I'd played rough enough with boys that I wasn't afraid of them in the way many girls are. Having said that, I also knew enough to run when need be if I found myself outgunned. As I got a little older, I made the mistake of intervening when my brother was being bullied. Although well intended on my part, of course it likely only made things worse for him. Little did I know things were about to get worse for me, too.

Girls really can do anything!

3

Falling Face First

When the start of high school happened, my world gradually began to derail in slow motion. It took a number of years, but the train started veering off the tracks. All of a sudden I went from feeling good about my pint-sized tomboy self, to realising I was somewhat different. In primary school I was friends with everyone and did well at my school work. I was a prefect and a sports house captain. I could handle myself in most sports and every year I would win the age championships on the athletic field. Some kids hated swimming carnival day, but I loved going in all the races. I knew where I fit among all the kids I had grown up with and they all accepted me. It didn't matter that I was a tomboy because I had always been one. They knew it, I knew it, no problem.

Unfortunately, in the well-intended interests of giving me a quality education, my parents didn't send me to the same high school as all my friends. I went from a state-run primary school to the local Catholic high school. My new classmates were the same children that us public school kids had spent the past six years making fun of on the bus we shared. We saw them as stuck-up and fancy, while we were somewhat rougher around the edges. I'm not sure where we got this idea from, because it's not like we lived in the 'hood and these kids were from Beverly Hills. This was Coffs Harbour on the New South Wales Mid-North Coast, an area known for its beaches and tourism. It bore little or no resemblance to Compton.

Yet the division of us and them was so clear and I felt like a traitor being forced to change sides. My brother David was already two years into his time at John Paul College so I guess I had known for a while that I would be following him there. I must have been in some serious denial, because when the news came I was as shocked as if my parents had told me I'd been adopted. I tried everything to get out of having to change schools. None of it worked. I felt powerless and like it was unfair to the point of treachery. My poor parents were just trying to set me up well for adulthood, and I carried on like it was the end of life as we knew it. Yet at twelve years old that is how it feels to be taken away from your friends and plonked down alone in enemy private school territory.

The first day of Catholic high school started with mass in the chapel. I walked in already feeling like an outsider as all the other kids had immediately formed into their cliques. They were excitedly talking after being reunited for the first time following their Christmas holiday break. I knew no-one except a girl I'd met once, who was the younger sister of my brother's friend. I sat awkwardly alone, incredibly uncomfortable with this new feeling of knowing no-one and having no idea what was going on. My family wasn't religious and I had never been to mass before. Suffice to say I had no clue what genuflecting was. I tried to look cool but I didn't know whether or not I was supposed to copy the other kids and bend down. It was a strange altered reality that felt horribly unsettling, like somebody had made a mistake and put me in the wrong place. I wasn't Catholic, and I wasn't supposed to be there.

This new feeling of being other was magnified by the dawning reality that, in high school, girls are meant to behave like girly girls. They are supposed to dress in a certain way, wear their hair in particular styles, talk about specific things and share similar interests. I quickly came to the clanging realisation that I was not on a mission like the other girls to see how far above my knee I could wear my skirt before a nun noticed. Nor did I want to regularly flick my hair like some type of horse swatting away a fly with its mane. I wasn't into discussing make-up or boys, and I couldn't have cared less about going shopping for new outfits together on Saturday. My difference crept over me like a slow chill that I didn't see coming. I had started my school holidays basking in the sun of positive self-image and had awoken in the cold winter of feeling secretly uneasy and out of place. It was something I didn't let anyone see. Growing up in the motel meant I had always made friends easily, so high school saw me fit in quite well with lots of different groups. Underneath, though, I knew things had changed in a way that made me feel less comfortable than I always had before.

I was already freaking out because of the uniform of the Catholic high school. It was a maroon and blue tartan skirt with a sky blue blouse. Hmm, yes, glorious. My mum had taken me shopping for it and I was aghast at the new top I had to wear. It was an awful material and seemed super low cut to me. It was very girly in a way that I wasn't used to. Yet the worst was yet to come—fawn coloured socks. Oh, how I hated those ugly brown socks. Even my incredibly limited fashion experience told me that sky blue socks would match this snazzy tartan ensemble, but no, apparently light brown was the perfect counterbalance to all that maroon and blue.

I just didn't get it. The new school, the new uniform, the new religion, the new rules about being a girl. The reality, that it was time to let go of being a little tomboy and face the fact I now had a one-way ticket to becoming a woman, hit me in the face like an unexpected ocean wave. I was looking up towards womanhood and couldn't see many women that I related to or wanted to be like. There just didn't seem to be any fully grown versions of me walking around in my vicinity. I liked being female and was happy to grow up, but the road forward didn't seem as clear for me as for the other girls.

If Google existed back then, I would have felt way more comfortable with where the path ahead might take me. I could have seen pictures of women who didn't fit the traditional mould of femininity such as P!nk or Ellen DeGeneres. The penny would have dropped in my early teenage mind that there are lots of different kinds of women. At that point the only women on television who I felt I related to were female athletes. They were women, but in a real kick-ass kind of way. They were strong, they were valued for their achievements and they didn't have to wear stupid fawn-coloured socks.

Sport was the way I knew I could express myself and feel good about who I was. But I felt a bit confused about where

I now stood with the boys in high school, once it became clear that athletic prowess was not prized by them the way it had been in primary school. One thing that boys apparently didn't value were girls who had the ability to beat them up. If one of the poor guys had sidled over and asked 'Do you want to go out with me?' it might have resulted in the delivery of a quick Karate chop and a Year 8 boy doubled over behind the bus shelter.

As the middle years of high school passed by, I knew there were ways that I was a little different and that difference was no longer necessarily a good thing. Where I had once felt totally at ease in my own skin, I was now aware that I didn't fit in the femininity box that other people wanted me to. Nobody told me that school dynamics were going to change so much as I got older and I didn't like the way they had altered. It was the start of an inner conflict that would soon be reflected in the rest of my world.

♦

As I completed Years 10 and 11 things started to change for me, though not in a good way. There was a great deal of conflict at home—between my mum and my dad, between my brother and me, plus an ever-increasing tension in my relationship with my parents. The complications of the past had created conflicts in the present. After years of awards and trophies, the day dawned where I knew that no matter how hard I tried I couldn't fix things at home. The more it sank in, the less alluring the shine of new medals became.

After watching the disappointments that alcohol leaves behind, I carried a raging restlessness. It was the kind of anger that would manifest itself as a self-destruct button if left un-channelled. I had to burn it out through physical exertion and pursuing achievement or it would ignite in the shadows and raze me to the ground. Instead of channelling that energy into my martial arts training, I gradually stopped training altogether. I was rebelling and hanging out with people my parents didn't like. As an adult I can look back now with crystal clear hindsight and realise why they were so opposed to me spending time with a guy who had recently been released from prison. I was hanging out with people who were into partying. This led to an exponential increase in familial discord as I became harder to handle and control.

Once heavily invested in being a good kid, I was now being a teenage jerk thinking that I knew what I was doing and not wanting to play by anyone else's rules. Things were spinning out of control but I felt powerless to stop it. I was losing the best parts of myself and replacing them with a self-destructive doppelgänger. I liked being wild for the first time and the outlet it gave me for the frenetic vibrating energy I felt inside. That is until it all got out of hand.

Things at home quickly reached boiling point, then blew up in my face. This resulted in me living elsewhere with friends. At such a crucial time in my schooling, with the pressure to prepare for the final year of high school mounting, my emotional state started to crumble. It was hard to explain to a fairly unsympathetic Catholic nun that I hadn't finished my assignment because I wasn't living at home and things were falling apart in my personal life. I missed more and more days of school, with the work piling up and my once-good grades slipping.

I acted out the conflict I felt on the inside. I spiralled downwards because I couldn't see any way out of the situation

I was in. I felt too far gone with my school work and too much was happening outside school to tackle the HSC the following year. I had originally wanted to study law at university but my grades deteriorated due to falling behind in completed work. It was getting to the point where I doubted I would be able to even finish school, let alone get anywhere near the high university entrance score I had hoped for in years gone by. It just didn't seem in any way possible from where I was standing.

My family situation felt much the same, eroded to the point where I didn't know how to repair it. I had gone further and further off the rails and lost the person I had once felt so confident in being. As the Christmas holidays between Years 11 and 12 passed, the pressure built to the point where there was no option but for things to change. I couldn't keep going the way things were, as they were only getting worse. Everything was messed up at school, at home and inside me. It was all rapidly reaching breaking point and something had to give. That thing had to be me.

I wasn't there the night my friend had a drug overdose that almost killed her. We thought it was cool to hang around much older friends with chequered pasts. Despite what we naively believed, nothing good was going to come from those friendships. As teenagers, you think you know what you're doing and believe you have a certain invincibility due to your not-yet-fully-developed brain. We knew the people we had become friends with were into all kinds of trouble. The teenage rebel in me liked just being in the same social circle as them. What I didn't want was to become one of them. My friend was dating one of the guys, who had introduced her to heroin. They had taken it together, she had overdosed, stopped breathing and then had to be resuscitated. It had left her with serious permanent brain damage. The party was officially over.

◆

Everything changed for me when I left for Sydney and entered the Ted Noffs Foundation where they help struggling teens make a fresh start. I had my seventeenth birthday there and stayed within their program for many months, eventually moving into their supported housing in the Darlinghurst area of inner city Sydney. I wasn't sure what I would do next, but I was glad to be out of the situation I had been caught up in. There were rules in the program that provided structure—you had to study or work, you had to be sober and you had to do what you were told. After having spent the previous years rebelling you'd think I would have found it hard to fall into line. At this point I was too lost and scared not to comply. I needed help to get back on track and they were willing to help me find solid footing.

My original loose plan was to go back to school after a year off to sort things out. My parents offered for me to move home but I didn't feel that I could go back. This caused a great deal of conflict and led to a period where we reached a stalemate, an impasse where neither side agreed with the other's solution. I needed them to sign some official papers so I could access government support, but for their own valid reasons they didn't want to do it. That meant I was in limbo without any way to immediately financially support myself. I was broke and getting a fast reality check about what it was like to go from having something to having nothing.

Growing up living in a motel meant that I'd had some definite perks, but we were in no way spoiled kids. My parents were frugal and sensible spenders which meant we didn't get the fashionable labels or newest cool big toys every year. We got what we needed, which meant I didn't have high expectations about living a luxurious life. What I didn't understand was how much everyday life cost—the daily tally of expenses, from food to rent and beyond. I suddenly found myself stuck between being supported by my parents and having to support myself. Any remaining hint of childhood privilege left me during those days. I had no money and no way to get any, even though I needed some fast. I was out of options and it was humbling to have to rely on the donations of others to feed myself.

Big companies would often make charitable donations to programs such as the Ted Noffs Foundation so one morning I found myself staring down a bag of Coco Pops the size of a bar fridge. No packaging, just a giant plastic bag of cereal delivered by its manufacturers. Now all I needed was milk, and lots of it. Yet what started as sugary puffs of joy quickly turned to the dull brown milk of repetition, as I made my way through that bag which must have been equivalent to one hundred normal sized cereal boxes. Still, I was happy just to have it.

Soon I found myself at the Salvation Army being given a few bags of groceries from their pantry. I was grateful for the generosity of the kind lady helping me fill a few bags, but I felt embarrassed at the same time. I knew there was nothing wrong with asking for help, but it hurt nonetheless as it became a reality.

Later, as I unpacked the cans of such delicacies as 'Franks and Beans' (which I hadn't even known existed until then), I found some Wagon Wheels chocolate biscuits. That nice woman had snuck them in without me seeing when she was getting the bags ready. I cried with happiness at this small act of kindness that made the situation less painful and brought me some joy. She saw that I was still a kid and gave me a treat. Every now and again as an adult I sentimentally eat a Wagon Wheel as a reminder of those days and so I never forget that small act of kindness. I've made sure to pay it back many times over.

The Salvos also gave me some food vouchers to use at the local supermarket to see me through. I swallowed my pride and went down to Clancy's on Oxford Street armed with a piece of paper and a small pencil. I was determined to make those vouchers stretch as far as I could by getting maximum value from every cent. I wandered around the aisles, putting things in my basket, adding them up and then replacing them if I found a better deal. I looked for what was on special and what I could combine with my limited cooking abilities to make the most of a meal. I felt sheepish recalling my lobster birthday dinners when I was younger and regretted that I hadn't participated more in Mum's efforts to teach me how to cook. Parents do know best and I wished I had listened when she told me cooking was a skill I would need. I just hadn't known how soon I would be needing it.

I desperately needed to change my situation so I got a job at a local cafe on Victoria Street in Darlinghurst and learnt to make coffee. It was 1993 and nobody knew what a barista was back then. Being rushed off my feet at work all day was a new feeling. While I loved being busy and making some money to look after myself, it was still a shock to the system. The coffee scene in Darlo is no joke, with many a thrown cappuccino after a failed beginner's attempt. I quickly learnt the difference between a piccolo and a latte, becoming a serious coffee drinker myself in the process.

I started earning enough to support myself (and therefore eat less Coco Pops) but only just. The rent we had to pay in the supported accommodation was tiny so the conditions weren't exactly glamorous. My furniture was either home-made or old beaten-up hand-me-downs. I made myself an improvised wardrobe that would have made MacGyver himself proud. I wired together two matching towers of four plastic milk crates stacked one on top of other. Then I ran a metal rod between them at the top, which made my clothes rack resemble the London Bridge. I had turned the milk crates on their sides with the opening facing the front so I could put all of my folded clothes in the boxes like shelves, while I hung the rest on hangers wardrobe-style from the rod in the centre. My teenage ingenuity creating furniture out of thin air made me feel as magical as Harry Potter, but it was also a massive reality check. I didn't have any money or any cool things like other kids my age. I didn't have a full secondary education or work skills. I was in a new city and didn't know many people. Things were clearly not looking up.

The difficulties of a fresh start were many but there was also an exciting freedom in this new life. I had replaced the pressures and struggles I faced with a new set of challenges, that were more about figuring out how to get by and grow up quickly. My only responsibility was to take care of myself and I was on a huge learning curve of finding out who exactly that person was now. I had gone so far away from myself that I wasn't sure who I was anymore. As the dust settled around me I started to adjust my vision. The first thing to come clearly into focus was something

I had always known on some level but not had a clear context for—that I was gay. My coming out to myself wasn't exactly dramatic in that I was just accepting who I had always been. It was a simple truth, like looking around a room one day and saying that's a chair, this is a table and I like girls. It just was. In the city, I finally saw my people and knew instantaneously the name for who and what I was. I knew that I made sense here in a way that I didn't at a Catholic high school up the coast.

Simply adjust the focus and the picture becomes clear. It wasn't a conscious choice I made. I was born this way and I was cool with it. Plus it wasn't exactly a giant shock to think the little blonde tomboy might not grow up to be straight. My self-discovery involved about as much thought and surprise as I imagine heterosexual people feel when they become aware of their own sexuality—not a lot. I just was. It was simply something true about me and there was nothing more to it. I felt lucky as a teenager newly coming into my sense of self to see positive reflections in the adults around me of what it meant to be gay. I wanted to make a life for myself that made sense with how I felt and aligned to who I was as a person. When I was younger, I had never envisaged myself with a lovely husband and three kids. That was a nice life to want and I was happy to dream it for my friends, but it would have felt to me like getting a right-handed person to write with their left.

Soon enough I made some friends and moved to a big share house in Redfern. I got a job working as a singing waitress in Darling Harbour and proceeded to immediately abandon any sense of public embarrassment I had ever felt. I would run wildly around this American-themed restaurant named Bobby McGee's in a gypsy costume. My character's name was Claire Voyant.

Get it? Augh, sigh. Anyway, I liked the job because I got to crack jokes and be silly while working at a fast pace and being social. I did split shifts and long hours, trying to get a little money in the bank by earning tips. I bought my first CD-player stereo and thought I was living the high life.

Yet I knew that working in hospitality wasn't for me in the long term. I had some regular customers who worked for Village Roadshow and they would jokingly ask what a girl like me was doing working in a job like this. They made me think about my future and planted the idea that, despite not finishing school, I should aim as high as possible. They suggested I come to work for them but I was too scared to take them up on their offer. I didn't want to tell them about my education or lack thereof. I felt like a high school drop-out who wasn't good enough to dip my toes into the corporate world. I was subconsciously telling myself a limiting story about what I was worth and who I could be. I missed an opportunity because I didn't yet know who I was and instead chose to believe the wrong part of my thinking.

I worked at the restaurant with an interesting guy named Peter who doubled as a doorman doing security in bars. We would talk about martial arts training and he started to spark my interest in it again. I felt as bad about giving up martial arts as I did about leaving school. Peter and I did some training together and he suggested I get into working in nightclubs, so I followed his lead which soon found me working as a 'door bitch' at some of the gay bars on Oxford Street. I was young but they gave me a go anyway. It was probably because they didn't consider my age and there weren't many women willing (or crazy enough) to work in the role.

The nights were late and the hours were long, in that they often went by in slow motion. It was a social job where I met lots of people but I had this front of being tough that I had to put on so people wouldn't mess with me. I hid behind that facade for years, as it made me feel more confident and less like an intimidated teenager. I suppose I came across as being older than I was. I didn't ever want to let anyone see that I was scared in some of the rougher situations. I could hold my own, or so I thought . . .

♦

Gay bars are not known for their violence or fights, but every now and again we would find ourselves getting into physical security situations. I was usually happier to talk my way out of things, both for my sake and the sake of the drunken bar patron who would likely regret it in the morning. I was nineteen and thought I could handle myself well, but was not fully aware of how dangerous the work could be. We had knives pulled on us, gunshots in the street, drug overdoses and assaults to contend with. The danger of the job was something I counterbalanced with the lifestyle it gave me.

I landed a high-profile job at a bar called Gilligan's. I always worked on the door with the same partner, a great guy named Mark who has been my best mate for more than twenty years now. I also met Kate, my first real girlfriend, while working there. Kate taught me so much about love and life. She has also been one of my dearest friends for two decades. We all worked in bars and knew how hard it could be, though we usually had some fun. Mark and I loved having big lines of cool people waiting to get in on the weekends. It was all very fashionable and seemed glamorous to allow access to one of the trendiest bars in Sydney. That made up for the long hours of working solo on weeknights, when it was much quieter. It was on a night like that, when I was working alone, where I found myself at a crossroads that would change my life forever.

There was a couple who were clearly intoxicated and seemed unaware that they had not yet made it home before beginning their night of passion so I had to ask them to leave. Unhappy and argumentative, the woman threw a punch at me and I pushed her away. This was followed by the man jumping me from behind, grabbing a fistful of my hair as we fell forward. He had one hand on my face and the other locked behind my head clenching my hair. Intense panic registered as he started to eye-gouge me. I was absolutely terrified as he pushed his thumb behind my eye and tried to pull it out. It was excruciatingly painful and the nails of his other fingers were cutting into my face as he screwed up his fist.

Time slowed down with the searing pain of his thumb cutting, forcing and tearing at my eye inside the socket. His determination and sheer violence shocked me as I felt a chilling fear that I would lose my eye. This man wasn't just scuffling with me, he was 100 per cent trying to permanently injure me. It wasn't a fair fight in any way—two against one, they'd started it and I'd been attacked from behind with some nasty street fighting tactics. This was no martial arts class. It was naive, but nobody had told me this was what real dirty fighting was like. No warning, no chance to fight back and no rules.

Using the full force of both my hands on one of his, I eventually pulled his fingers out of my eyes. I tore his other hand off my hair as I felt chunks of scalp get ripped away with it. I wiped blood and watery tears out of my scratched eyes. They felt like they were full of sand. My vision cleared just in time to see a punch fire past my face. I only just got out of the way as another one launched. Now this crazy guy was trying to knock me out. I could barely see as I backed away and narrowly avoided his swings. I couldn't see where his partner had gone and I was worried I'd also get hit from behind.

There were people gathered around yelling for the fight to stop. One of them came from nowhere and pushed away my attacker. He tumbled backwards and then launched himself at the man who'd stepped in to help me, screaming and calling him a 'faggot'. Now, this was all happening at the front door of a gay bar at Taylor Square on Oxford Street. Many gay men in this area were known for going to the gym a lot and being quite muscular. Unfortunately for my attacker, he had called the wrong gay man a 'faggot'. My tall and muscular saviour promptly ended the violent onslaught (now aimed at him) with one swift punch. That was enough to stop the eye-gouging guy in his tracks. I don't know the name of the brave man who helped me, but to this day I wish I could thank him.

As my black eyes healed and the cuts faded, I still felt shaken. It was my sense of self that was most damaged. The person I thought I was, and how I had perceived myself as a capable martial artist, had also taken a beating along with my face. I felt unsteady on the inside. If I wasn't good at protecting myself and confident in my abilities, then who was I now? I suddenly carried an insecure fear that was new and desperately uncomfortable. In the days that followed I would have given anything to go back to how I felt about myself and my place in the world a week before the fight. It was like realising you're standing out in the open with no clothes on, all of your protective coverings removed.

I had to make a choice at this time in my life that I knew would affect the way I lived the rest of it. I was at a crossroads where I had to decide who I was going to be from that point on. Option A was to let the fear and doubt this assault had created permeate all my self-belief and turn me into someone else. This new harsh voice in my head was telling me I'd have to give up martial arts because they hadn't worked when I'd needed them. It told me that I was just a scared little girl. I'd have to accept that I was vulnerable and therefore not as confident as I had been before. Words like *weak*, *scared* and *unprepared* ran cruelly through my mind. I was beating myself up. I didn't want this to be my new reality and the thought of having to feel this way forever terrified me more than being eye-gouged.

Then there was Option B, which meant admitting I was afraid and then finding someone to teach me how to deal with it. I could choose to keep doing martial arts but take it to a whole new, much more realistic, level. This scared me because it seemed like a harder and more confronting road. It would be easier to just let the bad experience I'd had make me run away and hide. Would I even be able to find a teacher capable of showing me how to defend myself for real, while at the same time not have to pretend that I was super tough? I knew that admitting you're scared was frowned upon in many a martial arts circle, but that now seemed ridiculous given the reality of self-defence. I needed an instructor who could make me physically capable, but also mentally capable of dealing with my fear.

I had to choose between these options because the attack had rocked me to the point where I knew I could not be the same person. I believe that the hard, painful parts of life can destroy us or force us to grow. At our crossroads, we make a decision, be it conscious or unconscious, about how we emerge from our challenges. Sometimes, in not deciding, we passively slide into having made a selection. So many times I have dragged myself away from tough times feeling broken by circumstance and needing time to recover. Yet eventually, I always seem to want to get back up when I'm knocked down. Even if I have to scrape myself off the canvas after one of life's inevitable knock-out blows. Somewhere deep inside we all have to access the little voice that says, 'Get up, you can do it, just try; okay that didn't work very well, so just try one more time.' The getting up is the hardest part, but if you don't, the staying down is permanent.

If you don't choose to get up, staying down might become permanent.

YOU CAN'T HAVE COURAGE WITHOUT FEAR

ROUND 2

CROSSROADS TO THE UNEXPECTED

Moving so fast that I was a blur in my gun grading test.

4

Standing Back Up

Staring down that crossroads, I had to choose to get back up. I felt a potent combination of nervousness to try something new but I was also jumping out of my skin at the excited thought of it. I went looking for a style of martial arts that would teach me to defend myself in real-life situations but also enable me to continue with the traditional martial arts training I had loved. In other words, I didn't want to learn to street fight from a bunch of thugs with no moral compass. Reality or sport-based fighting styles often lack much training in the traditions of Bushido, the warrior code. It's so important for someone learning physical skills that could be used to hurt another person to also learn self-control. If you train with the wrong kind of people, then you can learn more than enough to be dangerous to yourself and others. I was a firm believer in the idea you are who you surround yourself with, so I wanted to choose carefully. I was hungry to develop my self-defence skills but I also wanted to grow as a person. I could never have imagined how much growing there was to do.

I went looking for a school that had many different facets and I found that in a style named Ukidokan Karate. It is a combination of nine different martial arts with a threefold goal—to create a classically trained martial artist, who could compete in combat sports (like kickboxing) yet could also realistically defend themselves in the street. Many martial arts only deal with one element of this trifecta. Ukidokan tackled them all because it was derived from the life of martial arts training, competitive fighting and real-life self-defence belonging to one man, Benny 'The Jet' Urquidez.

Benny Urquidez is an American famous in his field, much like the 'Rocky' of kickboxing. For decades he remained an undefeated world champion in multiple weight divisions. His kickboxing record was legendary as he had zero losses. Of his sixty-three world title wins, fifty-seven of those were by knockout. The holder of nine black belts and a living martial arts legend, he is renowned the world over as a true pioneer. Famed for his interesting fighting style, he was known as the people's champion. I recognised his face from a picture I had seen in a martial arts book my Uncle Tony gave me for Christmas when I first started martial arts as a child. Benny Urquidez had an easily recognisable face, with his intense eyes and an intriguing air of mysticism to him.

When I curiously stepped into the Sydney school which taught his Ukidokan system, I met Sensei Glenn Coxon, who was Ukidokan's first Australian black belt. I was excited to discover this was who would be teaching my first one-on-one class. He had travelled to the United States to train many times with Sensei Benny and was the only person teaching Ukidokan in the Southern Hemisphere. He explained to me that even though I had martial arts experience, in Ukidokan everyone starts at white belt. This meant that each student, from a world champion to first-time beginner, was treated the same and started from scratch. I liked this approach, as it seemed humble and took away the pressure to perform. This was replaced with the freedom to learn and make mistakes. When you're not expected to already have the answers, you're free to learn things you didn't already know and ask questions, which isn't always encouraged in martial arts training. I was excited at the thought of having a fresh start in a new style with a new teacher. Sensei Glenn regaled me with stories of his training with Sensei Benny and all it had taught him as a person. I marvelled at these almost mythical tales and hoped one day to have my own.

I was so nervous the first day I went to train, repeatedly apologising for my lack of fitness. My memory of that training session is as clear as the bright sunny day it was. Sensei Glenn taught me basic strikes and blocks in a private session room at the front of the dojo (martial arts school). I fell in love with the movements all over again, just like I had when I was ten years old. From the start when we bowed to each other as a sign of respect, to the sweat that trickled down my arms as we trained. I had found my

It's never too late to start fresh. Surround yourself with who you want to become.

way home. I didn't know exactly why, but the familiar feeling returned immediately—without a doubt that this was the thing that I was meant to do with my life.

I still have the notebook where I wrote down everything I learned that first day. I have written so many notes over the years that I've ended up with an almost encyclopaedic knowledge bank. I started taking notes on everything I was learning in every area of my life. I still do it today. When I read a good book, I write down all the best parts. I don't want to read it and let it go, but instead I try to study it and take the most valuable knowledge with me. You never know when the new thing you've started reading about might become a pursuit that spans decades. Write it down people, write it down.

There was one unexpected part of Ukidokan that truly changed my life—this was internal training. Not only was I being taught all the physical moves, but also the psychological, emotional and spiritual elements as well. It was a part of martial arts training I had never experienced in such a significant way before. I already loved the moral code of martial arts that encouraged discipline, perseverance and courage. Yet I had never seen such a formal structured method for developing the warrior mindset to grow as a person. In doing the physical training, there were so many opportunities to develop yourself mentally. The harder I trained, the more unavoidable it became to face the challenges that were in my own mind. Sure, the physical training hurt, but the truly strenuous part was learning how to use courage when I didn't feel brave, to be resilient in the face of adversity, to change my thinking from negative to positive, how to have a clear grateful mind, and to face myself as a person head-on. This was where things really changed for me.

My martial arts journey became less about physical techniques and more about finding out who I was. It became a way of discovering what I was made of. At first I was unsure and kind of scared to find out. I was afraid I might not like the truth I uncovered. What if you find out what you're made of and you don't like what you see? Yet this was the mission I had chosen to undertake. I wanted to take a good hard look at myself so that I could work on the parts I needed to improve. Training gave me plenty of opportunities for growth and a vehicle for fostering a new, more grounded self-belief. There were plenty of challenging situations being thrown at me in the dojo, but they were showing me what I was capable of achieving.

I had only been training in this new style of martial arts for about six months after the eye-gouging incident when Sensei Glenn suggested to me I should compete in a tournament. In the style of martial arts I had done as a kid, we weren't allowed to compete, so this would be my first time. Flashes of winning trophies *Karate Kid*-style whizzed through my mind but so did a fear of failing. I wanted to fulfil that childhood dream of winning a tournament, but I was also scared I would lose. To take a risk or stay safe by sitting on the sidelines? I decided I would rather know what I was capable of, than never know because I was too afraid to try.

My first National All Styles tournament was nerve wracking, but I competed successfully, winning both types of sparring and also kata (where you perform classical movements without an opponent). In my second tournament I became the NSW Champion and, before I knew it, my third competitive experience was at the 1996 National Titles held in Perth. I couldn't really afford to go over to compete, but I had this weird feeling that I just had to do it.

The Australian Titles in Perth was a huge tournament with hundreds of martial artists from every style you could think of, all competing at one event. I was so nervous and took it all super seriously. I felt proud to have the New South Wales patch on my uniform but also an odd combination of hopefulness mixed with fear that my dreams wouldn't come true. This was an emotional cocktail I would become very familiar with over time, but these initial experiences with it were intense. I was discovering that I could maybe handle the pressure and I might even thrive on it a little. When others were freaking out, I seemed to get laser focused. I found if I could get myself through the first anxiety-inducing part of arriving at the venue, getting ready and waiting (oh, the endless waiting), then when my time came I would do everything in my power to perform at my best.

I won both the continuous sparring (like kickboxing but with light contact) and kata (as a first-time novice). I was so excited and the two trophies I won were a metre tall. It wasn't quite like Daniel-san in *The Karate Kid*, but it was pretty darn satisfying nonetheless. Later that night, through my exhaustion, I called my mum and dad to tell them that I had won. Martial arts had gotten my derailed teenage train back on the tracks and I was happy that this was a way for me to prove it. My parents couldn't have been happier for me and when I spoke to Dad I was so glad I had done something he could be proud of. Winning that tournament was the last thing my dad and I ever spoke about.

◆

The morning of 10 December 1996 I had been shopping for homewares at IKEA with Kate and Mark, as we had all just moved into a house together. We walked in the door and I laid out the blue rug I had bought. Just as I sat down on the couch, my phone rang. It was my brother David, which was unusual as he wouldn't usually call me in the middle of the day.

I knew as soon as I answered the call that something was very wrong. My blood went cold and I almost held my breath, a very specific feeling of time slowing down that only those who have had a phone call like that will know. David told me that Dad had died suddenly. He had gone to work and had a massive heart attack. He had passed away alone, which ripped my heart out. It was such a shock that I slid down onto the floor. Dad hadn't been in poor health prior to that day, except for feeling a bit sick the night before. I couldn't believe what I was hearing.

My whole world stopped. I was in shock. I sobbed and was absolutely inconsolable. There was no thinking clearly and nothing I could do to change what had happened. I felt completely powerless and small in the world. My dad was gone and I would never get to see him again. I was devastated that I had called home that past weekend to speak to my mum and when she asked if I wanted to speak to my father, I had said no. Not for any particular reason, but I had just assumed, as we all do, that there would be another opportunity. I was still shrouded in the cloak of believing that we have all the time in the world together. That one phone call had forever ended the buffer between me and the painful truth about how quickly life can change.

In the months that followed, my martial arts training kept me afloat. At first I would spontaneously burst into tears during a session and run to the locker rooms unable to control the emotions that erupted out of me. Sensei Glenn showed kindness and understanding to me as I timidly came back out to train with red puffy eyes. He knew I needed to be there, training out the feelings that as a twenty-year-old I was struggling so hard to manage. Over time I came to appreciate how valuable it was to have a solid foundation like this in my life to keep me steady. I had an outlet for my energy, a healthy distraction from my sadness and a safe place to process the anger that emerged from my dad's sudden passing. Such an unexpected and unfair life event left me standing in a wasteland of turbulent emotion and I had no choice but to walk through it. I felt so torn by the contradictory feelings that had run me aground. At the same time I missed the father whom I had dearly loved. I felt destroyed by the fact I would never have the opportunity to fully repair our relationship as adults. It was a war that waged inside my mind which made me feel broken by the intense drumming of the emotions I couldn't resolve.

I was lost and heartbroken. He was gone. It was forever.

5

Worst Becomes Best

In the year after my dad's death I trained every day, often twice a day. I needed it like oxygen in order to keep moving forward. Martial arts training has saved me more times than I can recount. Undeniably in a physical safety way, but mostly in terms of my own emotions. At the hardest times in my life, martial arts have been my safety net, the life preserver I've clung to, the map I've used to navigate and the ladder I've climbed to pull myself back up out of the pit. This is true because I made it true. At a vulnerable point I had decided to go looking for something I loved that was good for me on the inside and out. Then I laid it brick by deliberate brick as the new foundation of my life. It gave me so much more than a simple sport or a hobby. The internal training gave me tools to deal with how I felt and a way to survive it.

I kept working in bars and being faced with opportunities to use the mental and physical aspects of martial arts training.

Basically, drunk people yell at you a lot, so I learnt to not take things too personally. At times they would have to be removed from the premises, so I became fairly adept at restraining folks who might regret their actions in the morning. Violence is never a good option for anyone, because it always comes at a price. Whether that debt is paid in blood, in court, through shame or tears, there is an unavoidable cost.

It's better to resolve things with words whenever possible. I was taught that this was the mark of a true warrior—to not have to resort to a physical confrontation. It was good to be able to defend yourself, but it's not good to get into fights. Not being able to handle your emotions and then taking them out on someone else by hurting them is a sign of weakness. Sometimes people like that need saving from themselves and it's not the martial artist's job to teach them a lesson physically. It's better to talk the other person out of starting a fight that neither of you will ultimately win.

Unfortunately, I didn't always get to use my words. When a glass is unexpectedly thrown at your head and an upended marble table lands on your foot, the time for talking has already passed. This altercation started with a simple request for a group to leave the bar at closing time and descended within seconds into a full-blown fight. I dodged the flying glass but as I turned my head away I felt the table slam down hard on my left foot. My first thought was of the Karate grading I had the next day for a new belt. I knew my toes were probably broken, so I wouldn't be able to do the test. Plus, now I was having to deal with a group of drunken people wanting to fight because they were outraged we would dare to close the bar at 2 a.m. Alcohol and irrational behaviour are a quality mix.

Luckily my buddy Mark was working with me that night so he helped me herd these somewhat violent cats through the crash doors. I could feel a squelching feeling starting in my boot but was distracted by the table-thrower trying to jump back over his friend to take a swing at me. Unfortunately for him, as he launched himself at me, his throat ran straight into my hand as I pushed him away mid-leap. That at least put him back out the door which we quickly locked to end the drama. As I walked away from the doors, the squelching in my shoe turned to a sloshing sensation. Uh oh, I was definitely bleeding.

It took Mark and the duty manager about five minutes to convince me that they needed to check my foot before I left for the night. All I wanted was to go home. I knew something was up, but was trying to tell myself I could deal with it in the morning. Wrong. The boys made me take off my boot. I was wearing black socks with a grey heel and toe that night. As I removed my left boot I saw that the sock was now bright red with blood. At this point I started negotiating about not having to remove my sock. It's the kind of illogical thinking that is triggered by being frightened. The urge to close your eyes and pretend things aren't really happening. It makes no sense and often just makes things worse.

Before I removed my sock, I had convinced myself I'd just split the end of my left big toe open vertically. I told them that was all it was, but they weren't having a bar of my 'X-ray vision through the sock' diagnosis. Eventually the bar manager made me take it off. As I slid the sock down I saw that my foot and entire sole were covered in blood. That made me extra nervous, as it was a lot more haemoglobin than I was expecting. I gently peeled the sock off over my toes and the shock of what I saw stopped me in my tracks. My big toe was completely smashed and chopped in half below the nail, only hanging by a thread on the left side. The table had guillotined it off through my boot, which made sense as I looked at the marble table in front of me and saw the diagonal edge that sloped away from the top. My stomach turned over.

Mark went completely white as he looked at my foot and I'm sure I did, too. My toe was all disfigured, blue and bloody. The top half of it was sitting up and to the left of where it should have been. I couldn't quite comprehend that there was nothing I could do to re-attach it. This injury was so out of my control and I struggled to fathom what I was seeing. The detachment was an unnaturally jarring sight, like something I had only seen in movies. The real-life gore disturbed me and everyone else who saw it.

So off to the hospital it was then, instead of going home. I was relatively calm until the doctor started putting needles into the open end of my toe. I screamed when they pushed an injection down deep parallel to the bone. At that point I went into defence mode which turned out to be a lucky thing. I flat out refused the first doctor's suggestion that they stitch up my toe in the emergency room, under only a local anaesthetic. There was no way I was staying still for that to happen. They would have to knock me out or I was worried I might try to knock one of them out mid-procedure. My gut was telling me stitches wouldn't be enough. I knew all of the nurses and student doctors being sent in to look at what was apparently an unusual injury were surely not a good sign. I got worried about how I would do Karate in the future because when we kick we often balance on the tips of our toes. My thoughts raced and I worried that training would be over for me, which just made my anxiety worse.

As it turned out I needed microsurgery to re-attach the medial plantar nerve and the artery in my big toe. Afterwards, the surgeon told me it took him fifteen minutes of digging to find the other end of the nerve, as my toe was so badly smashed. Luckily, I also had plastic surgery while I was under anaesthetic, and amazingly you can't tell my big toes apart these days. The nerve sensation took a few years to return but my toe is now looking pretty again. I joke with new friends that I've had plastic surgery and, after some quizzical looks at my face and chest, they always ask shyly where I had it. Then the great toe comparison begins.

After I got out of the hospital I was on crutches for weeks and in quite a lot of pain but that didn't stop me training. I was so irrepressibly into it that I would hobble down the few blocks from my house to the gym and then drag myself backwards up the stairs to the third floor. I would sit on a step with my crutches beside me, then lift myself onto the next step where I'd stop and pull my crutches up. I repeated this for flight after flight of stairs until I got to the top, all flustered and in pain, but so happy to not have to miss out on my passion.

Not training wasn't an option even in these circumstances, so I would sit on the dojo floor and do all the moves I could perform with my upper body. For the leg movements and kicks I had to visualise what my body would do if I could move it. It was hard to imagine at first, but after a while I could close my eyes and feel how my feet would move. I learned to summon a clear image of my feet delivering kicks. Sensei Glenn taught me a complex senior level kata sequence while I sat on the floor. He would perform the movements standing in front of me and I would picture myself doing the same movements. It got tricky when it came to turning and changes of direction, but

I discovered how to feel the movements even if I couldn't physically perform them.

During all the idle time I had recuperating, the greatest value of training was that it gave me something to focus my mind on. Too much time alone to think wasn't my friend, as underneath I was still dealing with the difficult sadness of my dad dying. Martial arts, even while sitting down, gave me a focused purpose that kept me upright through those challenging times. It would prove to be a life-saving precedent many times over the next two decades.

◆

Once my foot healed I got into my training with a newfound vigour. It was a fresh passion brought on by experiencing what it was like to not be able to fully participate in the activity that I loved. The more I learned, the more my confidence grew. I discovered a whole new world based around using leverage to control a person's body, rather than having to strike them. I loved this concept. At 5 feet 6 inches tall, the odds were always stacked against me if I had to defend myself against someone bigger and stronger.

Leverage taught me about how the body worked and the direction that certain joints did not move in. That is, if you rotate a joint past its intended range of motion, then the person it belongs to will move their body to compensate and stop the joint being damaged. Essentially, you can move them the way you want them to go. My favourite principle along these lines was learning 'where the head goes, the body goes'. So if I could control a person's head position, there was a good chance I could stop them from hurting me, or someone else.

Leverage is better than force.

I had an opportunity to test this theory one night when I was leaving a bar. As I was walking out onto the street to leave, I saw a man yelling at and hitting a woman I had been introduced to by friends earlier in the evening. I've always felt the need to try to stand up to bullies, and didn't feel right about turning a blind eye to a domestic violence incident. Just to be clear, I don't advocate people playing the hero and intervening in unsafe scenarios. You can only ever do what feels right and safe to you. Someone who felt their personal safety would be at risk can still help by witnessing from a safe distance or calling the police. In my fast assessment of the situation I felt like I had to do something.

The abusive boyfriend had the woman up against a wall and was raising his hand to hit her, so I grabbed him in a very tight grappler's body lock from behind. I gripped him so he couldn't move his arms at all and the wind got knocked out of him. Luckily he was so confused by being restrained that he didn't resist a whole lot. I moved him away from her and spoke hard in his ear, telling him that it was time to stop, that I didn't want to fight him, but I would hurt him if he swung at me when I let him go. Those sound like fighting words, I know, but working in bars and dealing with aggression in so many different contexts had taught me that people who fight weaker opponents are rarely courageous in picking their battles. I wanted him to doubt himself. The way I'd immobilised him by locking his arms was hopefully an indication that I might just know a little bit about what I was doing. As strongly as I could smell his rage, I could also sense his weakness of character.

I marched him away from the woman and held him until he settled down a bit. He was angry but he agreed it was over. When I let him go, I also pushed him away to a safe distance and readied myself in case he attacked me. He wheeled around and saw me for the first time, yelling abuse and threatening me now that he was free. I was prepared, but not in an aggressive way that meant he would have to fight me in order to save face. I told him to walk away and leave the woman alone. This seemed to be the one thing he couldn't do, as he made a beeline for her.

My only goal was to stop the assault, not to get into an assault with him myself. As he pushed the woman back into the wall, I had to intervene again, this time by pushing him into the bricks beside her. He spun around towards me and as he did I used what I had learned about leverage to go with the motion. I grabbed his neck and pushed his head down so he couldn't punch me. I slammed it down hard, which bent him at the waist and forced his hips back against the wall. This gave me the leverage to keep pushing downwards until his head was between his legs with my full body weight over the top of it. Now his head was down, his body went with it so he wasn't able to attack me due to the wall wedging him in place. He couldn't go back or forward. This guy who had thought he was so tough a few minutes prior now looked folded over ridiculously like a clam that had been snapped shut. I gave him some harsh words again, telling him it was over or I would be forced to end it this time.

Next thing I knew, the woman who had been assaulted started yelling at me to let him go. I was unfortunately not surprised by this and a flash of sadness ran through me. I knew the couple would leave together. Eventually I let him go and he showed his true colours by bridging up like he wanted to fight but then backing down. In the security game we called guys like this 'walk and talkers'. They would yell and make a big scene as if they were tough guys but then would use this smokescreen to walk away. Fine by me. At the end of the day, ego is less important than your safety.

The years that I worked in bars had developed a keen sense within me of when to get involved and when to stay safe in the face of violence. The reality of fighting was brutal. I had no interest in being around knives and guns, or ambulances and hospitals. Unfortunately I knew more than most twenty-year-old women about violence and fighting. I had learned some of what was out there to be scared of in the world, and the boundaries of situations I was able to handle. Reality had given me no room to kid myself about what my martial arts skills could or could not do. I knew where I stood and I knew where other people did, too, from the average person to the violent criminal. It was a brutal education in the darker side of humanity, but one that would be valuable as a martial artist.

My eyes were continuously being opened. I was no longer as shocked by what I had seen, but intrigued and hungry to learn more in the face of the truth. This was very much the case when three American fighters who had been trained by Sensei Benny came to visit our dojo. One of them was a world champion fighter named Pete 'Sugarfoot' Cunningham. I was blown away by the way he moved and his skill level. It made me realise just how much I had to learn.

When the smallest of the three fighters kicked a punching bag, it was harder than I had ever witnessed anybody hit before.

These guys were undeniably world class professional kick-boxers. I had an opportunity to spar with them and loved every minute of it. We flowed in a way that was exciting and I felt like I improved by experiencing each passing round. Afterwards I couldn't believe it when they took me aside and told me they thought I had the potential to be a world champion myself one day. I was majorly humbled and amazed. It's not often you hear something like that. They ignited a spark in me to go deeper into my Ukidokan training and I knew that one day it would lead me to the United States with Sensei Benny. The thought excited and terrified me. Yet it was inevitable, given that he was the only person who could give me a black belt in his family martial arts style. If I wanted to reach a high level, I would one day have to go to the US and ask him personally for a high rank. That day would come sooner than I had planned.

What hurts now might lead to the best rewards later.

6

The Bodyguard

Life and love soon took me to the North American continent for a few years in my early twenties, when I moved to Toronto, Canada. I was on a working visa and out of my young comfort zone. It quickly became apparent that not finishing high school had seriously limited my employment options. I waited tables to make ends meet and went back into the security field, but this time I moved towards doing close personal protection for music industry celebrities. I was hired by a company called Star Security that looked after singers and bands who came to Toronto. I had worked with celebrities before, but this was a whole new league of VIP.

Never one to be overly impressed by fame, I had always treated famous people as just people. In my eyes, they were normal folks who happened to be doing a very public and quite stressful job. Perhaps they just seemed like regular people because of the numerous trips to the bathroom I made with them. It was easy to be impressed by a singer like Sheryl Crow doing an unplugged performance on stage, but as the female in her security detail it was my job to escort her to the ladies' room. Hearing a celebrity tinkle takes the shine off a tiny bit.

It was also my job to make sure their often overexcited fans didn't become so overwhelmed by the occasion that they did something silly or inappropriate. Unfortunately this happened a lot in public appearances. Some fans bordered on obsession, even frighteningly so. During an autograph signing plus meet-and-greet at a music store with Sheryl Crow, I was scanning the waiting line of fans when I noticed a particular man. He had that slightly strange quality that set off my spidey senses. This is where women's intuition in personal protection comes in handy—my gut told me something was a little off about this guy. We spoke to him about why he was there and he explained that he was going to marry Sheryl that day. Simple as that. Perfectly rational in his own mind, with a scary air of determination. Upon further investigation we found he was known to police for stalking Alanis Morissette. So we decided it was best if maybe he didn't get to the front of the line and within arm's length of the person we were there to protect.

The level of crazy regularly depended on the type of fan that particular singer attracted. Naturally, Ladysmith Black Mambazo didn't bring out the wild fan behaviour I saw with Black Sabbath or Marilyn Manson. Some people had trouble obeying the rules of engagement, finally being so close to someone they idolised. If they were told it was acceptable to take a photo but not touch the singer, the more that famous person became the most irresistible tactile object known to man. Of course, there is only so much uninvited touching that a celebrity can handle and they all had different tolerance levels. When Ozzy Osbourne reached his ceiling and then continued to be groped by grown men lost in their super fandom moment, he hit the emergency eject button. We had to rush him out the back door of the venue, with the rest of the team left to deal with the disgruntled sea of fans who had missed out on meeting their idol. There's always somebody who takes it too far.

Sometimes we had to protect the celebrities from themselves. I once gently suggested to U2's Bono that he and Helena Christensen might want to move a little to their left. The singer and supermodel were watching someone else's performance from the pit at the front of the stage. They had unexpectedly wedged themselves between the stage and a barrier, which kept back the crowd of thousands. The problem was they were right beside a pyrotechnics cannon that I knew was to be used in the performance. I guess they thought I was being overzealous when I strongly suggested they needed to move. In the end I was yelling over the music at a confused Bono that they needed to move *right now*. Luckily I convinced them just before a huge spray of sparks emerged only a metre from where those prized faces had been.

Then there were the times when all I could do was watch and cross my fingers that everything would be okay. Usually, when a band is on stage, my eyes are on the crowd and not the performers. But Anthony Kiedis of the Red Hot Chili Peppers had massive energy when he was on stage, so he and his antics commanded my attention. I could only watch nervously during a performance in downtown Toronto as he climbed huge stacks of amplifiers and jumped off, before heading for the frame of the massive outdoor stage. Not only did he climb two storeys high to the top of the frame, but then he hung from it, while I mentally prepared for a VIP medical emergency. As I walked him to the waiting car afterwards, it took all my self-control not to give him a hard time for almost giving me a heart attack. I knew I wasn't there to be his mum or anything, but I sure didn't want to end up with the person I was there to protect splattered all over the stage like strawberry jam.

◆

Life in Toronto was fun but it also had its challenges. I was away from my friends, family and my martial arts school in Sydney. If I wanted to train then I had to do it myself. I struggled at first but found an unexpected burst of motivation in the most unusual of places. I will never forget walking into a Blockbuster video store (yes, that was back in the day of actual VHS tapes) and for the first time finding something called the Ultimate Fighting Championship (UFC). As a kid growing up in martial arts, there were always debates about what would happen if this style went up against that style. It was like kids talking about who would win if Spider-Man fought Batman. Debates raged on about who the victor would be between a boxer and sumo wrestler or a grappler versus a ninja, but there was never previously a way of knowing the actual outcome once and for all.

In my hands I held a sports video of all different martial arts styles testing themselves against one another for real. Granted it was not everybody's cup of tea, but I was fascinated. The UFC was very small at that stage and nobody I knew in Australia had ever heard of it. It began as more of a sideshow spectacle than the multi-billion-dollar prestige sporting behemoth it has become today. Naturally I rushed home to watch it as fast as my little Karate legs would carry me. From that first day, as I watched all the old martial arts debates get settled on the screen, I became an instant fan.

As I saw a small-framed Gracie Jiu Jitsu fighter defeat all the other styles, one thing became very clear—that I had to learn how to fight on the ground. I was so excited to learn whatever I could about grappling and found random people to show me what they knew. This led to some weird situations where I'd end up wrestling with guys in their apartments and garages. They knew something I didn't and I was desperate to learn. I went to Jiu Jitsu schools and got tapped out in ways I didn't even understand, but it was all blowing my mind.

To fight on the ground with submission holds and chokes was a revelation to a traditionally stand-up striker like myself. The more I came to understand leverage, the more comfortable I became as a smaller person dealing with a larger opponent. The more I studied, the more what I had already learned in Ukidokan started to open up. Grappling was part of my Ukidokan training but I was more comfortable on my feet. Being on the floor was something I had not hugely focused on until that point. Now with fresh eyes and acting like a mad scientist, I spent hours breaking down techniques and creating new endings. It was like I had been stumbling through learning a language and all of a sudden I had become fluent enough to have new conversations. I started to actually *understand* what I had already been taught in a whole new way.

Within a year after this point I got a call from Sensei Glenn, inviting me to meet the Australian Ukidokan students in Los

Angeles to train with Sensei Benny for the first time. I was so excited I almost dropped the phone after that first sentence and headed straight to the airport. When I calmed down I was asked to do my brown belt grading test, which is the belt immediately preceding black belt. I jumped at the chance but soon the reality hit me that I would have to do all the training alone to prepare. Prior to that time I was used to training with my friends in our nice comfy dojo in Sydney and being spoon-fed new techniques by my instructor. Now in Canada with no support crew, the training was all left to me. I spent countless hours in a freezing basement practising alone. If I wanted to make a good impression and do well when I trained with Sensei Benny, then I was going to have to prepare myself, by myself.

I made charts of what I had to practise and stuck them up all over the wall. Some were about being creative with my technique but many were simply blocks of hundreds of repetitions I knew needed to be done. To thoroughly understand a move, you have to repeat it many hundreds of times just as a base, then as the repetitions stretch into the thousands you earn the ability to stop thinking about the movement and can start to *feel* what you are doing. The starting point is memorising sequences, then coming to know them well, but to genuinely own your material takes a long time. Having other people to share that time with breaks things up. It was a whole new experience to be putting in the hard yards cold and solo in a sky blue painted basement in Toronto. I both loved and hated it at the same time. I've always tried to remember that repetitive hours of hard work don't have an immediate reward but if you stick it out, there might just be an unexpected pay-off down the road. This has been the case for me so many times that I know it to be true.

Finally I was going to have a chance to meet this martial arts master I had heard so much about. I trained like my life depended on it. I had devoted years to learning his martial arts system and was about to perform it in front of the man himself. It felt like I was going to play piano for Mozart. No pressure or anything. Much.

The hours of hard work you do alone will pay off in the future (even if only because you're proud of them).

7

Do You Feel Fear?

The first day I arrived in California I was wired with nerves. I met the Australian group at Sensei Benny's dojo called the Jet's Gym in Los Angeles. I couldn't believe I was actually finally walking into the place I had only dreamed of going. We all warmed up and dived right into training. I worked out with the instructors and shared with them some of what I had been practising, both traditional and new. Sensei Glenn asked me a lot of questions and seemed interested in what I had developed in my private subterranean Canadian martial arts workshop. There was a buzz in the air, an electricity, as we waited for Sensei Benny to arrive. I half-expected him to appear in a puff of smoke like a magician. I couldn't wait to meet him and now I finally knew how all those overexcited music fans had felt when meeting someone who meant so much to them.

Suddenly we were called to stop what we were doing as Sensei Benny walked into the room. We all bowed, as is tradition when the most senior teacher arrives. I felt a lump in my throat when I first saw this man who had become somewhat of a legend to me. There was something almost mystical about him. He moved so smoothly through the room, with an air of calm and confidence that was rock solid. His energy was almost tangible and as I bowed to him for the first time, my eyes welled up a little. The emotion was out of respect, not idolisation. Sensei Benny's martial art had given me something to believe in when I had needed it most and my gratitude flooded over me. This was a big deal juncture for me in a way I hadn't expected, which just made me more committed to doing well in my grading test.

Sensei Benny and Sensei Glenn greeted each other and quickly disappeared, leaving the students to train. I was excited and nervous, with no idea what was going to happen next. It was like Christmas morning and doomsday all at once. My senses were super heightened with the thought of the challenge ahead. I was unsure about how hard the test would be or what I would have to do. I'd heard Sensei Benny was a hard man to impress and a traditionalist at heart, which meant none of this was going to be easy. I was jumping at noises and my eyes darted around the room. I was ready for anything, or so I thought.

Without warning I was quickly summoned next door to a restaurant where Sensei Glenn and Sensei Benny had been having a meeting. I ran over there then tried to slow down as I entered the back room where the instructors were seated in a large leather booth. Images of the film *The Godfather* flashed through my mind as I was told to sit down. I was so thrilled to finally have the opportunity to talk to Sensei Benny in person. As I slipped into the booth, I had all the eagerness of a puppy. I was met with Sensei Benny looking at me very seriously, with almost an icy glare. No warm introduction, no smiles and not the happy meeting I had envisioned. It felt like when you see someone run enthusiastically straight into the jarring stop of a sliding glass door. One minute everything was great, the next everything was very much not. I was instantly thrown off balance mentally and felt confused, as if I had inadvertently done something wrong. Sensei Benny was letting an awkward silence hang in the air between us as he looked me over with hard eyes.

'Do you feel fear?' Sensei Benny said to me.

The way he delivered this line almost made my heart stop. He looked me dead in the eye and said it almost as a challenge. I was knocked sideways in surprise at the way our first conversation was beginning. Of all the myriad ways I had imagined this moment, it had never included him being cold and serious towards me.

In my best attempt to gather myself and seem nonchalant, I replied, 'Yes, everybody does.' I didn't want to let him see that I was somewhat afraid of what was to come. I didn't want to be singled out as being scared at all and I absolutely didn't want him to think I was intimidated because I was a woman.

Sensei Benny let my answer hang in the air for a few seconds as it turned sour like week-old milk. He shook his head and said, 'No, there are people out there who have no fear. Some fear no man and others aren't psychologically capable of feeling fear.'

I felt foolish about what I had said. I resisted the strong urge to recant my answer and just agree with his. I had a massive rush of wanting to tell him that of course I knew that and he was correct, but it wouldn't have mattered anyway. This wasn't about being right. It was about him seeing if I would be honest or if I would hide my real feelings. It wasn't a hard question but where and when he asked me made it even trickier to answer.

What I didn't understand at the time about that conversation was that Sensei Benny is a person who gets straight to the heart of the matter. He would rather aim directly for your truth and see if you firstly even know it and secondly have the courage to speak it. I had attempted to be honest, but had added a disclaimer. I didn't yet have the knowledge of myself or of him to understand that the best thing to do was just say the truest thing, with no smokescreen around it. This is always the best policy, but at times saying the truest thing can be the absolute hardest thing to do.

I didn't know the grading test had already begun. It started the second Sensei Benny saw me. This first conversation was a way for him to see who I was, if I was self-aware and who I would be in my dynamic with him. Silly me for thinking the test would start when we stepped onto the training mat. Martial arts was never just about the physical training for Sensei Benny, so he was looking at my all-round character. This gave him an idea of how I would carry myself in the world and handle all the things I knew how to do physically.

That first time we spoke was a decidedly unsettling experience. We talked for about ten minutes and he basically asked me what my intentions were. Sensei Glenn had taken stock of where I was now at in my training, including all the new learning I had done. He had suggested to Sensei Benny that I might be ready for my black belt test, rather than the lower-level brown belt exam which I was expecting. Another student named Toby was there to be graded for his black belt, so it was put forward that I should do the same test. But Sensei Benny wanted to meet me first and see if I could 'hold water', as he put it, which meant assessing if I was strong enough mentally and emotionally to get through the experience. So it was decided. I would be given the opportunity to do the Shodan (first level) black belt test.

The freaking out on my part immediately began in earnest. That one small conversation had dented my confidence already. Despite this test being a huge honour, my head started flooding with a deluge of reasons why maybe I couldn't do it, why I wasn't ready and why I might fail. I wanted so badly to do this, but I was also afraid to do it.

It's so easy to psyche yourself out before you even start something. We convince ourselves we are not capable of things, mostly because we are scared to fail. Most people are afraid to fail, especially publicly, let alone in front of those who they respect most. When the risk is too great, the natural inclination is to avoid.

We've all watched someone defeat themselves without trying, whether it was at the idea of asking someone out on a date, changing careers or losing weight. We fast-forward in our minds to the end part where things didn't turn out the way we had hoped, then apply that feeling to the present. Nothing kills a dream like imagining it being crushed. This is the key time where a dose of courage helps. To do or not to do the hard thing, to begin or not to begin. Yet the only people who are able to realise their dreams are the ones who start. It's impossible to finish if you don't start. We all know it, but do we live by it? How many things are there in your life that you *could* have done?

When I was offered the opportunity to do my black belt test, I had to consciously choose to start it. I had to say yes to the challenge, even though my head was giving me all the reasons in the world why I wasn't going to be successful. Call it chutzpah, blind faith or just a few brave seconds when I knew that I would

regret taking the easy road. I decided to do it and give it everything I had. Little did I know how hard the road ahead would
prove to be.

◆

The black belt grading was a week-long test, during which I spent
the vast majority of the time thinking that I had failed. Sensei
Benny didn't make me feel any better about it as he glared at me
from behind his clipboard while I attempted to perform the techniques he required. It was so stressful and gruelling that I lost 10
kilos. I was already quite fit so I'm not sure where I lost it from
exactly. I ended up covered in small bruises from the knocks of
daily training, which made me look like a purple leopard. There
were days of drills and constant assessment where I was told by
the most senior instructor that I moved like a white belt beginner.
I tried not to let that statement get to me, but of course it did.
Was I actually that bad? An unfamiliar self-doubt crept in and
permeated everything I did. A move that I was usually very confident with somehow became awkward and hesitant. I felt like
I didn't have the right answer to anything I was asked and started
to doubt the things I knew well. It seemed I was now standing
on slippery ice instead of solid ground. What I didn't understand
was that was exactly where Sensei Benny wanted me.

On Friday, towards the end of the test week, we had a full
formal day of martial arts examinations. The kickboxing or
sport element in the boxing ring would be tested the day after
on the Saturday. As we warmed up for Friday's Karate session,
we were told to put on our hand wraps, which is usually done
for boxing. I dutifully complied, thinking that the test days must

have been swapped around. Then Sensei Benny proceeded to test us for hours on our Karate curriculum. I was completely confused about why I was wearing hand wraps, with the bandages constantly coming undone and distracting me. After the fiftieth time they got tangled, I asked to take them off. Sensei said no, looking at me as if I'd asked a ridiculous question. Even as I did high pressure drills against a circle of much bigger opponents attacking me one after the other, I had to leave the wraps on. I was so distracted by having to quickly gather them up every time they came loose. I would be just starting to tuck them away when the next guy would attack me. It didn't make sense and it was messing up everything I was trying to do.

Sensei Benny has never been interested in what I call my 'best day abilities'—if I could perform a series of moves perfectly, he would watch it once and then ask me to do it backwards, left handed or blindfolded. Knowing the moves well enough to perform them correctly was usually the black belt standard in most martial arts, but it was just the beginning for him. One of the central premises of Ukidokan is to be able to *control your emotions under pressure*. So that meant Sensei Benny was always interested in applying pressure situations. He constantly kept me off balance to see what I could do with my 'worst day abilities'.

I later found out the hand wraps had indeed been totally unnecessary for the Karate test and served no purpose other than to deliberately distract me. Sensei Benny wanted me to be uncomfortable and stressed. He had planted that seed from the instant we met. Sensei wasn't very interested in watching me execute hours of perfectly pre-rehearsed memorised movements. He wanted to see how well I actually knew what I was doing and how I would react when things seemed to be going wrong.

It made sense because if you have to defend yourself for real, there's a good chance you'd have some difficult emotions to deal with at the same time.

How good are your 'worst day abilities'?
Make it so you shine on the tough days, too.

There were three levels of learning knowledge for a teacher like him. The first was to *memorise* what you had been taught and I saw many students get stuck at this phase. The second level was to *know* the techniques well, which required a good understanding in addition to memorisation. The last level was *owning* what you had been taught, so that it became part of you. This meant you could do it upside down and back to front. The goal was to understand what you had learnt so well that the knowledge became fully yours to use in any given situation. Under great pressure, you will always go to the things you know best.

The pressure went through the roof when we were tested on a defensive movement involving a simulation of being held up at gunpoint. It was a sequence for disarming an attacker standing behind you. I had performed it countless times, and had an understanding of how to avoid being shot, moving with your opponent, trapping the gun and ultimately disarming the attacker. In training we usually used a rubber pistol that looked real enough. On test day, Sensei Benny brought out a high-powered metal air pistol that fired copper pellet balls. He made a point of slowly loading it directly in front of Toby and me. We knew we were about to have the pistol pointed at our backs.

Sensei test-fired it away from us towards a wall and I felt a cold chill as the pellet ricocheted around the gym. It bounced off one wall, then off another wall on the other side of the gym and kept going which made me extra nervous. That gun had some real power to it.

Sensei Benny selected Damien, another one of the students who was also doing a grading, to be the attacker holding the gun. He told Damien that the second he saw us flinch he was to fire the pistol. If he hesitated, he would fail his own test. The pressure on all of us went up exponentially. We were told that if the copper ball was fired into our backs, it would cause a penetrating wound to the skin, but would not go through us like a bullet. *Oh well,* I thought, *that's a relief, not.* The gun had some major ballistic force and I knew Sensei had methodically demonstrated it right in front of us so we would understand just how serious the threat level actually was. Sensei Benny had been stabbed and shot at in real life, so this was a scenario he expected a black belt to be able to deal with.

Toby had to go first and luckily didn't get shot. Sensei Benny has a way of making you feel an intense amount of pressure just by looking at you, so he made sure Toby was under maximum stress during this important part of the test. He was so churned up by the experience that his eyes welled up a little afterwards. Then it was my turn.

The first time the air gun was placed in the middle of my back, I was in such a hurry to disarm my attacker that once I got him to the ground, I let go of his arm in order to strike him. Unfortunately, this was the arm that had the gun in it. I recovered the weapon but couldn't believe I'd made such a simple mistake. The nerves and pressure were real and it was affecting me. Sensei Benny shook his head. The whole point was to get the gun, and I had blown it.

I had one more chance to do it properly. True to form Sensei was going to make it even harder for me to get it right second time around. This time I felt the gun's muzzle at the back of my skull. I visualised flinching as I turned and poor Damien firing that copper ball into my eye. Being permanently blinded was not like a cut that would heal. A real trepidation now swept over me. This was not a game or a safely controlled pretend experiment, this was really dangerous. I had the option to call things off at any point and I knew nobody was forcing me to do this. But having had encounters when I worked in bars with people carrying weapons, I needed to know that I could handle this pressure successfully. I decided if I was in a life or death situation when I had to disarm someone with a gun to my head, I would need to know I could do it. I also hoped this was as close as I would ever come.

My fear made me move super fast and Damien hit the ground hard face down. I had him in an arm and shoulder lock that would have broken both if I'd needed to. I put my full body weight on his back, pinning him through my knee as I stripped the weapon out of his hand. Now that he was disarmed, I knew why Toby had felt so emotional. The rush of adrenaline also brought a rush of emotion. Although this part of the test was under controlled circumstances, the threat of injury was very real. I knew my fear didn't make me weak, but was completely logical and sensible. We were expected to learn to face our fears head on.

I was still emotional at the end of testing on Friday. All of the mistakes I'd made that day were racing through my mind like

Fear doesn't make you weak. Courage is built on being scared.

a movie. I went to Sensei Benny afterwards to apologise for my poor performance. I knew I was capable of doing much better than I had demonstrated, plus I was upset because I didn't think I had done well enough to pass the test. I was disappointed in myself and as I spoke to him frustrated tears rolled down my face. This meant so much to me but it wasn't going very well. The fact that I was now also crying about it made me feel embarrassed that he could see I was so emotional. Sensei listened to me intently with the same stern face that I was now coming to think was his only expression.

When I was finished, he reached his hand out towards the side of my face and for a second I worried he might give me a clip over the ear for being so silly. Instead he waved for me to move towards him and although he'd given me no reason to ever think he would hurt me, I was a little scared. He beckoned me again and I was surprised when he pulled me into a gentle hug. He softly said to me, 'Just come back tomorrow.'

I was at once comforted and confused by his response. Even if I was failing, did that mean he just wanted me to complete the testing? Did it mean I'd done a good enough job to continue? Was he feeling sorry for me or trying to encourage me? I was so utterly confused by Sensei. I kept reminding myself that I had to learn to control my emotions under pressure and the pressure had never been so great. One thing was for sure though, no matter what the outcome if I didn't go back tomorrow I would never have any chance of finishing either way.

♦

The next morning was the infamous Saturday Breakfast Club which was full-contact kickboxing sparring, during which we would be doing the combat sport element of the grading test. I'd heard legendary stories about how hard these sessions were and I had been dreading it all week. If there was ever a time to get a taxi to the airport, it was unquestionably Saturday morning. I had no idea exactly what to expect, but I was expecting it to be painful. I wasn't used to hard contact ring sparring yet and knew that many of my opponents that day would be experienced fighters who trained under Sensei Benny. All the confidence I had at the start of the week was gone. All the excitement about my newfound grappling skills had left, too, as I knew none of that would help me against bigger kickboxing adversaries. All that was left was my exhausted body and almost broken will. Not the best weapons to have in your arsenal. I was still emotional from the day before and knew that I would likely be out of my depth. I had come incredibly close to giving up so many times during the week, at one point having a phone pulled from my hand as I wanted to call Sensei to tell him I quit. But Sensei Benny had told me to come back the next morning and when your Sensei tells you to do something, you are expected to do it without question. This would be the hardest part of the test and I had to do it when I felt at my weakest mentally and physically. So there I found myself anyway, in the boxing ring.

We spent an hour going through all kinds of intense drills and exhausting exercises which left me feeling like I had almost nothing left in the tank. My arms were like lead and my legs were numb with tiredness. That's when I found out the first hour had just been the warm-up. I was in shock, as I had given my best effort already and the main part was yet to come. I had no idea how many rounds I would have to do in the ring. I almost broke down at the thought of getting hurt, which at this stage would most likely happen because I was too tired to raise my hands beside my head in defence. The only thing between my face and their strikes would be the heavy sixteen-ounce gloves I would have to hold up as a guard. I started to feel afraid and wanted to run. The urge to quit shot through me like electricity in a last sensible effort by my brain to save my body from harm. But I had come this far and knew that even if I failed, there would be a certain satisfaction in just surviving. If Navy Seals have 'Hell Week' to measure themselves by, then I had my own week of hell in this grading test. To get through to the end would be an achievement in itself.

The first sparring round I had was against a much bigger Australian fighter who had moved to Los Angeles to train with Sensei Benny and pursue his professional fighting career. As the bell sounded, my adrenaline dumped into my bloodstream leaving me feeling like I was stuck in wet cement. I could barely raise my gloves and was moving in slow motion. I had never experienced this extreme fight-or-flight reaction in my body chemistry before and it made me panic. It continued for another few rounds, while all I could do was hang in there and try to stay calm amid my panic. I attempted to dodge shots and occasionally fire back with whatever energy I could muster. It felt like a bad dream. With Sensei Benny watching from the side of the ring, that terrible feeling I was failing threatened to completely overwhelm me again. It was a heady mix of disappointment and embarrassment that made it even harder to perform physically.

Opponent after opponent, round after round, I struggled through and occasionally had flashes of success. Most of the time I was discovering what I was doing wrong the hard way. One of my toughest opponents was a female American fighter, coincidentally also named Nadine. She was a student of Sensei Benny's sister Sensei Lilly, who was also a world champion kickboxer. Nadine was a lawyer and attacked with the same precision I'm sure she used in the courtroom. She was slightly shorter than me, but very fast and tough. With my back to the ropes I tried to attack, but Nadine ducked down and popped up over my gloves with an overhand right punch. I heard my nose crack and a lightning bolt of blinding pain mixed with surprise. This was no longer just sparring. I had to fight and I had to fight right now. I battled Nadine the best I could through my exhaustion. I felt like she got the better of me, but I gave absolutely everything I had left in the tank.

Sunday saw the end of the grading test week and a celebration barbecue at Sycamore Beach, up the coast past Malibu. I was nursing some bumps and bruises from the day before at Breakfast Club. It's called that because afterwards everyone goes next door and has breakfast together while Sensei talks about internal training. Basically it's a chance for everyone to make peace after the intense feelings that hard contact brings up. It was team bonding after you'd just punched each other in the face. It was odd but it was perfect. I had sat at breakfast with ice packs attached to me in a number of places and melting ice cubes on my bruised nose and knuckles. We were a close-knit group of people with a shared understanding. I loved every minute.

My opponent Nadine from the day before came up to me at Sunday's barbecue and said she had something for me. My pride was a little bruised as I wished I had done better during our time in the ring, but I had a huge sense of respect for her. She hadn't let me off lightly, but instead had pushed me further than I thought I could go. I felt overexposed but also grateful to her because she had taught me a lesson about what I could handle. She had taken me swimming out in the deep water. It was tough for me to know that she had seen me at my worst. I felt a little diffident as she was much more experienced than I was. What happened next blew me away. Nadine gave me a pair of her 'Jet Fighter' kickboxing shorts which meant you were part of Sensei Benny's fight team. She said that she wanted to honour the heart I had shown in the ring against her. These weren't just any shorts, they were the ones she had just won her last fight in, complete with little blood spatters to prove it. She wanted me to have them.

There is a tradition in martial arts where you pass your fighting spirit on to someone else through something you have used in training. That is also why we don't wash our Karate belts. The sentiment is that your spirit is captured in the hours of training, the effort, the sweat and strengthening of character born from exertion. The same is true for fighting shorts. I was so touched by the gesture and I promised Nadine I would fight in those shorts myself one day.

I thanked my new friend and as we talked about the grading, I explained that it didn't matter I probably hadn't passed, because I had managed to make it through the whole week. I knew I would just come back next year and try again. I could have taken the easier road and just done my brown belt grading but I'd made the choice to go all the way. The real learning had been in just coming back each day to complete the black belt test, whether I was ultimately successful or not. Sometimes it's more about finishing what you started and resisting the urge to quit. If you give up, it means you can't finish. There is something to be said for simply staying the course.

It was right after those words had left my mouth that Sensei Benny called the group together and asked me to stand at the front. I was taken aback when he announced that I had actually passed the test. I was being given only the twenty-first black belt in the world to be awarded by Sensei Benny in Ukidokan Karate and Ukidokan Kickboxing. Everything suddenly became clear, from the harsh words to the disapproving looks. What mattered was my belief in what I could achieve and not letting that be swayed by the opinions of others. It had come down to how badly I wanted it. Sensei explained that succeeding didn't mean you weren't afraid along the way, or that the path should be easy. Quite the opposite, actually. The journey was about being willing to go through the hardest parts in order to reach the best parts. Stop halfway and you will never find out what might be at the end of the long road.

You can learn to control your emotions under pressure. If you give up, you rob yourself of any chance to succeed. *Just come back tomorrow.*

YOU ARE WHO YOU TELL YOURSELF YOU ARE

ROUND 3

CHANGE YOUR THINKING

Learning lessons with my eyes wide open as
Sensei Benny and Sensei Sara watch intently.

8

You Are Who You Say You Are

From my first meeting with Sensei Benny I knew that he was a special human being. He had a way about him that was unlike anyone I had ever met before. He had the presence of a man who had achieved more than most and was quietly confident in who he was. Sensei modelled what healthy self-esteem looked like and encouraged me to treat myself with a new level of inner regard. He taught everything in a unique way that would often hit me like a ton of bricks. The meaning and complexity he wove into things is what made them stick. Even simple truths became powerful when he aimed them at me, like when he explained that *you are who you say you are*. You are who you tell yourself you are. You are who you believe you are.

Now I'm not talking in the sense of wishing you were rich and famous, then fairy dust sprinkles over you, followed by a puff of smoke and all of your dreams magically coming true. I'm talking about your own positive and negative self-perception about who you are and what you're capable of. Your beliefs about yourself dictate how you respond to your life and the place you make for yourself in the world. Maybe you tell yourself you're only smart enough to do the job you've got now and shouldn't ever try to reach any higher. Maybe you stay in a relationship with someone who doesn't treat you the right way. It could be that you have a dream but you have already decided it will never happen for you. If you're the one deciding you deserve less than the best, then that is usually what will happen. I knew from experience that telling myself a negative message in my own mind was like holding up a cement ceiling above my own head. Sensei made it his mission to teach me how to tell myself a positive message and to get out of my own way.

The way he spoke at times reminded me of Yoda from *Star Wars,* in mystical riddles that didn't make sense until the student had learnt enough to understand the teacher. He was always challenging and testing me. I knew I had found my own Mr Miyagi in him, a teacher whose skill and wisdom were unique. Over the next twenty years Sensei Benny taught me many truly life-changing lessons.

My dad had only been gone a short time when I met Sensei, so naturally he became somewhat of a father figure to me. He had said to me early on that I could choose to call him Benny or Sensei. He was giving me the opportunity to decide the direction of my connection with him. Did I want to be his friend or did I want a teacher? To this day I have never once called him 'Benny'. This is despite the fact that we are very close. I love him dearly and he stays at my house when visiting Australia. It's not about being forced to be overly formal, but instead about maintaining a valuable tradition. Showing him this respect has never cost me more than an extra word when speaking to him, but to remove it would cost me more than I could explain.

There are lots of martial arts traditions that I keep alive in our student/teacher relationship. Whenever I first see Sensei, be it at the gym, in an airport or a restaurant, I will always bow as a sign of recognition before I give him a hug. I know it sounds more like something you'd see in downtown Tokyo, but for me it's a small reminder to always know my place with him and not become overly chummy. The formal part of our connection provides a valuable structure that sets it apart. I have many friends, but I will only ever have one Sensei.

An uncommon trait about him is that he was never interested in being referred to as a master (or Shihan). At his stage of experience he surely qualifies for revered martial arts master status. Yet he is happy to humbly be called a Sensei, which is more like a humble teacher. I think being pigeon-holed as a master for many people means not having the flexibility to also be a student. Sensei always tries to maintain the white belt mentality, meaning he is always open to learning more. He values being a student more than he needs others to show him greater reverence by making him a master. He asked me never to place him on a pedestal because he is just a person, as fallible as any of us, though having said that he has never let me down. Sensei Benny knows exactly who he is.

One of the most important lessons I ever learnt concerning respect was about showing it to myself. It is easy to say and harder to live. The more I became aware of paying homage, it highlighted the ways in my life I wasn't treating myself as

I would have liked. A wise woman once said to me, 'Show yourself the respect you deserve.' In hearing those words said with love, I knew I wasn't showing myself that same level of love as I was showing others. I saw how much other people were struggling with this, too. I watched the same battle manifest itself in so many forms around me. It shows in what (or how much) we eat and drink, who we have relationships with, what we say to or about ourselves and ultimately what we believe we are worth. I had to ask myself if all the choices I was making were in line with the good things I wanted for myself.

I took a hard look at both the small and large decisions I was making in my life. I started to see more clearly where I was showing true esteem for myself, but also where I was lacking perspective. I imagined my younger self and how I would treat her. When you think of little kids, hopefully you attach feelings of love and kindness towards them. Our relationships with our adult selves are so much more complicated than this simple loving kindness. Who wants to have their lives run by someone who isn't on their best behaviour? So I decided to gauge my decisions and behaviour towards myself on how I would treat a three-year-old version of me. I would never give her a brutally harsh verbal critique, give her big servings of unhealthy food, make her work ridiculously long hours or let her be around people who weren't good for her. I had to admit that despite some of my behaviour to the contrary, she was deserving of all my love and kindness. The more I thought of the type of gentle advice I would give to myself if I were a kid, the softer and more supportive my inner voice became.

How would you treat three-year-old you?

◆

All of the lessons I was picking up about respect were having an effect on the way I viewed where I stood in the world. Getting my black belt had forever changed the way I thought about what I was capable of achieving. My grading test had taught me that if you work hard and don't give up, then you can eventually succeed at things that seemed impossible. I took stock of the areas in my life where I didn't feel a sense of achievement and found I was the only one holding myself back. One area stood out for me like a neon sign in Vegas—my abruptly halted education.

I felt a bit ashamed about not finishing school. I didn't want to be a high school drop-out with limited options for the rest of my life. I wanted more for myself.

When I came back to Australia at twenty-three with my freshly minted black belt, I decided I had to go back to school. I was brimming with the enthusiasm of a fresh achievement in Los Angeles that made me feel strong enough to face my demons. I knew it wouldn't be easy to take what in some ways would feel like a backwards step in moving forward. Having spent years supporting myself meant the idea of studying full-time was daunting because it would limit my income. But the thought of never addressing the issue was far worse than having less money in the bank. So I swallowed my pride and enrolled to do a bridging year at Randwick TAFE.

That year was tough and I was way out of my comfort zone. Being uncomfortable for twelve months was a challenge, but I told myself that it was short-term pain for long-term gain. At the end of that year I would have completed my high school equivalency and would be free of the self-imposed drop-out tag forever. I wanted to give myself a more positive trademark for internal use. The old one was way past its expiry date.

I spent countless hours at TAFE studying and looking out the window past the Randwick Racecourse to the giant white UNSW sign atop the library at the University of New South Wales. I knew it was one of the best universities in the country and I dared to let myself dream I might go there one day. It kept me focused and pushing forward when things got challenging.

I nervously waited for the end of year results where a university entrance score would be awarded. I had to furiously battle all of my old limiting self-beliefs as the suspense made them flood back into my mind. Part of me had felt like leaving school must have meant I wasn't smart or good enough. I was afraid my results might prove that to be true.

When I finally saw my score, I was elated to see it was in the mid-90s out of a possible 100. I was accepted into UNSW to study criminology and social policy. My excitement soon became diluted by a new set of fears about whether I would be able to succeed at university.

On the first day of induction at UNSW, I swear I must have been the happiest new student on campus. I felt like a big nerd with my brand new notebooks and pens but I was old enough to appreciate the opportunity I now had. A big group of senior students noisily barrelled around a corner to welcome all the first-year students and show us around. As they ran towards me, I felt a small tear slide down my cheek while I stood in the middle of that university lawn. I had made it. I was going to get a tertiary education. Granted I was nervous and concerned about how I would pay for it as a mature-age student without a full-time income, but I was just so excited to be there.

Then the heavy workload started and the fear of failure kicked in. As I handed in my first essay to be marked, I was worried that I might be in the wrong place. What if I got good grades at TAFE but would get poor marks at university? What if I had just tentatively returned to a positive self-image around my education and then it all comes crashing down, heartbreakingly, in the first few weeks of uni? I used the 'three-year-old' concept to tell myself it would be okay if I didn't do very well on my first essay, that I would try harder next time and get better with practice. I told myself it wasn't the end of the world and that my value wasn't solely tied to one mark, on one assignment. Gulp.

A week later, all these thoughts spun in my head as I waited outside the lecturer's office to pick up my essay. Once it was in my hand, I was so nervous I had to walk a few metres down the hall before I could even take a squinty look. As I turned the papers over, I saw I'd been given a high distinction, which was the best possible score. I did a little victory dance down the hallway. Okay, so maybe it was a medium-to-large-sized victory dance as all of my fears about not being good enough fell away. I was meant to be here, I was going to be able to handle it and might even do well.

I was so heartened by that first result and it set the standard for my whole degree. Once I knew I could do it once, that meant I could do it time and again. I used all the perseverance and discipline I had gained from my martial arts to push myself through to the end. I knew all I had to do was just come back tomorrow. When I graduated I became the first person in my family to earn a degree and it was all thanks to the lessons I learnt from getting my black belt. Achieving one milestone had made achieving others seem possible if I was prepared to work hard and believe that maybe I could do it. The seeds had been planted and I was watching them grow.

Treat yourself with the respect you deserve.

9

Nudist Camp

There are some experiences that have the power to change you forever. They can be a brief moment or a whole new direction that dictates where your fate will take you. Martial arts have always been that for me, the directing force on the compass needle that altered my life's course. Many of us have made the seemingly random choice to take up a sport or hobby without realising the long-term effects it might have on our lives. Maybe it just changes what you do on a Saturday afternoon for six weeks, or as in my case it may change you so deeply that your entire life would look different had you not pursued it.

I owe all the best things that have ever happened to me to my martial arts training, either directly or by association. I am more grateful for it than I can ever express and feel blessed to have been able to take the journey I have. Whether you believe things are pre-ordained or not, it still blows my mind that I met a teacher like Sensei Benny and had the opportunity to spend decades learning from him.

Every lesson Sensei Benny taught me in the gym has shaped who I am in my everyday life. I have been willingly coloured by it, all the while knowing how rare it is to find your true teacher. He always taught me to give away my knowledge and not hoard it for myself. So I have devoted myself to teaching everything I was lucky enough to be taught, as I saw how many people around me wished they had their own Sensei Benny/Yoda/ Mr Miyagi.

Sensei Benny wanted to teach me and I was hungry to learn what was on offer. It felt like arriving at a Las Vegas mega buffet when you've prepared by not eating all day. The only spanner in the works was that Sensei lived in Los Angeles and I lived in Sydney. As a university student I wasn't exactly raking in the big bucks, so international travel required some serious saving. I was desperate to get back to the States and have another dose of Ukidokan. After many months I managed to save enough cash to go on a training visit to see Sensei Benny.

I arrived at the Jet's Gym in North Hollywood, California, full to the brim with enthusiasm, but with a fairly empty wallet. My trip had only been made possible by Sensei offering to let me stay at the gym. I was so happy to be there that I didn't mind sleeping on the floor. A roll-out padded mat in a back room was a small sacrifice compared to what I was gaining.

Sensei Benny grew up in the San Fernando Valley, which was not necessarily the most economically flourishing area of Los Angeles. He knew what it was like to not have much money as a young person. Without me having to tell him directly, he knew exactly where I was at. He saved my pride by taking the lead and looking after me. The first day I was there he had one of his senior students named Majid take me to the local Dollar Store to buy some food. I left with grocery bags filled with discount cans of tuna. Now, I don't particularly love tuna, but it was on sale and I knew the protein would fill me up. During my stay I ate so much of that damn fish that I still cannot eat it to this day. It was humbling (aka it sucked) to not be able to go next door to the restaurant and eat with the other fighters. Instead I would retire to my back room and enjoy yet another portion of questionably tasty tuna. The feelings of not having much, just made me more determined to pursue my passion.

I had saved enough money for the trip and my mum had generously given me the funds for one private lesson with Sensei Benny. Every day I trained in the group classes at the gym, but I was excited to learn from him one-on-one. Knowing I could only afford one session, I made sure I was well prepared and took my notebook with me. I wanted to remember everything he said and did. Sensei expected it. We both knew this would be the food I would take away and digest for a year.

I nervously warmed up before our scheduled 11 a.m. start so I would be fully ready when the time arrived. When we started, we started fast. Sensei took me on a journey through all of the techniques I knew and many I was learning brand new that day. We stopped to discuss certain points, because Sensei wanted to teach me why we did things and not just get me to copy the movements. Real confidence comes from experience and understanding, where false confidence comes from copying a move but not understanding how to use it.

When Sensei Benny slid his small circular focus mitts on his hands I knew we were doing some boxing training. He would never let me hit these pads hard, instead insisting that I focus on accuracy and precision. That just increased the pressure and I was so stressed about doing everything right that my mind was getting in my way. It was written all over my face. Sensei went from telling me to relax and have fun, to suddenly stopping and looking at me sternly. He said, 'You're wasting my time, my dear.'

I was shocked and disconcerted because I thought he was saying that I was making so many mistakes it was pointless for him to train me. Geez, I didn't think I was that bad. Instead Sensei explained to me that we had precious little time together. All the minutes I spent beating myself up meant that I was mentally disengaging from being connected with him. Every time I made a mistake I would start thinking about how I'd just blown it and checking out from what I was doing for a short period. The voice in my head was giving me a harder time than Sensei ever would. He had to wait for me to stop talking to myself negatively inside my head before he could get my full attention again. It was an unnecessary waste of his time because he didn't care if I made mistakes. He expected it. Sensei said I would get more out of our session by just giving myself a break and the freedom to make a truckload of errors. He told me that my mistakes were mine and were a part of me just as much as my strengths.

Sensei gave me something to do so I could counteract my initial reaction when I made an error—I should smile at it. He then

Don't waste precious time beating yourself up.

asked if I would give myself permission to make mistakes. I knew logically that I would make errors for the rest of my life and there was no point giving myself a hard time about it. He told me that learning required the freedom to get things wrong. Otherwise we miss the point, which is to grow instead of trying to be perfect. He had been watching me criticise myself and it was a waste of both of our time together. So the new plan became to quickly reset my mind when I made a mistake, by looking Sensei in the eye instead of getting lost in my own thoughts. What a relief that was. It felt great to not have to waste so much time on self-criticism.

Sensei taught me to learn in a way that was so engaging it felt like time stood still and nothing else existed. When we finally bowed to each other to finish the private session, I looked up at the clock. It was after 4 p.m. which meant that instead of the one-hour training session I had paid for, Sensei Benny had given me more than five hours of his time. We had both forgotten to eat lunch or use the restroom. This was a new level of connection and absorption in learning and I wanted more. I was hooked and knew that my future lay on a shared path with his. I was blown away by how generous he had been with me. That taught me just as much as the actual session.

◆

Being in that Los Angeles gym with all the professional fighters was an immersion in another world for me. I was just a little blonde Aussie girl in my early twenties, trying to hold my own in a new place full of seasoned veterans. I did my best to play it cool, but I often felt like I was swimming out of my depth. It was vaguely familiar water and rapidly becoming more so, but

I was still in way over my head. Plus, I was in a foreign country. Granted it was an English-speaking Western country, yet things were different than at home. Like saying hello to someone in the gym. Back in Australia at my martial arts dojo, we would bow to each other Karate style. In LA the gym was a combination of martial artists and fighters competing in combat ring sports, so there were all kinds of ways to say hi.

I will never forget the first time I met a champion African-American fighter named Thunderwolf. I heard him from across the room before I saw him. His personality was just as big as his imposing muscular frame. Thunderwolf was standing beside the boxing ring coaching someone as I was introduced to him. He stuck out his hand and I went to shake it, but at the last second I saw he was holding out his closed fist. As we brought our knuckles together, I gave him my first ever official fist-bump. I couldn't have gotten more Caucasian if I'd tried. But I was young enough to also feel super cool in that moment, like I was in a scene from *Rocky*. I even self-consciously ran through it in my mind later, hoping I did the fist-bump right, using the correct amount of force and nonchalance, etc. Oh boy, so uncool.

Having watched how much pressure I was putting on myself in the gym, Sensei told me I was taking everything too seriously. I was surprised as I thought that was kind of the whole point. Clearly he was older and wiser, knowing dedication always has to be counterbalanced by some fun. Sensei demanded I go out and have a good time. He asked a group of the gym's female fighters to take me out one night. While it was a nice offer, I immediately started to panic because I was so short on spending money. It was a tough spot to be in, because I didn't want to miss out but I also couldn't really afford it. I knew I should just say something, but my pride got in the way. I didn't want anyone to pity me. Sensei gave me an ultimatum by saying that he was going to call the gym that evening and if I was there, he would come by and kick me out. I knew he meant it. So I did as I was told and went out to dinner with the girls.

They took me to Mel's Diner on Sunset Boulevard. I loved the classic American feel of the old-style booths. It made me feel like I was on an episode of the television show *Happy Days*. I scanned the menu for the cheapest option and went with a burger. I felt confident I could get through this without having to say anything to blow my financial cover. Then the bill came. I had forgotten about tipping on top of the bill. The girls generously covered it for me but I felt bad about it. A horrible humiliating feeling rose inside me and I made a silent vow to myself that this would be the last time I felt this way.

I knew the reason I didn't have much money was because I had spent the past four years studying, not because I was lazy or I'd blown all my holiday cash on piña coladas. I was young and on a mission, with a budget that didn't allow for too much flashy spending. Still, I couldn't shake the murky feeling of shame that was slowly creeping up my spine. I told myself one day I would be successful and order whatever I wanted from that restaurant's menu. Each time I have gone on a trip to LA since, I always go back to Mel's Diner and fulfil that promise to myself (and my belly).

The next day Sensei Benny and I spoke about what had happened at dinner with the girls. I felt uncomfortable as the words left my mouth, explaining the tipping situation or lack thereof to him. I tried to resist the urge to cover up my embarrassment. I trusted him and as much as it made me cringe to admit it, I also cared what he thought of me. It's tough to feel vulnerably exposed that way in front of someone you look up to. That was when he casually dropped into the conversation that he was going to take me to a nudist camp. I tried to keep a straight face or at least not panic. My mind raced from a feeling of confusion, to wondering if this was some type of California hippie thing. I was a believer in dutifully doing what your Sensei tells you to do, but this was going way too far. A sense of worry began to rise in me, that I might have misjudged him.

Sensei looked at me seriously and said that our training necessitated being in a nudist camp. I had sudden visions of high kicks being performed with people's personal squishy bits flying everywhere. I had an ominous feeling of doom that this must be what it feels like to be in a cult when they first mention the Kool-Aid. *Oh no, what have I gotten myself into? How do I casually run for the exit without seeming rude?*

It was then that Sensei smiled at me and said, 'Don't you know you've been in a nudist camp this whole time?'

What he meant slowed started to dawn on me. He explained that the point of our training was to get to our own truth. Most of us wear layers of armour to protect ourselves emotionally, just like the layers of clothes we wear. We hide all the parts of ourselves we don't want other people to see. Everyone knows that everybody else is naked underneath, but we keep popping outfits on top, hoping nobody will see what's underneath. I didn't want him to see I was abashed about not having enough money at dinner, so I threw on another emotion-smothering jacket, thick scarf and a jaunty hat. It didn't work on him because he just wanted to see the truth that was there all along. Sensei wanted me to understand that there was no need to cover up who I was emotionally with him.

'You are who and what you are, imperfections and all,' Sensei said.

He just wanted me to get to that point, my own truth, and get there quickly. To strip away all the layers we use to cover and protect ourselves so I could just be my real self with him. I'm sure I drove him crazy when he would ask me a question and I would tell him what I 'thought'. I would talk around things so much, taking him on a complex journey around the walk-in wardrobe of my mind. This detour would go on for many minutes when I could have just gotten there in one sentence. Sensei operated on a straight-shooting, deep level that I wasn't used to. He was very patient with me, but he made it clear that all he wanted was my truth, not the way I was used to interacting with people. He didn't want to shoot the breeze with me unless that was the relationship I wanted with him. I didn't. I wanted to grow and learn, so he taught me to get to *the truth under the truth*. To get metaphorically nude instead of covering myself. No small talk, no self-protection, just the nitty-gritty facts.

It was a strange concept at first, to remove all the everyday noise from talking. All the niceties and justifications that I wasn't even aware I was using. As comfortable as they are, we use them to talk around the truth or to give standard answers to fit with convention. When Sensei Benny asked me if I'd had a good time having dinner with the girls at Mel's Diner, the automatic response was a standard yes, followed by a chat about what it was like. Though in the nudist camp of conversation with Sensei, it went straight to the truth of the experience—I'd had fun but I felt awkward about not having much money and felt too vulnerable to say it out loud. It sounds simple, but when the buttons of fear and insecurity are pressed, it can seem impossible to call a spade a spade. The situation made me feel uncomfortable enough, let alone to actually draw anyone's attention to it. No way. My pride wouldn't let me. I was too young and needed to feel safe. I wanted to fit in. I'd rather have sat under the table and subtly reached my hand up to grab a french fry every now and again.

To get down to the awkward deeper truth about dinner wasn't necessarily a huge achievement, but it felt like one to me. I was used to the little fortress of emotional armour I wore, that stopped anyone seeing how fragile and sometimes scared I was. Or so I thought. My age gave me a false veil over my eyes that let me think other people, especially those older than me, were buying what I was selling. Of course they could see through it, if they actually looked. As classic as it sounds, I was acting like a tough girl because I wasn't very tough on the inside. I'd have done anything to not admit it and feel exposed by openly telling that truth.

There we go, now clothing is optional. It felt like having the real conversation with Sensei Benny about how I'd felt at Mel's Diner had whipped the pants right off me, leaving me standing there trying to cover my butt as the breeze blew. He metaphorically matched me, though, making it okay to just stand there and let things be what they are naturally. The only difference was that we had spoken the words and tolerated verbally standing together exposed. I felt mighty uncomfortable, but also oddly free.

From that day, and for many years to come, I would often repeat to myself—'The truth is the truth, whether you say it out loud or not.' It just is. No matter how many clothes you wear over the top, what's underneath remains the same. Whenever I would divert from this simple idea, things would come undone.

The worst times in my life were made drastically more difficult by not speaking my deepest truth for fear of the consequences. Sensei Benny taught me that the fear of saying something out loud is common because once you speak it, you make it real, which means you have to do something about it. Nothing good ever came from failing at this, choosing instead to give in to the fear of being truly seen. The best connections come with the strongest nude honesty. Sensei sure had a memorable way of making sure I didn't forget it.

This new level of honesty with Sensei Benny was like operating on a whole different frequency. When we spoke, we got quickly to the point. If I wasn't fast enough, he would let me know. Naked truths were flung about rapid fire like throwing knives hitting a wooden target in fast succession. There seemed no need to talk around anything anymore. I was excited by this new way of being and wanted to engage this way with everyone. I soon understood not everyone was as keen as I was to blast straight down the barrel to the bold truth. Many a time there was the sound of crickets chirping and a tumbleweed drifting by, after I had dropped some clanging piece of honesty to an unsuspecting victim. I was like a baby deer overexcited to walk and constantly splattering myself all over the grass.

Your truth is the truth whether you admit it out loud or not (so you may as well face up to it sooner rather than later).

10

Why Are You Crying?

Finding yourself in a nudist camp, so to speak, means there is little point trying to cover up how you feel. This was both empowering and awkward for me. Being connected to Sensei Benny on such an unusually direct and honest level made me feel close to him and like our bond was becoming deeper. I had so much respect for him, and the change being created in my life meant a great deal. Because he was so special to me, naturally I wanted to mean something to him, too. Sensei Benny had many devoted students and I felt the uncomfortable urge to try to stand out from the crowd. My hope to have some significance in his eyes made me feel childish. I wanted to be a good student. I wanted him to be proud of me. I also wanted to have the maturity to not care what he thought but the truth was, I cared about him and his opinion of me.

At times I would watch how gentle and fun Sensei Benny would be with the other young women in the Los Angeles gym. He had excellent boundaries so nobody would ever take his kindness out of context. The girls would come for the kickboxing classes or private lessons with him and he would be so gentlemanly and soft towards them. I was a little jealous of the easy, fun rapport they shared. It looked so much less restrictive than the teacher/student decorum that always existed between us. I knew it was there for an important reason, but it wasn't easy. There was part of me that wanted to have a relaxed bond with him and I didn't completely understand why he didn't have that with me. We got along very well and clearly liked each other, but he was always hard on me in a way he wasn't with the other girls (or most of the guys).

What I didn't comprehend at the time was that the way Sensei showed our relationship mattered to him was by being tougher on me. He knew I was there to change my life, not just to get a workout in. As our relationship developed I came to understand that he was hard on me because I needed him to be. I needed someone rock solid in my life, who I couldn't charm or sway. I needed him to be the boss. When I was strong, I needed him to be stronger. If he had relaxed the connection between us, then I fear I'd have valued it less in some way. Perhaps I wouldn't have taken heed of his lessons in quite the same manner. I was so hungry to learn, that being my friend would have been an impediment to that education. He was first and foremost always my teacher, and he had the wisdom to know I needed that far more than a best buddy. Sensei would cheerfully praise the more casual students he trained, but would rarely praise me. The more he withheld his approval, the more I craved it. He knew it and I knew it. I was young and insecure in the face of performing in front of a legend. There were times with Sensei when I'd have given anything for a pat on the back and a 'job well done'. Uh, no. None for me.

I'd gathered from winning trophies that I wasn't too bad at this whole martial arts thing, so I'd gotten used to some acknowledgement from people. Not from Sensei Benny, though. When my early twenties self couldn't hold on any longer and would go fishing for some type of reassurance that I was good enough, he would never give me what I wanted. It broke my heart a little bit each time because his opinion mattered so much to me. I was young and still figuring out where I stood. I'd try a different approach with him, thinking I was being all cloak and dagger, saying things like, 'I've been working really hard on that technique all year and was looking forward to showing you. Is it at a good enough level now?' Yep, real slick there, Champion. No way he would have seen through that carefully crafted smoke screen.

Sensei Benny would reply with, 'It doesn't matter what I think' or 'Do *you* think it's good enough?'

This drove me crazy. I knew he was trying to demonstrate that only my opinion of my own performance was important. Still, I couldn't help that for years I wished for a gold star or a high-five even. The youngest most insecure part of me desperately wanted Sensei to tell me I was good enough. The more I wanted it and the longer he withheld, the more I assumed it would likely never happen. Sensei had the patience to go on like this forever. He was a master of maturity and at times I felt like an infant around him.

Sensei was just about the only person in my life who didn't say positive things to me about my martial arts. Other people's opinions seemed almost inconsequential, but his held incredible weight. By deliberately saying nothing, it bordered on feeling downright mean at times. Why be so hard on me when at any moment he could scatter some praise my way, and it would have been like Christmas morning in my eyes? His well-intended Grinch-ing continued into a decade-long recurring theme and a battle I could not win. The less Sensei said, the more it niggled at me. It was like wanting a new boss or partner to let you know you were making the grade, but they just leave you hanging in vulnerable territory. For years on end. What started as a casual small wondering on my part, over time became a bigger deal. It was like a tiny itch that Sensei deliberately turned into a rash. He let me sit in the uncomfortableness of it, knowing eventually I would have to soothe myself. The less he said, the more I wanted to know. I believed deep down Sensei approved of me, otherwise I would not have been there in the first place. But there was always a part that needed him to tell me. To my face. Please?

This dynamic was slow torture to a little achiever like me. It was like being starving hungry and in the company of one of the world's greatest chefs, who served delicacies to others right in front of you but never offered you a taste. It was maddening but it also made me understand just how hungry I was.

My focus eventually shifted towards feeding myself. I starved for so long that I could no longer look outside myself for nourishment. As much as I wished Sensei Benny wasn't so hard on me, I also knew that if he had given in and fed me, then I would have missed the point. It would have been far easier for him to give me praise and keep our relationship festive, but those would have been the actions of a friend, not a teacher.

Now that I'm out the other side of the lesson I look back in awe at how long he was prepared to stick to his guns with me and not give in. It was all so that I would grasp what was such an important concept for a young woman to understand. Sensei explained it to me in one concise sentence, '*You must love yourself more than anyone else could ever love you.*' It sounded like a syrupy cliché when I first heard it, but when I held it up to the light of my need for outside approval I knew it was a truth I had to try to live by. Easy to write on a greeting card, but harder to do in real life. You can't look outside yourself for something that needs to come from within you. Sensei Benny held out until I *finally* stopped being concerned about his opinion. I had to stop caring about what he thought so I could focus on my own thoughts. His kindness looked like cruelty at times, but I knew and trusted his heart. It would have been more fun to take the easy road, but I valued Sensei's ability to take the harder road with me. He saw clearly what I needed and gave me a tough lesson that was for my benefit. I had to learn it again the hard way at a big time in my life that I will tell you about later, but I did get it eventually. Medicine tastes bad on the way down, but the healing it creates is worth it.

Luckily the hard lessons were always counterbalanced with good times. I needed only to look at the warm welcome I received with every visit to Los Angeles and the generous time that Sensei would spend with me. I honestly enjoyed his company and all the ways I could see he was hugely invested in teaching me both as a martial artist and a person. I loved the physical training sessions but there was so much more to it. He made sure his students were always learning emotionally, no matter how long he had to wait for them to absorb a lesson.

This is what set Sensei Benny apart from all of the coaches I had trained with, and made him special. He had thought long and hard about his role and took it deadly seriously. He knew it ran so much deeper than just the physical. When it came to the techniques that he taught, Sensei was lethal and knew that passing those skills along came with great responsibility. Teaching effective martial arts techniques was like handing the student a gun, then as they became more advanced, it was like loading the bullets. He felt it was wrong to hand someone a weapon without making sure they had the strength of character to not go on a shooting spree. He knew martial arts attracted all types of people, including those who are aggressive and like to fight. He wasn't in the business of teaching thugs how to beat people up.

If you wanted to train with him, you had to be prepared to talk about your feelings. This wasn't usually high on a hoodlum's list of priorities. Sensei knew the importance of dealing with your emotions and many of the unavoidable ones brought up in training were uncomfortable. He had no interest in teaching people dangerous skills and then sending them out in the world without the emotional skills to handle themselves.

Sensei would often say that Ukidokan was 'only for the brave' and this didn't mean it was just for tough guys. Being hard as nails on the outside was the easier part, but he was looking for a whole other kind of bravery. I once watched Sensei, in a crowded room of mostly male fighters, ask an ex-Israeli army soldier and champion fighter if he cried. There was a long pause of awkward breath-holding from the guys in the room, before the soldier answered the question with a clear, 'Yes, Sensei.' The whole crowd collectively exhaled. There was no space for tough guy posturing, only for the truth to be told. It was a revelation. Sensei Benny was unquestionably masculine and tough, so he was the perfect person to model what it was to be *a real man*. For me, he was demonstrating what real strength looked like, regardless of gender. It wasn't about pretending you didn't feel things, but instead having the courage to admit how you honestly feel. His goal was to train warriors who were connected to their own hearts. This was how he could arm his students with the proverbial gun, but they would never use it unless they absolutely had to.

◆

Sensei Benny was determined to teach the hard lessons necessary for me to make peace with who I was. He loved putting me in challenging situations where I would learn my truth, and learn it fast. The higher the pressure, the greater the lesson to be absorbed. He was neither interested in nor impressed by how well I did against an opponent or how skilled I was. Those things were just the basic starting point, almost a given. He was all about how I dealt with things when I was as uncomfortable as possible. Constantly having the odds stacked against me made training with Sensei Benny very tough physically, but more so mentally. I was used to being one of the more skilled people where I trained, so it wasn't always easy making the adjustment to coming off second best. It was embarrassing. It's hard when you're accustomed to being good at something and are then constantly put in situations where you feel like you're not. It messes with both your ego and your confidence. It was a hard road that many times made me question myself and why I was doing all of this. But I trusted Sensei and knew he was taking me on this painful journey to ultimately make me believe in myself. He broke me down in order to rebuild me, but many times the lessons left me in tears. All of the easy parts of training were quickly forgotten. The more difficult the lesson emotionally, the deeper the impression it made on me.

One of the most tearful lessons I ever got was at the hands of Majid Raees, one of Sensei's top world class students. He had also travelled from overseas to train with Sensei. I had heard his story of risking it all to travel to America to learn from his hero and I applauded him for all he had sacrificed. Every time I went to LA, Majid would outclass me by a mile. He was very good and supremely confident. He knew exactly how good he was and sometimes that rubbed me the wrong way. I was usually relatively sure of my skills, but something about him got under my skin.

On a particularly tough day in the gym, Sensei Benny made me get in the ring with Majid. I knew it was going to be challenging, as always. But this day was different. It was bad enough feeling like I was losing the entire time, but in addition Majid was mocking me. My blood boiled as he acted like I was a beginner who had no right to be in the ring with him.

I was getting angrier and angrier with each round that passed. Majid was deliberately sticking out his chin at me and provoking me to try to hit him. When I threw a punch, he would make me miss and then hit me with a good shot of his own. He was laughing at me and constantly making fun of me. As my embarrassment rose, it turned into rage.

To make matters worse I was fearful I would be badly hurt in this training session. Majid was throwing kicks at full speed and power that were whizzing past my head. Each time I felt genuinely scared for my safety. There's being hit hard by someone who doesn't know what they're doing and then there's being hit by an expert. I was evading the kicks by a few millimetres each time, and I wasn't sure if it was because he was missing on purpose or that I was making him miss. If it was the latter, I was afraid that the next kick might connect with my face and knock me unconscious or worse. A small part of me was hoping I would get knocked out, just so I could leave the ring and this horrible session would be over.

When I faced Sensei Benny in the corner between rounds, I was so angry that I was crying. I guess I was hoping for some sympathy or for him to be on my side because Majid was being so damn mean to me. Um, not so much. Sensei looked at me and said, 'Why are you crying?'

'Because Majid is being such a jerk,' I replied, but saying that just made me cry more. I felt silly and like a little girl for being upset at something that I was clearly taking so personally.

I turned away and wished I could stop the tears. It was just making me feel over-exposed, on top of what was happening in the ring.

Sensei made me look at him and when I went to turn away again, he held onto my boxing headgear so that I couldn't. Tears and other bodily fluids streamed down my face as I tried to pull away. He held my face only inches from his and confronted me with, 'Why are you *really* crying?'

I responded much along the same lines as before, blaming my opponent's bad behaviour for my poor performance. But I knew that was only the surface excuse.

If I was being uncomfortably honest, the true reason I was crying was because I was being humiliated in front of Sensei Benny. I felt ashamed that I was reacting in a way that made me feel vulnerable and childish. So I covered it up with an outburst of anger. I was angry at myself for not being braver or tough enough to handle the situation. I was frustrated that I wasn't better than Majid, or emotionally strong enough to deal with the way he was treating me. I was mad at myself for being so upset and letting him rattle me. It was like getting beaten up at school by a bully who not only hurts you but takes your pride home with him.

Sensei Benny had taught me that physical contact in training brings up a lot of feelings in people. The ring is like an emotional microwave that speed cooks the feelings we struggle with in daily life. A person who gets punched in the face and doesn't have an emotional reaction to it is likely a sociopath, so it's quite normal to have a strong response. Sensei said there were four emotions we all face in the ring: fear, anger, frustration and anxiety. I was sure I was feeling all four at once. I was afraid I'd get hurt. I was angry at Majid. I was frustrated with not being able to perform, and I was anxious about what Sensei Benny was thinking about how bad a fighter I must be. It was the perfect storm of emotions to make for a horrendous sparring session.

I was completely emotionally captured by my opponent. I was reacting to what he did and how he was treating me, instead of doing what I was trained to do. I fell apart mentally and that made my technique fall apart physically. I was so busy being upset that I wasn't able to focus on what I was doing. All clarity went out the window, closely followed by my self-control.

As the rounds continued, I was crying as I was sparring. Turns out you can multi-task in a boxing ring. I kept exchanging shots with Majid as the tears flowed and all Sensei Benny said to me from the corner was, 'Change your thinking.' He said it over and over again which only made me more frustrated because I had no idea how to do that. I exasperatedly thought to myself, 'If I knew how to change my thinking I would, so why don't you just tell me how to do it?' I wanted out of there so badly, but Sensei made a point of not letting me quit by leaving the ring. He made me stay in there until the final bell.

Change your thinking.

Afterwards I was so angry that when Sensei sat me down with Majid to talk I didn't even want to look at him. I ranted about how his bad behaviour had ruined my performance. I was uncharacteristically angry and couldn't stop myself from venting it. They both let me say what I needed to say. When I was done exploding at Majid, Sensei Benny told me that he had asked Majid to do that to me on purpose. I was shocked and hurt that Sensei would do that to me. At first I didn't understand why someone who meant so much to me would deliberately cause me pain. I didn't want to be let down by him. The tears started again as my hurt got the better of me.

Then Sensei Benny looked me right in the eye and said, 'Is that all it takes to break you?'

I wanted to throw up as I uncomfortably admitted it was true. Majid laughing at me was all it had taken to break me mentally. It was a truth I couldn't run from. It left me with nowhere to hide and I had to face the reality that I had behaved immaturely and without perspective. He made fun of me and I fell for it. I could have just ignored it and taken care of business, but instead I took his taunts personally and made them my reality. This was the kind of stuff that Sensei was worried about us buying into in everyday life if we had our proverbial guns loaded. He needed us to have an emotional handle on ourselves enough that we wouldn't start firing if someone called us names. I felt like a fool, but I could see his point. He needed me to build a thick enough skin that I wouldn't use what he had taught me to lash out at someone physically if they hurt me emotionally.

The hard lesson Sensei was teaching me that day has stayed with me ever since. Afterwards he explained to me that *the only thing you can control in response to a hard situation is your thinking, your reaction to it*. If you can't control the circumstances or outcome, you can control how you respond. We always have a choice when it comes to whether or not we connect with something negative.

These were difficult lessons to learn, and they made me feel like a child in the company of adults. I knew I had a lot of growing up to do before I could avoid getting emotionally captured—both in the ring and in my life. I had spent years learning the theories, but theories don't count for anything unless you live them. Making mistakes and failing to live up to the best of yourself is how you learn those lessons at a deep level. They hurt the most, but they reveal your weaknesses and show you where you need to grow. Sensei Benny was adept at creating situations where I would have a chance to grow up a little more and understand who I was.

> Often the only thing you can control in a hard situation is your reaction to it.

♦

Sensei sat me down one day and asked, 'So, who are you?' His tone was matter of fact, as if he had just asked me where I left the TV remote. To him it was a reasonable question for which I should be able to provide a simple answer. Much awkward mumbling on my part followed and I proceeded to answer him with a series of random facts about myself like my age and hair colour. When I started to ramble about being an Aquarian and liking long walks on the beach, he stopped me and said, 'Don't tell me who you *think* you are, tell me who you *really* are.' He wanted me to go deeper, to move away from the outward signifiers that label us as this or that. Sensei was so used to operating on the level of getting straight to the point that he patiently waited as I flailed around in my own confusion about myself. As basic as it seems, it's a hard question to answer well. When I ask the same question to people now, they usually react exactly as I did that first day—with uncomfortable answers that often end in a response of 'I don't really know'.

The more Sensei led me down this path to being able to name the things about me that made me who I am, the more challenging it became. Having blue eyes didn't make me myself. He wanted both the bold statements and shy truths. He wasn't looking for the outside stuff, he was asking for the unique balance of traits that comprised my inner make-up. It took work to get past the superficial and down to the bones of it all. He called this the 'I Am Concept'—to be able to speak out loud the truth of who I was. He was looking for things like, 'I Am . . . a talented martial artist.' Okay, I can feel your eyes roll from here, because I had the same initial response. We are socially programmed to react negatively when someone tells you things they are good at or things they like about themselves. Trying to say these things out loud made me discover how difficult it can be to just speak without judging or editing yourself. We all have things we like about ourselves, but we don't usually sit around telling one another, right?

Sensei Benny was creating a safe space for me to discover my strengths. After being taught to not need his approval, I would have to be shown how to properly access my own. I needed to learn what I liked about myself and make peace with speaking that aloud to a non-judgemental person, so that I could hear myself say the words. It was the whole 'speak the truth out loud to make it real' idea again. It's amazing what you think you know clearly in your own mind, until you have to actually let it pass your lips and be spoken. Words stumbled out falteringly. I would say to Sensei, 'I Am . . . kind' with almost the tone of a question. At first I would offer up statements and to an extent wanted him to reassure me of the answer. It all sounded so arrogant and self-aggrandising coming out of my mouth that I could feel myself turning red with embarrassment. He pressed me for clear, confident answers. He made me write them all down (always with the writing things down) and create a list of my strengths of character. This was a tangible way to change my thinking.

When I now teach other people the I Am Concept, we start by writing down five I Ams. Many people get stuck after two or three, having never thought this way about who they are before. Sadly, when I ask them to tell me some things they don't like about themselves, a fast flood of ten usually hits me within seconds. We are conditioned to spend time thinking about our negatives and not taught to devote time to thinking about our positives. When you last made a mistake, did you beat yourself up? I know I have wasted hours, days and even years focusing on the things I have done wrong or don't like about myself. Let me also ask you, when you last did something well, how much time did you spend contemplating what it was about you that made it so good? Most people allot time to mulling over their weaknesses and find it almost offensively challenging when it's suggested they spend time thinking about their strengths.

The real challenge comes when I ask people to turn their five I Ams into twenty-five, then fifty, and to reach for a goal of one hundred. It's not easy to write a triple-digit list of all the things that are cool about you. That takes some serious work. You have to go mining for gold through analysing experiences and reaching out to others. It's a way to clock up minutes and then hours of positive self-reflection. We could all use a list of how awesome we are. Maybe not desperately today, but there might come a day in life when you feel so beaten down by circumstance that a list of your strengths is a life-preserving remembrance of who you actually are. If your marriage ends, if you lose your job, or find yourself floored by grief from the death of a loved one. These are the times when you can wind up adrift so far away from your centre that a list of your true self, written in better times, is a priceless reminder.

Now some of you are still going to be feeling that you don't need to write a lame old list. Sounds a little too hippie self-help for you? Let me reframe so it's not about you. Think of your child, any little person you love or if there are no kids around just think of the person you love the most in the world. Do you love them with so much kindness that you would devote a little time to writing an I Am list for them? Would you do it if your kid came home from school crying after being bullied? What if your best friend had just broken up with their partner? That is the time they need a safe place and a way to counterbalance the negatives. One of my students has a large sheet of paper stuck on the inside of her son's bedroom door, and every night they spend a few minutes talking about his day and adding an I Am or two to his list. His mother's gift to him is a childhood where every day he sees a tangible account of his good qualities. Not a bad place to come home to after a hard day. So if that sounds like a good idea to you in regards to someone you love, why on earth wouldn't you give yourself the same gift? Because it's you? Because you don't need it, right? Well, I used to think that, too.

Here's the trick with some of these simple exercises Sensei Benny asked me to do—they're so simple that in my foolish pride I thought I was smart enough to understand them without actually needing to do them. Sensei would check back with me over the years to see how much progress I had made on things like the I Am Concept. To my own chagrin I had to admit I hadn't followed through on creating an extensive list. I thought I understood it on the first day he taught it to me. It seemed so easy that I felt it was for *other* people who needed it more. But Sensei would remind me to persevere, and after actually putting pen to paper I came to understand I needed it more than I had realised.

The deeper I looked below the surface, the more the real truth of how I felt came forward. As I was writing down the good I Ams, I also started to see my not-so-good feelings more clearly, too. I knew I struggled with how I felt at times, but the picture was becoming clearer. I had been running from some occasionally grim feelings about myself and the world. I was in my early twenties and only a few years after the death of my dad, so my inner psyche was still sporting a raw black eye and bloody nose.

After a long conversation with Sensei on the side of the training floor in the gym one day, I surprised myself by admitting that I didn't like being me. As much as I wanted Sensei to believe I thought of myself in a positive light, the truth was I'd been carrying a sadness I could not shake. My mind was at times a noisy place full of unhelpful thoughts careening around me. It was like trying to mentally run across the eight busy traffic lanes of the Sydney Harbour Bridge during peak hour. So many loud horns and screeching tyres up in there. At times I felt things so acutely I worried my feelings might run me over. I was sensitive to the point of being tormented by thoughts and I wrestled with how to make peace with the sadness I had experienced. I'd developed a good external skill set, but internally I was agitated, restless and about as far from being a mini Yoda as you could get.

Admitting this out loud felt like an earth-shattering revelation to me, while Sensei only responded with kindness and a strong reassurance that I deserved so much better than to feel that way. He could see what was going on internally from a mile away. Getting the words out triggered a little shame, yet it also made me feel free. We all want to be seen in a good light by those we admire. I didn't want to hide behind a veil of trying to appear strong. I had spent too long being trapped there and knew I needed something better. The only way forward was to lay bare how I was feeling.

Sensei Benny made sure I knew it was okay to feel the way I did, understandable even, but he encouraged me to not get too comfortable in that place. If I couldn't say it to myself, then I couldn't change it. Now that I had acknowledged it out loud, it was time to do something about it. I'd made it real and now I needed to start looking for a new place to inhabit in my mind. He suggested I tell myself a different truth.

He had me imagine how I would like to feel. It all boiled down to one simple mantra that I was to hold firmly in the forefront of my mind—'I like being me.' Sensei asked me to make myself a sign and place it in a position at home where I would see it all the time. He had me promise that I would keep the sign there until I made it come true.

It felt weird to write a note to myself reminding me of how I didn't yet feel, but I believed he knew what he was doing. I fancied up a little orange Post-it note with the words written on it in green Texta. I put it on the monitor of my computer (yes, it was that long ago I had a monitor the size of a cardboard box). That sign sat there for years as I did the work necessary to make myself believe it. I looked at it thousands of times and the message became ingrained deep into my mind. I liked being me. I was telling myself how to feel. Being me was becoming an excellent thing. I had strained at it like the stuck lid of a pickle jar, until one day I found I was no longer trying so hard. The jar had opened with ease and I hadn't even noticed. I was free. I'd been trotting around all happily liking myself without even thinking about it. The sign was now made redundant.

I loved that little orange note, though. It found its way into my desk drawer, where it would welcome me with a cheerful accidental reminder when I was fishing around for a pen. I still have it as a small treasure I keep to make sure I remember how hard won my happy feelings were. I had done the hard work to change my thinking and I never wanted to forget it.

Decide that you like being you and love yourself more than anyone else could ever love you.

11

Be Teflon

I woke up to hear the rhythmic beat of a punching bag being pummelled in sync with Latin hip hop music. I looked at the time and grimaced when I saw 6 a.m. I was jetlagged and staying at Sensei Benny's gym on my second training trip to Los Angeles. Disgruntled to be awake, but excited to start the day hearing the sound of a fighter training, I wondered who it was. After getting dressed, I unlocked the door to the small healing room I had slept in. The Jet's Gym was in a location where it wasn't advisable to go walking alone at night so the doors were always locked after hours. Who was in the gym so early, and why?

When I went out to discover who was training, I found my old friend/nemesis Majid, training as if his life depended on it. We acknowledged each other respectfully but very briefly as I could see he was super focused and drenched in sweat. This wasn't the time to interrupt him for a catch-up conversation.

I learned later that Majid was there because Sensei had struck a deal with him. Majid would get to train with Sensei, but he had to be at the gym every morning at six to train by himself. Every, single, morning. Alone. This went on for many years. Now that takes a whole new level of dedication. It's fun to train in a gym full of people, but by yourself day after day for a long period of time would have been very isolating. Like many sports, fighting often involves a crowd cheering for you, but all of the hard work is done far away from encouraging eyes. In Majid's case, his daily hard yards were even removed from the eyes of his coach. I commended his work ethic and commitment, but I also knew Sensei wouldn't leave him to his own devices for no reason. There was always a deeper meaning behind everything he did.

The price Majid was expected to pay for Sensei Benny's time were the early hours of solitary sweat he put in every day. When Sensei Benny told me about this deal, what blew me away was the unspoken understanding between teacher and student. He had made an agreement with Majid and fully expected him to honour it. When I asked how Sensei knew Majid had held up his end of the bargain by training at six every morning, he replied, 'I don't know. I never checked up on him.'

Initially I was a little confused by Sensei's response. If it were me, I would want to make sure the requested training was happening. Not Sensei, though. He had no interest in what people told him they were going to do. He only cared about what they actually did. He would always say, 'Don't tell me, show me.' Sensei wasn't interested in having Majid tell him that he had been at the gym every morning. He was only interested in *seeing* if he had done the work or not. The truth would show in how fast he improved from all of the extra training, so Sensei had no need to check up on him. Majid had to train for himself, not for Sensei Benny. If he were to become well known for his skills, he had to be prepared to put in those lonely hours with no applause and no praise from his teacher. It was just expected. He honoured what he had been taught by sacrificing the time it takes to practice and actually learn it.

That type of effort creates champions and Sensei had done the hard yards himself to gain that knowledge. Just getting on with it when there is no-one else around to encourage or reward you, only because you know it will make you better one day. The point is that you know it is benefiting you. Sensei could have easily teamed Majid with a training partner, but it was the dedication in isolation that was necessary. Majid went on to fight for a world title with a skill set that was beyond question and all those years of hard work under his belt.

◆

Dedication and practice make you who you are. In martial arts, we are talking many years of hard work. You can have a natural talent in one area, but be weak in other aspects. Let's say you play golf and have an excellent drive, but you're not so crash hot at putting. You can't magically become good on the green. You have to spend hours there repeating the same skill over and over until it becomes second nature. In martial arts, even if you are good at most things, there is always an element so frustrating that it can make the toughest man cry. Sparring is usually the fastest way there, but for many people their frustration comes out when they try to master classic boxing equipment like the speedball.

You've probably seen a speedball in movies where the boxer stands underneath a small bag and hits it in an upwards arc against a horizontal wooden platform. It rebounds in a semi-circular rhythm that sounds like *thuda-da, thuda-da, thuda-da.* Think timeless images of Muhammad Ali turning his fists so fast they were a blur. It's old-school but it works for many reasons. The basic premise is to teach speed, timing, rhythm and endurance in the shoulders that allows a boxer to keep their hands up despite weary arms. I discovered another reason why this simple piece of equipment is invaluable for training boxers—it is often incredibly frustrating to learn. Rarely does anyone just walk up and start doing it very well. Skill on the speedball takes time. Picture Clint Eastwood in the film *Million Dollar Baby* watching Hilary Swank take sad little beginner swings at the speedball. It can be painful to watch, and even more painful to hear, as someone is learning the speedball's rhythms.

On the same trip to Los Angeles when I uncovered Majid's training deal with Sensei, I was in the punching bag room working the speedball. Or at least I thought I was working it, until Sensei Benny came in and almost laughed. He stopped me and said, 'No, try it like this,' then dazzled me with some moves I had never seen before, that he had clearly been doing for decades. It felt like sliding all the way down Everest to the bottom again when you were already halfway up the slope. I thought I was good, until I saw what good actually looked like. *Okay, starting from scratch. Again.* So I began copying the pattern he was showing me, first in a slow thudding beat and then awkwardly in a faster sequence.

Sensei taught me about ten new advanced things to do with the speedball and as always, when he was finished, I madly scrambled for my notebook. I tried to get it all down before I forgot the details. This was the recipe I would take back to Sydney and spend the next year following, over and over. I didn't want to miss a thing he had said and always did my best to describe on paper the mental movie I had just taken in my head, in the hope that my notes would bring it back to technicolour life at a later date.

For the rest of that trip I worked the speedball during the day but lived on it at night once everyone had gone home. I put the same song on repeat to remind me to persevere. This was back in the days of CD players and I had a single of the Aaliyah song 'Try again'. The sentiment behind the song was that if you failed you should pick yourself up and just give it another go until you get it. I knew going into my visits to the Jet's Gym that I was sure to encounter many points like these. I had to maintain a positive attitude where I would just keep on trying, no matter how bad I thought I was on any given day. I was used to feeling on top of things in my training at home, but in LA I was the small fish in a tank full of sharks. Frustration, intimidation and feeling out of my depth were guaranteed. So I listened to that song hundreds of times while I drummed out new rhythms on the speedball. I attempted to show Sensei Benny my amazing new skills and he only smiled and told me to keep practising. So practice I did, until my hands hurt and my eyes watered. That became my gauge for speedball effort. Until there were tears streaming down my face from staring so intently at the same spot for hours, I wasn't trying hard enough.

The speedball was such a valuable tool because it taught me there was no point getting upset about not being good at something, but instead I should just get on with the work of becoming good at it. I knew bitching about how frustrating the speedball was wouldn't make it any easier. Sensei Benny would always say, 'Where there's a bitch, there's a want.' He taught me to look beyond the frustrated bitching and find the want. Like if someone is sounding off about how stupid and pointless the speedball is, chances are it's because they *want* to be better at it than they are. Whenever I hear people complaining about things or getting angry, I try to remember this idea and look for the truth about why they're actually upset.

It's a real challenge to go deeper than the surface of the behaviour we are presented with and look for understanding of what drives us. There are so many opportunities to take things personally if you only splash around on the surface. Even in the face of appalling behaviour, thinking about where it's coming from can be a circuit breaker to reaction. Unfortunately, people usually just bounce off each other like reactive pinballs, especially in an argument. Oddly enough, this also happens in the ring.

One of the most common things that occurs in sparring sessions is that people take getting hit personally. It's a strange situation given that two people have both signed up to make contact with one another, so it's not like they're upset because they didn't know it was going to happen. Even when you're expecting a blow, we still perceive what is happening through the filter of our own emotions. What starts as a friendly situation can quickly escalate into frayed tempers and lack of control. Why? Because one or both of the participants took it personally. Maybe they didn't like the way a body shot was thrown, the power they got hit with or the look on your face. Something kicked off a frustration in them, so they fired back a little harder. This, of course, then sparks the exact same reaction from the other person, so the next thing you know it is, well, on.

Naturally what invariably happens is each person blames the other for starting it.

I once had a sparring partner absolutely drop their bundle and try to knock me out. We unexpectedly went from calm seas to a furious storm in a matter of seconds. After everything I'd been through with Majid I'd learnt not to take things too personally in sparring, so I didn't immediately connect to what was happening. Instead I just made sure I didn't get hurt. When you get emotionally involved with a situation like that, you often become less able to deal with it effectively. Chances are that it's not personal, and half the time it's not even about you. It's about their filter, their reactions to things within themselves, so there isn't much point getting all thrown off your game, too. I weathered the storm of my angry opponent until the end of the round, when the gloves came off and I was screamed at. I was more than a little confused about what had happened, until in the middle of the screaming came, 'What the hell were you laughing at me for?' Ah, there it was. The want behind the bitch.

> Laugh at your mistakes and find the joy even in the most painful times.

I knew that feeling of being totally frustrated and losing my temper. Early in my training I would often get frustrated because I took it all so seriously. Sensei had to slowly teach me to laugh at myself. Literally. He would make me laugh out loud at those stages when I was all pent up with my own annoyance. He taught me that even when it all got very serious I still needed to have fun as a pressure release. In the middle of a serious training session Sensei would make us dance in the middle of a circle. It was pretty hard to take yourself seriously or think you were tough while publicly getting down with your bad self. The more you resisted doing it, the more emotional and difficult things became. If you just laughed instead there was no need to beat yourself up mentally. Over time, if I made a mistake my knee-jerk reaction became to laugh instead of cry.

Now back to my angry opponent, who hadn't yet gotten the hang of that lesson. After some quick consideration, I remembered that halfway through the round I had been a little frustrated about making a mistake and had laughed out loud at myself. My opponent had thought I was laughing at them. They read my reaction through the lens of their own experience, and clearly they didn't like being laughed at. I will never know why or what that represented to them, but I knew it was a big trigger. It wasn't like they'd felt a little annoyed. No, instead they'd tried to separate my head from my shoulders. Luckily, along with the ability to laugh, Sensei Benny also taught me how to apologise. So instead of bracing up the walls of my ego by telling myself their reaction was their problem (and that they were a major jerk), I explained that I was actually laughing at myself and said I was sorry for upsetting them. It didn't matter that they had read the situation inaccurately. All that mattered was that my actions had inadvertently hurt them. We parted as friends but that day stuck with me because it made me wonder how many times I had taken something personally that didn't have much to do with me.

◆

Sensei Benny walks around covered in Teflon. Not literally, but that's what he calls his ability to not react to other people. I look at Sensei, now in his mid-sixties, and the way he moves in the world letting very little stick to him. He is a master of this and one day I hope to be like him. He knows how to not take things personally in everyday life, so that they don't upset his inner equilibrium. He maintains a steady state of mind by conscious choice. By comparison, I watch in amazement at how easily upset we all get over the smallest things. Someone is rude to us when we order our coffee or drives too slowly in front of us on the way to work and most people get mad. Yet, in watching my teacher navigate his course so calmly, I can see there is another way but it requires operating on a higher frequency than where most of us spend our time.

Sensei Benny walks the talk, especially when it comes to being Teflon. At his level of physical skill he has to make sure he is quite hard to offend. I can only imagine how scary it would be for someone with his dangerous skill set to also possess a hair trigger temper. He would tell me stories about how he had an aggressive soul, but had to learn to temper it as he got older. In the face of being offended he would say, 'what's it to me?' If someone wants to say nasty things, it's more about them than you. Their words didn't mean he had to say or do anything about it. Rising to an insult is more a sign of your own weakness than anything else.

One Teflon moment I will always remember happened when we were on a movie set together in Thailand. During a break in shooting we went for a walk together to talk as we wandered through the film sets. We meandered past the facades of 1940s buildings and fake ships docked in shallow water. Eventually we came upon an older lady who was working intently by herself on one of the ornate stages. We watched the work she was doing and eventually said hello. A pleasant conversation ensued over the next five minutes or so, during which we found out she was a senior set dresser and Sensei explained he was the film's fight choreographer. Following the sharing of their job titles, Sensei introduced himself by name and reached out his hand to shake hers. I have never seen a mature lady with such a look of disgust on her face in response to a nice gesture. It was as if Sensei's hand were covered in some kind of bio-hazardous excrement. Sensei left his hand extended for ten excruciatingly drawn out seconds while he carried on talking as if nothing had happened. Eventually he gently smiled and withdrew his hand without missing a beat. Always the loyal student (and with the maturity of someone half his age), I got annoyed because I couldn't believe how disdainful this woman had been to him. The thing that upset me most was that it was oddly unjust because he was being so pleasant and polite to her. Not only had she been rude, but she had done so in the face of kindness. I said nothing but inside I was tossing around some low level outrage. After their conversation ended, he wished her well and we walked away.

As we rounded the corner, Sensei could feel my annoyance. When he brought it up, he let me vent for a few minutes about my surprise over how rude she had been and why her reaction had been so inappropriate. What I couldn't get past was that Sensei didn't seem fazed by it at all. I guess I had been subconsciously expecting that he was too polite to say anything at the time but might say something to me later. Wrong. He just said, 'What is her reaction to me?' and reminded me that it wasn't personal, even though my head immediately protested that it sure looked personal from where I was standing. Sensei said her reaction to his outstretched hand wasn't about him, it was about her. She had reasons we would never know, nor were they any of our business. Sensei chose not to connect to her reaction, because it was *her reaction*. He was Teflon and felt it was petty to allow something so small from someone he didn't know affect his mental state. Meanwhile, I had been annoyed on his behalf without even realising how foolish I was being. The instinct to protect the feelings of those you care about is healthy, but sometimes unnecessary. It was a small thing but it had a profound impact on me and how I saw interacting with people. I wasn't sure my sensitive self could learn to let all the crappy things people do bounce off me without sticking, but at least it gave me something to work on as I get older. Learn to be Teflon.

I liked the idea of not letting something stick to you if it's not yours. I invested in the concept that if someone was unkind to you, it did say a whole lot more about them than it did about you. These simple solutions seemed to work better the more time I spent in the ring. My ability to be Teflon was in direct correlation to the amount of time I spent under pressure myself. When I had to move through challenging feelings quickly in the ring in order to perform at my best, it made me more able to let go of or not connect to the tough parts in daily life. The reason? Practice. It always comes down to practice. The more times I did it in sparring, the more easily I did it outside of the gym.

The flipside of learning to control my emotions in the ring was being able to do what Sensei Benny called 'capturing your opponent'. An emotionally out-of-control competitor is usually not a good one. They overreact, they try too hard rather than pacing themselves, they leave themselves open and they make mistakes . . . lots of mistakes. I spent years of sparring being on the losing side of that equation, like when Sensei asked Majid to deliberately capture me. It's important to learn because in such a dangerous sport, you have to keep yourself together mentally in order to not get hurt physically. There's nothing worse than getting angry and charging at your opponent, only to then walk right into a blow that injures you, simply because you were pushing forward so hard. It's like driving while angry—it's not safe and one or both of you might get seriously hurt.

To balance out all the toughest times in training, Sensei Benny would always remind me to find the joy in what I was doing, especially at the worst points. When I had nothing left, when I wanted to give up, he would tell me to find even a tiny spark of joy within. Just the fact I had two arms and two legs was usually enough to shake me out of feeling sorry for myself and the pain I was enduring. Gratitude reset my mind to focusing on how lucky I was to have found my passion in life, even if in that moment it was painfully difficult. It worked as a high-speed mind changer at the worst of times. Find the joy in it, especially when you feel there is no joy to be found. Look harder, it's there under the coals. If you sift through them, you might just find that ember when you need it most.

Be Teflon—you can choose to just let it all slide right off you.

12

It Doesn't Hurt Less If You Close Your Eyes

I was fascinated by the mental warfare of training, both with my opponent and within myself. I needed the practical tools that Sensei Benny gave me far more than I needed the physical workouts. On each visit, it was virtually guaranteed that somewhere along the line I would end up in an intense situation either physically, mentally or more often than not, both. I wanted to grow and learn so badly that I was willing to make myself seriously uncomfortable in the process. What started as the discomfort of sleeping on the gym floor in my early twenties, turned into the kind of psychological gymnastics that left me sore for days.

Being around Sensei Benny required me to open my mind and have it tumble, flip and pike its way to a deeper understanding. Yet this was often done while nailing the kind of physical move that would have Nadia Comăneci attempting another perfect ten. It is amazing what your mind can make your body do under pressure. Sensei Benny would tell me the *'general controls the troops'*, meaning your mind has to be in charge of your body or there will be chaos. The greater the mental pressure, the most common reaction is for your thoughts to race in fifty different directions at once, like toddlers with an unlimited supply of red cordial. When the general is calmly directing the troops, then the battle is well organised and executed with calculated precision.

> The general controls the troops. Use your mind as a powerful commander to get the best from yourself.

In the ring, if your mind gets out of control then your body won't perform at its best. The same goes for losing control of your emotions at work or home—it's probably not going to yield a great result. Training is just regular life in a different context. Sensei Benny knew this and would deliberately put his students under pressure so that they had to learn to deal with it well. We each have an innate ability to deal with stress, some better than others, but every person has their breaking point where the wheels start to fall off the wagon. The more times you go there, the further away that point becomes and the better you get at keeping your cool. Just like you can't learn to swim by sitting on the edge of the pool and watching, your mind needs to practise staying calm under pressure. Fun? No, not while it's happening. Useful life skill? The best.

I'd often be surprised by what my mind could talk my body into doing. When the general's orders come loud and clear, the body's troops complied. The troops get better at it over time, to the point where little protest is heard in response to tasks that once would have caused an entire platoon to go AWOL. In martial arts and many other pursuits, you have to make peace with experiencing pain in your body. Exertion hurts, plain and simple. If two people compete with the same skill level, but one of them is better at pushing through pain, then that person will likely come out on top. This is especially important in the ring, where you never want to show pain on your face in case it encourages your opponent. When I first started getting hit in training, I would cry at what I now think is quite a light contact level. Eventually, I taught my brain to send my body a different message about pain.

With time, the ability to be hurting, and not let on, does go from impossible to normal. If you're going to get hit either literally or metaphorically by life, *it doesn't hurt less if you close your eyes*. If you see a shot coming and you close your eyes pretending it's not happening then when it hits, the impact is often worse. If it's going to hurt either way, you're better off being brave enough to keep your eyes open and face it head on.

Pain feels basically exactly the same whether you show it on your wincing face or not. Sure, yelping and throwing your most agonised look out to the world might help you feel a little better, but it doesn't make much difference to your actual internal pain factor. Your mind can *choose* to feel your burning lungs or aching muscles, without the need to display it. That doesn't mean you pretend it's not happening. Instead you acknowledge it to yourself, but make a conscious decision to just let it happen without reacting to it. When you need to get the job done, sometimes you have to work unfalteringly through the pain. Making a big deal about it just becomes a waste of energy and distraction from the task at hand.

Realising you have a choice in what you react to felt like a switch clicking on. Suddenly I had some say in what I chose to respond to, both with other people and with my own thoughts. Sensei Benny taught me to meditate and every single time I would inevitably get an annoyingly itchy nose. It would drive me to distraction. I knew I could just end the irritation by scratching it, but there is something important to be gained by just staying in the saddle. At times, it's better to just let things be what they are without reacting to them. The same can be said of being bothered by another person. Only you can decide whether you will let them upset you, but so often we hand that power over to other people. I liked the idea of being Teflon like Sensei Benny, and was learning to actively practice keeping a balanced equilibrium without being unsettled by my own or other people's issues. This proved tricky at times because it's normal to make a big show of being in discomfort, so that others can see it. It's common but not always necessary or positive. I don't mean that the small child who falls over and skins their knee shouldn't cry. I am referring to a more adult phenomenon we have all witnessed where people neglect soothing their own discomfort in favour of publicly performing it. It's the friend who complains constantly to you about the simplest problem. The co-worker who is always whinging at the water cooler about everything. It's the guy at the gym who grunts his way through a workout and then dramatically drops his dumbbells unnecessarily loudly so everyone knows he was lifting heavy.

My personal favourite is when people finish a round of boxing on a punching bag and then proceed to theatrically lie down on the ground as if they have just crossed the Sahara on foot. There is usually only one reason a boxer would lie down in the ring and it involves an unexpected loss of consciousness. It's not a good look in my sport. If you let yourself flop onto the floor because you're tired once, then there's a good chance you'll do it again. Add a hefty dose of pressure with an actual opponent, plus the fact that you move faster in competition than you ever do in training, and you've got a massive reason to have a little sit down on the canvas. Best not to get comfortable with that, perhaps. No matter how tired you are, you will still be the exact same amount of tired whether you show it or not. That's the kicker, if you collapse you've allowed it to have total power over you. When you learn to have control over what you can make your body do, then it shifts the boundaries of what you can achieve. To truly go beyond yourself, first you have to get over yourself.

It doesn't hurt less if you close your eyes. Pretending it's not happening doesn't change the fact that it is.

I use an old-school drill to teach my students how to train their mind to push past their own initial emotional reactions to physical pain. It was how I came to understand that the *general really does control the troops*. The exercise involves holding a push-up position on your knuckles on a wooden floor. Yes, I know it sounds like some kind of illegal torture technique akin to water boarding. Remember, I did say it was old-fashioned. Let me also mention that historically martial artists did many things to condition their knuckles and hands, but none of them involved a manicure.

We start the drill by balancing on our fists with our whole upper body weight resting through the first two knuckles. This becomes painful very quickly as your blood rushes and hands gradually turn white. As the skin tightens, your hands begin to feel as if they will split open. This is the point where the urge to relieve the pain kicks in, first as a gentle suggestion but building to a booming voice in your head. That voice screams at you to stop, to immediately move your hands so the pain goes away.

When this exercise is first performed, students often give up when they begin to register pain. Fair enough, too, as they are not yet used to making peace with this oh-so-unpeaceful visitor. The trick is learning to wait it out, to hold on past that first impulse to quit. Over time you let the warning system of your mind sound for as long as your body will allow. Then when you choose to let go, it is on your terms. You become capable of riding the pain out until your arms shake and your hands are white hot. You learn that the only way you will drop to the floor is if you decide to or you hit your absolute physical threshold. Your mind can disconnect from the pain, feeling and acknowledging it but only observing without reacting to it. It's much like watching a toddler have a tantrum. Sure, there's a lot of noise, but you don't always have to go running towards the screaming.

As crazy as it sounds to deliberately put myself through pain in order to get comfortable with it, over the coming years I would owe my life to this skill. I learned how to tolerate physical discomfort by changing my thinking. My mind controlled the lengths to which I could push my body. I was once terrified of physical pain, but gradually became less afraid of it. So often things don't actually hurt as much as we imagine they will. The time we spend worrying about how much it's going to hurt is usually longer than the actual duration of the pain. We create imaginary discomfort in our minds. Sensei Benny taught me that *90 per cent of our fear is imagined*. We make most of it up. Don't believe me? How many times have you been eaten by a shark? Now weigh that against the number of times you've nervously looked over your shoulder while swimming. I've even irrationally done it plenty of times while alone in a swimming pool. We unintentionally invent things to be afraid of. We are all guilty of creating boogey men under our beds.

That doesn't mean there aren't plenty of legitimate things we should be afraid of out there. Even when the fear is real, it's easy for our minds to quickly expand it into a worst-case scenario. Our fear can quickly turn a stranger walking too close behind us into an imagined axe-murdering psychopath. In a flash our valid and manageable fear can become outrageous and all-consuming. We waste so much precious time turning simple situations into dire scenarios. We worry about invented possibilities that will likely never happen. Think about all of the people who are afraid of public speaking—what are they actually afraid of that makes them shake with fear? It might feel like it beforehand, but you probably won't *actually* pass out or drop dead on stage. Or when you invent worries leading up to running your first half-marathon, on race day it's unlikely that you'll come last or require an ambulance. How mean is it to scare yourself by making up menacing stories that probably won't come true? It is so much easier to just circumvent all the scaredy-cat noise our minds create. When you finally get that you're creating so much of your own fear, it makes life a lot less terrifying and things seem much more achievable.

> Most of our fears are imagined and will probably never actually happen.

Time and again Sensei Benny would create scenarios for me to understand how much of my own fear I created. He would tell me early in the morning that he was going to put me in the ring that afternoon with someone intimidating who I knew could crush me. Then he would watch me getting more tense as the hours went by, imagining all the things I was afraid of: getting hurt, being totally outclassed and walking away feeling like a bruised fool. I could spend hours squirming with the best of my made-up fears as I held myself hostage in my mental gym.

Each time Sensei set me up for feelings like that, I fell for it like a total rube. It was like lighting the fuse of a stress bomb and watching it burn away as I creatively came up with 90 per cent of the most frightening possible scenarios. It took me many years to figure out that Sensei wasn't just innocently mentioning training opportunities to me, but instead was leading me into the traps of my own mind. Sensei would drive me into the 'hood of my fear, and push me out of the car. He'd smile and wave as he drove away, leaving me to fend for myself alone in Feartown. It's not such a bad place to be, unless you fill it with imaginary gangsters all looking to bust a cap in your ass. The more fear you create for yourself, the more you have to call on your general to pull the panicking troops into line.

◆

There was an essential dynamic operating in the background each time Sensei Benny made me face my fears or learn to tolerate pain. Historically, there has always been a powerful obedience expected of true martial arts students towards their teachers. When given an instruction, a student is required to do it to the absolute best of their ability and without question or explanation. In the days of old, disobedience or lack of timely effort would result in brutal punishment or expulsion from a school. In modern styles that tradition lives on, with pupils being expected to loyally do as their teacher says no matter what.

This is how Sensei Benny regularly got me to do things I thought I couldn't handle. He knew that whatever he told me to do, I would simply respond by saying '*Osu*'. This has many meanings, but the sentiment I hold most dear is that 'I will do my absolute best or die trying'. No, not literally (thank goodness), but the idea is that you do all you can, until you absolutely cannot do any more. It's about being unwilling to give up on yourself. An instruction isn't up for debate with your teacher. It sounds harsh I know, but there is actually a real beauty in it. Sensei Benny constantly proved to me he knew the boundaries of what I was capable of far better than I did. My fear or pain would make me give up on myself too soon, when I still had far more to give. He would tell me to keep going, and in any other situation I would have argued the point and said no. With him though, 'Osu' was the only appropriate reply and the next thing I knew I had reached a whole new level. It was an external discipline imposed on me until I learnt how to impose it on myself. When thoughts of *I can't do this* or *I'm not good enough* would fly through my mind, all I had to say was 'Osu' and I would instantly start believing in myself again. Tell yourself you can and you can. Tell yourself it's okay to quit and you will.

My trust in Sensei Benny developed gradually over time to the point where I believed wholeheartedly in what he was teaching me. From the outside, it might have looked like blind faith, but I knew for a fact he would never ask me to do something that he wouldn't do himself.

I was so grateful to have found such a genuine and wise teacher. Having a Sensei is a beautiful thing. He always spoke from lived experience and passed on the knowledge he gained by going down the same road before me. He lit the path through the dark scary forest because he had already walked it. So when he told me to do something, I was often amazed by the result I created, essentially because he had suggested it was possible. I owed him a huge debt for the way he was changing my life but had no way to repay him except with blood, sweat and tears. He made sure I gave plenty of those, but he gave me so much in return. Many of the lessons were hard ones, but he was also very kind to me.

After all the years of hard training visits with Sensei Benny, one particular small kindness meant the world to me. I had been staying at the Jet's Gym again, as per usual. The day had come for me to fly back home, which at that point was Toronto, Canada. Sensei had organised for me to be taken to the airport by one of the junior students. I was sad to leave and waited for a chance to spend even a little more time with him before I had to go. Unfortunately for me, Sensei was having an in-depth conversation with someone (as he always is, the man doesn't do small talk). I waited as long as I could, but eventually knew that my time had run out.

As I walked over to him, I smiled when I caught his eye. In order to not interrupt him speaking, I circled behind him and placed the spare keys to the gym into his hand. As I went to walk away, he gently caught my arm. Without missing a conversational beat, Sensei turned my hand over, placed the keys inside and closed my fist over them. I figured he must have misunderstood what I was doing, so I opened his hand and again pressed the gym keys into his palm. As if nothing had happened the first time, he repeated his returning motion and held my hand closed over the keys. Knowing better than to argue the toss with Sensei Benny, I accepted the confusing gesture and went to collect my bags, thinking we could sort it out later.

Possibly the best workout of my whole trip was dragging my heavy luggage down the stairs to the gym exit. I was looking for the student who had been waiting to take me to the airport. I had five minutes to find them and then say a final goodbye to Sensei Benny. I couldn't find the student so I walked back over to Sensei. When I approached him, he said, 'Are you ready?' I replied that all my bags were downstairs but I couldn't find my ride. He said, 'I am your ride,' and motioned for me to go with him.

We chatted as we sped down the LA freeways in his big truck. I beamed like the kid who'd been picked first for the sports team. It felt like this person I so valued might also value me, not just as a martial artist but even also as a friend. After so much discipline and so many hard challenges in our training, it was just a really nice thing for him to do. As we drove, Sensei brought up the gym keys. He told me that they were for me to keep. Forever. He said I always had a home with him there, that I was welcome anytime and that it was a place where I belonged. He said I should keep them with me and always remember the meaning behind them.

I was so touched that he gave me those keys and had chosen to take me to the airport himself. He wanted that little bit of extra time with me, just like I wanted to spend it with him. This was the first time I knew for sure I had earned a small special place in his heart. I tearfully thanked him and told him how much everything he had taught me was having a profound effect on me. Then I placed the keys on my keychain. One of the keys had three little open windows at the top, similar to the pie slices on a Trivial Pursuit piece. For many years to come I would hold my keys in my hand and run my thumb over those little shapes, and every single time I would remember that day in the car with Sensei.

When I first met him, I knew that he would be my teacher for the rest of my life, but that was a commitment I'd made in my own mind. When he gave me my black belt, he said he invited me into his family. When he showed me kindness by giving me the gym keys, it was like an invitation to stay. I had found my place in the world, and there was no doubt it was practising martial arts with Sensei Benny.

BACK YOURSELF, FIGHT FOR YOUR DREAM. SHOW THEM ALL WHO YOU ARE.

ROUND 4

STRONG FINISHER

Why not me? My time to face my fears.

13

International Adventures

My martial arts journey has taken me to so many different parts of the world, including Australia, the USA, Japan, Canada and Thailand. Each place has taught me a different lesson and acted as a marker of growth. Even if I speak a different language to the people I'm training with, there is an unspoken understanding between us that we are the same.

In Japan the language barrier was huge, but I shared some unmistakably clear communication based on movement and shared passion for our training. I had the honour of watching a Japanese master of Karate demonstrate kata (patterns of movements that simulate a fight performed with an invisible opponent). The beauty and intensity of his skill brought me to tears. When I was later introduced to him, I stumbled my way through an enthusiastic explanation of the impression his kata had made on me. My Japanese is limited, so it was generous of him to pretend he understood my Japanese and English hybrid speech. It was hard to express even in one language the effect watching him had on me. It was how people must have felt watching Nureyev perform ballet or listening to a Chopin composition. This was my kind of beauty. It made perfect sense in my soul and moved me with its powerful grace.

In Japan I felt a real sense of the spirit of Karate. I felt it rumbling there when I heard the loud Taiko drumbeat marking the opening of an international Karate tournament. In a pitch black Japanese stadium, a lone drummer was illuminated by a spotlight as he slowly pounded out an ominous sounding rhythm. As he began to play I felt a connection to an age old warrior lineage. Although I'm a blonde Western girl, I knew my love for martial arts was something I shared with my Japanese counterparts. We reflected the same movements to each other no matter where in the world we were from.

◆

Martial arts has an almost magical ability to create common ground for people that crosses over language and social barriers. This was the case even when I visited the United States. When I stayed at the gym in Los Angeles I always had plenty of spare hours where I just floated around. Sensei Benny would often just grab me and get me to jump into a training session he was teaching. Sometimes it would be as a stand-in body so he could explain a technique, but often he would tell me to get ready to do some sparring. He wouldn't necessarily tell me who with or what was going to happen, but I always had to be ready for anything. I would gear up with all manner of padding and start to warm up, knowing that I would soon be in the ring with an opponent. On one of these occasions, Sensei put me in the ring to spar full contact with a young guy who was mentally challenged. I hadn't been expecting this scenario and hadn't been given any warning before getting into the ring. To be honest, I wasn't sure how to feel, and Sensei didn't give me time to feel much about it before we began.

As we started to move around I could tell he was a beginner and I had a feeling of wanting to take it easy on my new opponent. I know this is sensitive territory, so to be clear I need to explain that what I was feeling was a desire to look after him and make sure he had a good time, which was common when sparring with someone less experienced. I also felt somewhat uncomfortable being in this unexpected situation. Everything was happening so quickly without even the chance to say hello to each other first. Put yourself in my shoes and I'm sure you can imagine some mixed emotions.

I quickly discovered the feeling wasn't mutual as solid punches flew my way. Here was a capable opponent and I knew his strikes were strong enough to do some serious damage. I had to change gears and stop overthinking the situation. As the rounds passed, I made sure I focused on my defence and moved a lot so I didn't take too much impact. Sensei was telling me to work harder on my offence, but it just didn't feel right to me. Something in my gut said I didn't want to open up and go at full power, not because I didn't respect my competition, but because I did. I honestly felt that my intentions were caring, kind hearted and coming from a good place.

'Shame on you. Shame on you, Nadine,' Sensei said as he took my gloves off after the sparring session.

I immediately felt bad that I had possibly gone too hard on my opponent. Sensei must have thought I was taking advantage of the situation. He was looking at me in a way that made me rottenly uneasy and I felt the need to plead my case. But he shut me down and said, 'How dare you assume he needed you to take it easy on him.' I cocked my head to the side in surprise like a Labrador puppy. Sensei continued, 'He didn't need your pity, he needed your best.'

Right away everything came into perspective.

What I had thought was well-intended care for my opponent on my part, was actually an assumption that I knew what was best for him. I had already learned this lesson myself the hard way with all the guys who thought they were doing me a favour by condescendingly sparring with me like I was a girl made of glass rather than an opponent. Controlling their power was fair, but treating me like I was a delicate little flower who would crumble at any minute just served to make the sparring session a waste of time for us both.

Without even realising it, I had perpetrated a similar type of patronisation on my opponent that day. Sensei told me that my rival loved his training just like I did, that this was his opportunity to be brave and I was taking that away from him by reducing the level of threat I presented. He knew I was trying to help, but what I had actually done was the opposite. What my sparring partner needed was to be treated like any other opponent and Sensei had wanted me to give him my best effort. I would never have thought of myself as judgemental or unsupportive of anyone with challenges, but I had been forced to examine my own well-meaning assumptions. Although it came with a degree of shame, I knew this lesson was good for me.

> Only you can win the battle within your own mind.

As always Sensei used the opportunity to burn a hard lesson into my psyche—*In order for someone to be strong, you have to let them be.* You have to give them that opportunity rather than take it away from them, despite your best intentions. You just have to do your best and let go of the outcome for others. Sometimes defeat or a tough challenge is exactly what they need in order to grow in their lives. Sensei knew this situation would give me greater understanding of how to treat people and how I had been treated by others.

Another day in the gym, Sensei Benny spontaneously told me to put on my sparring gear and get into the ring to work with a blonde woman I had never seen before. Again we weren't introduced, but instead just told how many sparring rounds we were to do together as the bell sounded for round one. Within the first thirty seconds she tried to kick my head clean off my shoulders. All I could think was, 'Woah, who has Sensei put me in here with?' As another kick whizzed past my nose at lightning speed, I reminded my body not to tense up (because it makes your reactions slow). I quickly trawled through the go-to solutions from all my training for this type of situation. Years before I would have freaked out and emotionally overreacted, feeling scared for my facial safety and worrying why Sensei Benny hadn't warned me ahead of time about this crazy kicking woman. These days it seemed Sensei trusted me to react in a more measured way, no matter what kind of hot water he put me in. It seemed I had some of his tricks figured out by now and was harder to shock.

I had to quickly solve the problem of these intense kicks being rapidly fired in my general direction. The solution was to close the gap between my opponent and myself so that we were at arm's length and she didn't have much space to kick me. So I moved in and started to box with her. Immediately I could see she wasn't very comfortable defending hand strikes, so I guessed she likely had a Tae Kwon Do background. This was where I had started out my training as a kid so I knew she preferred leg techniques. She tried repeatedly to move away from me and gain the distance to kick again, but Sensei had taught me 'the mark of a warrior is that they know how to dance'. This means before you do anything else in the ring, you have to know how to move your feet smoothly to control your opponent. Every time she moved, I moved with her and negated her distancing. If I stifled her I knew she would get thrown off her game.

After a couple of rounds I knew I had captured her mentally as the frustration of not being able to play to her strengths was written all over her face. She wasn't used to being forced to box and the psychological toll of being out of her comfort zone was quickly depleting her skill set. I felt for her because I had been dragged into that deep water so many times myself. Yet I knew being nice to her and easing off my attack wasn't what Sensei wanted. I knew what it was like to be on the receiving end of the tough lesson when the roles were reversed.

After we got out of the ring, Sensei introduced me to her and I found out she was a recently crowned Tae Kwon Do world champion. My new friend humbly thanked me for the sore-faced lesson I'd delivered. We both already knew the value of not coming out on top because it's where the real growth happens—when you're freaking out, wondering what the heck you're going to do and how you got yourself into this mess in the first place. Yep, that's some fertile growth territory right there. In the case of my opponent that day, Sensei Benny had known (but neglected to tell me) I would give her a run for her money and likely use what he had taught me to take her out of her game. He knew this would be no fun for her at the time, but ultimately would be a good learning experience. It was a relief to finally not be the one having the difficult experience that day, but I knew better than to get a big head about it. If we had been in a Tae Kwon Do tournament, she would probably have schooled me but in the kickboxing ring things were in my favour.

◆

My travels also took me to Canada a number of times and launched different challenges at me with each adventure. Not everything I learned about martial arts there happened in training and not all the situations where I used my training involved physical contact. One day when I was taking a walk through a park I witnessed a huge gang of teenagers (I'm talking about forty) rabidly flowing around a fight between a few young guys. I was wandering along peacefully when I heard an unmistakably familiar tone of voice shouting in the distance. I knew there was trouble brewing from the way it activated a chemical reaction in my adrenal system. It's a specific pitch that sounds like dogs angrily barking. I had heard it many times while working in bars, knowing the tone usually heralds impending violence.

There was a large swarm of high school aged kids churning around a running battle. The two fighting teens ran ahead, only stopping to trade blows. They would be immediately followed by the crowd who would swiftly engulf them again, obscuring my view each time. It looked like one of the fighters was trying to get away from the others. That was a bad situation. Sensei Benny had told me that young men are often more violent when their friends are watching, so I knew this whole situation might get very out of hand. I'd seen enough scenarios where people's pride was on the line in front of their mates to know that's how things escalate quickly. They can easily go from a fair fight between two young guys to a group beat-down where someone is going to hospital.

The one guy who was retreating tried to get away but fell down. When the group caught up to him a number of them started to lay into him while he was on the ground. That was when I knew I had to do something. An unfair fight isn't just poor form, it's downright dangerous. My training had taught me to not run blindly into altercations, but to evaluate a situation for my own safety before intervening. I knew that if I ran in and got physically involved, then the crowd would likely turn on me. That wasn't good, but the kid was taking a real beating now. I started running towards them with a plan rapidly developing in my mind.

When I got to the edge of the crowd, I started yelling at the top of my voice sounding like a panicked teenager myself, 'Run, the cops are here. Run, run, the cops are coming.'

As soon as I shouted it the girls in the group screamed and started running, quickly followed by many of the boys. I changed direction and started yelling about the police again, pushing away some of the guys and saying, 'Quick, go, the cops are right there.' In the confusion of the pack, nobody realised I wasn't one of them. Most of the kids were now running towards the edge of the park, so I had a clear view of the core fighting group that was left. I rushed up to one of the boys on the periphery and yelled at him to get his guys out of there before the cops got them. He grabbed a couple of friends and started pulling them away, which now left me with the main culprits.

I dragged one of the attackers away from the guy on the ground and as much as I had the urge to keep him there until I could call some actual law enforcement, I knew that ending the fight took immediate precedence. I didn't want to grab him and become his new target, so I kept up the charade acting like I was on his side. I quickly told him he needed to get out of there, which much to my relief he promptly did. I did the same with the next one. The final attacker I approached from behind (the safest angle if I had to physically restrain him) and told him to stop because the kid had had enough. As I dragged him backwards, he quickly saw everyone else had left him there alone.

Two guys were now quickly moving towards me from the far side of the boy on the ground. I only had a few seconds to weigh up my next move. Suddenly the final attacker I was holding started to pull away. He was more interested in running after his friends than in attacking me. With more people closing in on me I had to let him go. Now I just had the two guys running back towards me to deal with. I readied myself and yelled to them that the guy on the ground had already had enough. 'Is he okay?' they replied and then started calling out his name but he didn't initially respond. These boys were actually the victim's friends, who had run away but at least had come back for him. As the boy on the ground came to, I gave him some first aid. He was now conscious and his nose was bleeding, but at least the beating was over.

♦

On my second trip to Toronto, I was again called on to push myself out of my comfort zone. This time it would be in order just to train. The winter there was freezing and my Australian beach bunny self is not a fan of cold weather, let me tell you. My natural state is to avoid wearing shoes all summer, rather than having to put on ten clothing layers just so I don't die of exposure when I walk out the front door. I had found a Canadian boxing gym where I was training with an all-female boxing team called the Toronto Newsgirls, led by the iconic Savoy 'Kapow' Howe. The only catch was that the gym was across town and I didn't have a car. What I did have was a bicycle and a burning desire to spend some quality time with a punching bag.

Riding a bike through the snow at night-time is neither easy, nor fun. Let's just say it's more along the lines of slippery and sloshy. It was relatively dangerous, but it was the only mode of transport I had to get to the gym. Every time I went on that sliding ride, with a bag full of boxing gear on my back throwing me off balance every chance it got, I remembered what I was prepared to do in pursuit of this thing I loved so much. Martial arts, Ukidokan, boxing, kickboxing, Jiu Jitsu, you name it, I would ride through snow to do it.

When I got to the gym, I was greeted by an old-school set-up like you'd see in the movies. The Newsgirls squad at the time trained out of the male-dominated Sully's Gym which was above a mechanic's garage in a slightly rough part of town. It was exactly what you'd imagine a boxing gym like that to be—the smell of sweat as you entered, the non-stop drumming of punches thudding on bags, skipping ropes rhythmically tapping the ground, round timer bells going off and a constant pumping beat coming from the stereo. I loved the classic feel of the place. It was loud, a bit grimy and crowded with young men releasing their aggression. So, in other words, just the place for a refined young lady like myself. Ahem, curtsy.

Coach Savoy Howe was a mini dynamo who gave everyone a fight name when they joined the Newsgirls. Mine was the 'Aussie Mauler', which in a Canadian accent sounded more like Aussie Molar, as in the teeth. Savoy looked after the women who trained with her, from novices to competitive fighters, making sure each felt welcomed and was treated with respect. She also taught me a lesson along those lines that lingered long after that first day in the gym.

A room full of fighters interacting with one another can closely resemble a fleet of bumper cars. As a martial artist, you are taught to be courteous, to give way to others and be considerate. In an old-school fight gym like Sully's, there of course wasn't a whole lot of traditional martial arts etiquette on display. The place was full of guys in their early twenties training to fight, who were all testosterone and arrogance. If you were training in an area that they wanted to use, they would literally come and take over the space. I wasn't accustomed to this kind of overtly inconsiderate behaviour so I let it slide a few times. That and I was a bit shocked wondering if what I'd thought had just happened actually did? It felt like standing in line and someone literally just barging in front of you without saying a word and acting like nothing happened. I didn't want to make waves when

I was the new person at the gym. It was what I imagine being the fresh inmate in the prison yard would feel like. You don't want to fight but you also know that if you let people push you around, then they will continue to and it will likely only get worse.

Savoy walked up to me and quietly said, 'You have to take up space. As a woman, you have to take up space or the boys will take it from you.' She was telling me to hold my ground, not in an aggressive way that would force a confrontation, but just in a quiet solid way.

As soon as she spoke those words my mindset changed, as did my sense of personal space in the gym. I just went methodically about my training, but without giving way to the young bucks. It was more about not letting them disrupt what I was doing, than reacting to them encroaching on my space. Savoy was savvy, she knew the best path was to stand strong without creating a problem and, sure enough, the issue would resolve itself. If we didn't move for them, they would move on. She taught me to own the space I was in, without apologising in any way for being there. Savoy herself was a powerful, subtle display of female self-confidence in a small body.

◆

Fighters the world over have to develop very strong self-confidence and self-belief. If left unchecked, this positive self-image can turn into a massive ego. The best exude superior confidence without even trying. You can almost smell it on them as they pass by. Fighters see this in each other, often letting on by doing what I call the 'fighter's nod'. It's a subtle acknowledgement and a way of silently saying, 'I feel you, I know you're there.' It's recognising your people, without even needing to speak to them.

When I travelled in Thailand with Sensei Benny, we received the fighter's nod in all kinds of places. Thailand is famed for Muay Thai (a brutal form of kickboxing that also involves knee and elbow strikes), so there's no shortage of warriors. Sensei Benny, often also his wife Sensei Sara and I would all get up at dawn every morning and go for a run in Bangkok's Lumpini Park. At the edge of the park sat Lumpini Stadium, one of the most famous Thai boxing arenas in Thailand, attracting fighters from all over the world. Sensei Benny was one of the first Westerners to ever fight in Thailand back in the day. This visit to the country was to make a movie, but I also happened to be training for an upcoming fight. All the torturous rounds we had done in the ring over the years had led me down the path of needing to test myself in actual competition. That involved a whole new level of commitment and effort in training.

Each morning Sensei would tell me what time to be ready and we would set out on our runs. The heat of the day was already present even as the sun was coming up. I've always been someone who runs quite hot, both literally and even generally at rest. I overheat in extreme weather and feel the cold at the slightest sign of a chill in the air. I would usually go running in a crop top and small shorts to counteract this, but the Thai culture leans towards modesty, so I always had to wear a shirt when we ran there. Combine this with the intensely hot temperature and about twenty minutes into every run I was struggling. I spent hours looking at the back of Sensei Benny's head as he ran far ahead, even though he was a couple of decades older than me. Occasionally I would see him raise the back of his hand to the side and his fingers would bend to wave me forward urging me to catch up with him. I would hit the accelerator even though I felt like my tank was already on empty. All of the training not to show pain or discomfort came in handy, yet I couldn't help but whimper out loud as I felt like my legs were turning to jelly. Even more disheartening was when I would finally catch up with Sensei and see that he wasn't even breathing hard. I wondered if he was actually some type of cyborg, sent back in time like the Terminator to stealthily kill me via dehydration.

Due to Lumpini Stadium being literally at the park, we would see many fighters from all over the world doing their morning runs. They would give us the fighter's nod as they passed, a silent acknowledgement that they knew why we were there. I was happy to be part of this culture and to be recognised as belonging to it. It was almost like an exclusive secret club. As we were running Sensei would point out commonalities and differences in the way these fighters carried themselves, both physically and energetically. He would mention the way one moved his weight as he ran or how another was trying to look like the top dog over everyone else. It was fascinating to hear the way he saw everyone from a different perspective to me.

When we would get to a hill, especially if it had other fighters part of the way up, Sensei would tell me to sprint to the top. He said when other people get to a hill, they often slow down and pace themselves because they know it is going to be hard. He taught me that when others slow down, I should speed up. Every. Single. Time. Once I got used to it (otherwise known as—I stopped wanting to cry every time there was even the slightest increase in road gradient), I started to notice the change in energy the fighters would have as I sprinted past them. Some wanted to go faster with me, but most instantly deflated. It was almost audible, the way some of their spirits would start to break. It's a familiar feeling to being in the ring when you're exhausted and suddenly it seems like your opponent isn't gassed at all. It's devastating psychological warfare and Sensei Benny was a master of this 'art of war'.

I pushed hard to keep up with this man who had remained the best in the world and undefeated for twenty-seven years. As we ran he would talk to me and teach me about what it meant to have the mind of a champion. I was suffering tremendously during those exertions, but I knew that if my head told my body to go, then my feet would follow. If my mind told my body it was acceptable to stop, throw up and sit down feeling sorry for myself, then that is exactly what my body would have done. It's somewhat disgusting, but in the ring Sensei Benny taught me to work so hard that I wanted to throw up at the final bell. He wanted me to give everything I had and leave nothing in reserve. In fact, I will never forget the sound of Sensei's voice impatiently letting me know a new round had started. We were training in the ring and he fully expected me to answer the bell, despite the retching sounds I was making in the corner. He had no sympathy for me, instead only a cold expectation that I would wipe my mouth and get on with the task at hand. If he had been too easy on me, then I would have been easy on myself and made excuses about why I needed to stop. The reality was I didn't actually need to stop at all despite the vomit. Sensei knew what it meant to be at his own limit, and that fighters rarely discovered the true boundary of their capabilities because they would take heaving as a sign they were finished. For me that familiar feeling became one of many that I was just getting started.

Although it was at times unpleasant, I was being taught how to just carry on no matter what happened and get the job done. Sensei knew the trap for many competitors was not being able to leave it all in the ring. It's a terrible thing to hear a fighter in the dressing room, having lost their bout, lamenting that they 'could have done more'. But it's an all too common refrain. The antidote is to train to completely empty your gas tank before the final bell with no excuses, not even regurgitation. That may sound harsh or crazy, but remember this was coming from a man who is one of the greatest fighters in history. He went undefeated for decades for a very good reason.

I pushed myself on those Thailand runs as hard as I could, wondering if the high temperature and humidity might cause me to faint. I felt glee and relief when we would round the corner towards the gate to the park where we began and ended our runs. One morning Sensei asked me to take my headphones out and give them to him as we neared the finish after a long hot run. I said, '*Osu*,' and dutifully complied without asking him why. When I handed them over, Sensei's face got serious and he pointed away saying, 'You go again. This time, no music.' My heart sank. I ran because it was an important part of training, but I didn't love running itself. One of the ways I made it easier was by listening to great music to stay motivated. Sensei could feel my overheated and tired hesitation. For a second I even considered telling him that I didn't think I could do it, but I couldn't say the words to him especially if I hadn't even tried. He came closer to me and said, 'When you run, you fight *yourself*. Competing in the ring your favourite song won't be playing to motivate you. You have to battle your inner voice that tells you to slow down. It is going to scream at you, but you have to overcome it.' That was all I needed to hear and as another '*Osu*' left my lips, I set off determined on my mission.

He was right, every footstep of the second half of the run was done to the awful soundtrack in my head of that inner voice yelling at me. I wanted to quit, I wanted to slow down, but I knew I had to do it. As much as it felt like it would kill me, I sprinted with all I had left as I got to the hills. I knew I had to do it even when nobody was watching. I had to do it for me, no matter how much it hurt. As I ran back towards the finish point, I guess I'd been expecting to see Sensei's face smiling at me. When I rounded the final bend, I couldn't see him. He wasn't there and as I walked, confused, back to the hotel, it slowly dawned on me—of course he wasn't there, this was about me and knowing the only voice that I would have during a round in the ring was my own. It wasn't that Sensei didn't care enough to wait for me, it was that I had to do it myself. I had to fight to gain the mental edge within my mind. The old chestnut resurfaced of having to be happy with my own efforts, instead of needing someone else to tell me what I had done was good enough. Sensei and I never talked about it again. He didn't ask me if I had finished the run. Like Majid having to train by himself at six o'clock each morning at the gym in L.A, Sensei knew I would do what he asked of me. The tough battle with my own thoughts was one fight I desperately wanted to win.

◆

Sensei Benny was always teaching me about the mental edge, whether it was running in Bangkok, putting me under pressure with challenging opponents in the ring or just by talking to me over a meal. Everything came back to knowing your own mind and the way our training brought that out into the light for all to see. The beautiful and equally difficult thing about the boxing ring was that it exposed the unequivocal truth of what you were made of. During the toughest points against an opponent, it's not possible to fake your level of heart or character. When fatigue comes to suck the life out of your muscles and break you, it's only your inner voice and what lies inside your heart which decides your fate.

> Practise being a strong finisher. When everyone else is fading, make it your habit to power through.

It's a special moment to see someone in any physical challenge rise up powered only by their mettle. It's the marathon runner at the Olympics who gets a second wind just long enough to stagger on wobbly legs over the finish line. It brings tears to our eyes because we know that effort comes straight from their heart. Sensei knew that type of mental fortitude could be fostered in training, just as he had been teaching me on our runs in Thailand. He wanted his fighters to know they had a turbo thruster pack of perseverance and will to win that they could bring out when they needed it most.

There's a quote I love associated with the great philosopher Aristotle, 'We are what we repeatedly do. Excellence, then, is not an act but a habit.' In line with this, Sensei Benny demanded bursts of energy that would further develop mental toughness at the end of every training round in the gym. In a fight, there is a clapper that sounds as a signal ten seconds before the end of each round. In training, every time I heard the last ten seconds signal, Sensei taught me to sprint with everything I had left. Being a *strong finisher* was non-negotiable. Putting in a solid effort during the round but fading towards the end was not an option. The more I practised finishing strong, the more it became normal. It became an almost Pavlovian reaction—hear the sound, give a huge effort. In a bout the idea was to finish every single round as hard as you could, to show the judges and your opponent who wanted it more. You could send your opponent back to their corner thinking you weren't as tired as them (when the truth was you were likely almost dying inside) and to steal the round on points if it had been a close one. Over time you learned to trust your ability to end the round hard and recover quickly due to your fitness. The harder you trained, the fitter you became and the more intensely you could compete. Your physical ability always came down to your mental edge.

Adjusting my mindset so that the end of an exertion was flipped around to be the time I pushed the hardest made me improve in unexpected ways. I decided that the *last one always has to be the best one.* If I had to do one hundred kicks, then the one hundredth kick had to be the best one I threw. Even if

Make your last one your best one.

it wasn't, I had to try like it would be. It became habit to try to finish everything I did with an exclamation point. I liked the feeling of putting my stamp on what I was doing, no matter how tired I became or how difficult the conditions. The more I pushed outside my comfort zone, the more I started to like it out there.

14

Why Not You?

I kicked John Cusack in the face. Yes, his million-dollar Hollywood actor's face. I'm not sure who was more surprised that day in Bangkok—me because I'd managed to get my foot up that high when he's 6 feet 2 inches, or John because he wasn't expecting it. I had done something I didn't think I could do. It wasn't the first time on that trip to Thailand and it wouldn't be the last.

'Johnny', as Sensei affectionately calls him, has been his student for three decades. Needless to say, he is very skilled and when you add that to very tall, you end up with a hard day at the office for little old 5'6" me. Luckily, John is one of the nicest guys you will ever meet and spending so many years training under Sensei Benny has given him the heart of both a fighter and a martial artist.

With the heat in Thailand being a particularly stifling affair, it would leave me feeling drained by about 7.30 a.m. On the day of the famous face kicking, we were training in the squash courts at John's five-star hotel. Now that sounds hot enough, right? But no, Sensei Benny had called ahead a few hours earlier and asked the staff to turn the air-conditioning off. By the time we arrived it was like a sauna in there, just the way Sensei Benny likes it. He didn't intend for us to train under normal conditions. The more pressure the better, be it distracting withering heat or being outgunned by a bigger opponent.

Now I couldn't offer John any challenge in the height department, but I could give him a run for his money on the fast track. The strategy with a taller, heavier opponent is to get in quickly to strike and then get away without being hit back. This requires both cunning and moving like the floor is on fire under your feet. To make the fight a little fairer when John and I were sparring, Sensei put him in a training device that involves attaching resistance bands to the hands and anchoring them to the fighter's chest. It looks like a chest strap with big rubber bands that disappear into the boxing gloves.

That meant every time John went to throw a punch, he had to try ten times harder and it slowed him down. Thankfully for me, when he did connect, it was much lighter than normal. After a few rounds we were both dripping with sweat. John looked like Godzilla tied up with elastic ropes, while I buzzed around him at speed having about the same slightly annoying effect as the Japanese army in the film. Well, that was until my foot connected with his jaw . . .

To this day I don't know how I managed to stretch that high. It was like a slow-motion Kung Fu movie scene where the actors are flying around on wires, doing multiple kicks that look like they're running through the air. But the truth is, it was only one kick. As soon as I did it, I clicked out of training mode and into reality that this man couldn't afford a black eye during filming. I had forgotten that he was a celebrity while we trained and he had a job to do.

Sensei Benny had the same attitude in the gym, treating everyone in the class equally. It didn't matter if you were a kid like me sleeping on the floor because you were broke, or one of the many famous people who trained there. Celebrity didn't rate highly on his scale. In fact, Sensei Benny is fairly famous himself, which is easy for me to forget, having known him half of my life. It was always an amusing reminder when people would freak out upon seeing him in the street, countless times stopping us for photos or an autograph. They recognise him from being in films or because of his high profile in martial arts. It always makes me smile because he is so humble, you would never know he was famous from the way he carries himself. He moves with the self-assurance of a man who has faced and defeated every possible opponent in the world, but he has the humility of a true martial arts master. Not that he will let you call him that.

◆

Sweat is the great equaliser. When we would all train hard together, there was never a distinction of what made people important in the outside world. I shed so much sweat locked in that Bangkok squash court with those two famous men who treated me as an equal. We were family, brought together by our love for the training and what it taught us about ourselves as people. Even as we punched and kicked each other, it was always with respect. When I caught John with that head kick, he didn't show it and promptly made me pay for my efforts. I fired back with a left hook that connected. Afterwards he smiled and jokingly held his jaw, telling me I'd caught him with a good shot. I laughed and said it was a miracle.

When training was over for the day, Sensei Benny and I caught a boat back across the Chao Praya river. I loved these times with him, satisfied from a good training session, when we would sit and talk. Once we got to the other side of the river, Sensei and I sat down and started discussing life. Never one for casual chit-chat, Sensei Benny always spoke on a deeper level. He asked what my dreams were for my future. I had learnt over the years since the first day we met, not to tell him what I 'thought' or to talk around an issue.

I answered the question with the best my young heart could muster. I don't even remember now what kind of standard average things I said I hoped for in my life. All I recall is Sensei's reaction. He looked at me as if I'd said that my life dream was to be a hobo begging for food by the side of the road. He asked why I didn't want more for myself. Why my dreams were so small? I had never thought they were until that point. I thought of myself as someone who strived to achieve. Someone who wanted a good life and was prepared to fight for it.

What I understood then was that I was looking *up* at what I thought a good life would be. I had placed an invisible ceiling which was the limit to what I could reach for, without ever consciously deciding it. Sensei Benny was looking *down* on that ceiling as someone who had reached so much higher in his life, and was wondering why I wasn't prepared to do the same. He was telling me that my ceiling was far too low, and questioning why I had one there at all.

If I wanted to be a fighter, he asked, why didn't I aim for being a great world champion? If I wanted to be successful, why didn't I set my sights on being rich and famous? If I wanted to be happy, why didn't I want to be the happiest person I knew?

Granted these seem like lofty, maybe even unrealistic goals out of the reach of most people. But they weren't unrealistic at all to Sensei Benny. They were the kinds of things that had happened to him in his life. To him it seemed a shame to hope for less for yourself.

This was the first time I'd seen my own self-imposed limitations from another perspective. If I was going to reach for something, why not reach for the highest branch on the tree if that was what I deeply wanted? That didn't mean Sensei only supported my dreams if they were huge. He just didn't want me to aim low, simply because I didn't believe I was capable of any more than that. My mental autopilot had not even bothered to consciously consult me before deciding I could only aim 'so' high. I wouldn't have thought of myself as someone who had placed limits on what I could achieve, but here was clear evidence that I had. It was a stark reality that made me uncomfortable, but that's how I knew it was true.

Sensei Benny looked at me and said, 'Why not you?'

I had no logical answer for him. What do you say to a world champion who has been in dozens of movies when they ask why you couldn't do the same thing if you chose to? It all seemed so realistic and possible to him. Why couldn't I have the kind of life others only dream of? I was stumped for what to say. The only options were: 1) because that's not what I desire for myself (which seemed reasonable); 2) because I'm not good enough (which made me sad); or 3) because I've decided that

I'm average without even realising it so I'm just going to achieve regular things and hope for nothing more (which made me want to throw myself in the river).

Sensei asking me that question was so deeply transformative because it was just so plainly stated. It wouldn't have had the same effect if he had been trying to pump me up and tell me I could achieve anything I set my heart on. Instead, to him, it was simply a given that I should reach for the exceptional in life. Why not me? I knew I had to start by changing my thinking.

A familiar theme began sounding in my mind. We are who we *think* we are. We are who we *decide* to be. We are who we tell ourselves we are (so long as we aren't delusional). We limit ourselves by what we decide is our truth or by what we feel we deserve. The insane part is that we do it without even consciously realising it. Knowing this, I made a decision to expect more for and of myself. My reality had been permanently altered.

The *why not you* conversation with Sensei stayed with me for years, uncomfortably gnawing away at my mind every time I made a decision about what I could or couldn't do, and what I wanted for myself. It was like my denial had been snapped and I couldn't put it back together. I couldn't un-know what I knew about the boundaries I'd set for myself to live inside. Sensei had pushed the point further by asking, 'What are you pretending *not* to know?' There were things I knew about who I was and what I wanted that I'd been hiding away in the back of my mind, too scared to bring them forward.

From that day in Thailand, it was like a spark had been lit inside me that was the dream of a bigger life. It smouldered until the heat from it became impossible to ignore. I had to admit my secret dreams to myself. But once I did that, the consequence

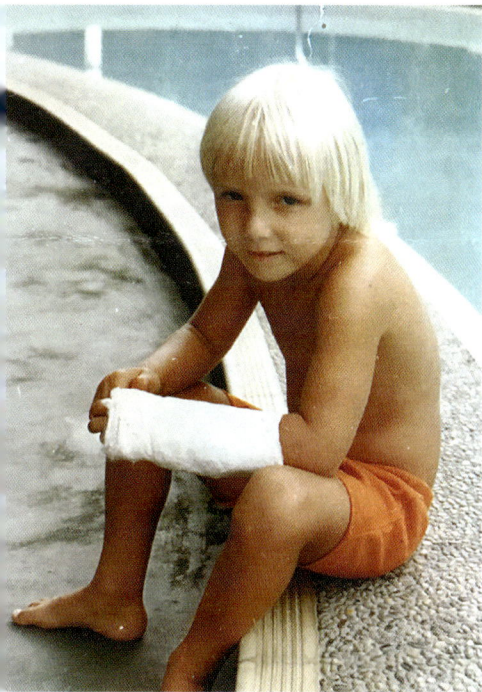

A broken arm for my birthday. No pool party for me.

A karate kid at ten years old. I still make the same kicking face.

The look on my flower girl face says it all.

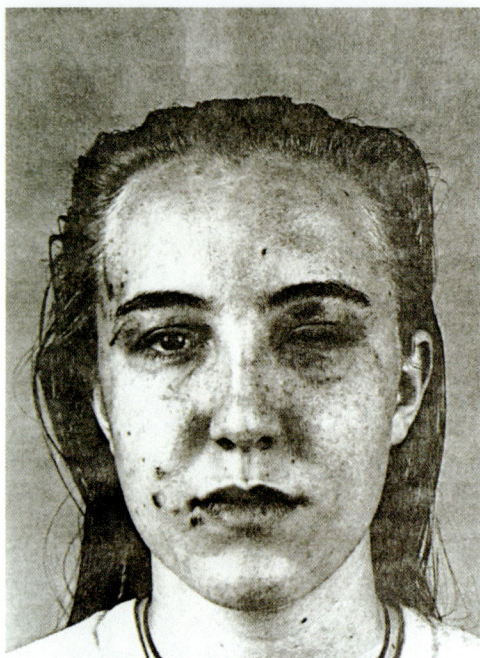

Police photo showing the results of being eye-gouged.

The first time I met Sensei Benny (with those Jet Fighter shorts behind us).

My black belt test with Sensei Benny watching me like a hawk.

My two favourite things together—Karate and the beach.

Sensei Benny, John Cusack and me on the movie set in Thailand.

My first title fight was a battle with my opponent and within myself.
(Simon Taylor Photography)

Sensei and Andy taking my gloves off after the fight. Let's just say it hurt. Lots.
(Simon Taylor Photography)

My *Karate Kid* moment—wearing the title belt and Sensei proudly smiling at me. (Simon Taylor Photography)

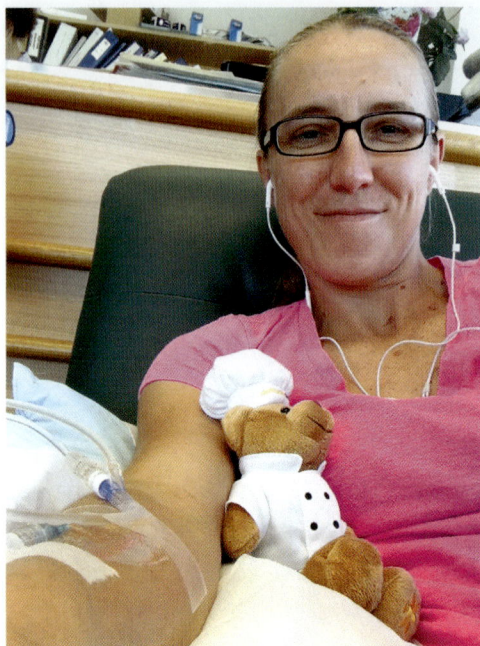

My first day of chemo. The pink shirt was to keep my spirits high.

Struggling to train halfway through my cancer treatment. Hair and eyebrows falling out but I had Paul and Sensei Benny behind me.

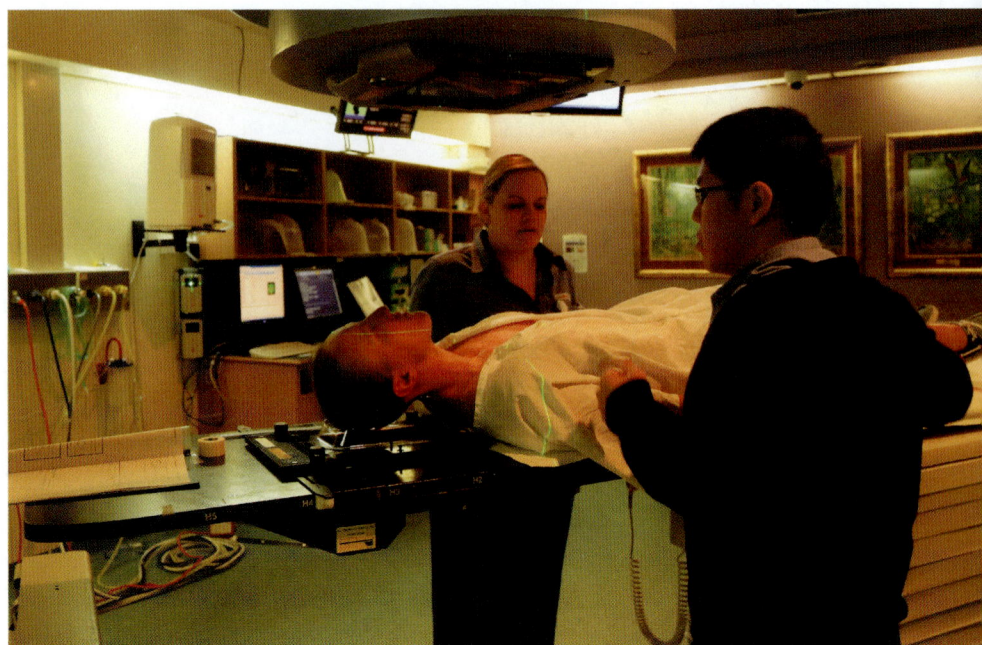

Strapped down under the radiation machine every day for a month.

After wiping away my tears I replaced them with joy as I left the hospital on my final day of radiation.

Speaking for the first time with a huge audience at TEDx Sydney at the Opera House.

The moment before I tried to break the board, with everyone's hands up in support. (Photo by JJ Halans)

Wearing some of the victory hardware. You never know what you can achieve unless you try.

would be that I had to do something about them or live in the knowledge that I had never even tried to make them come true.

♦

One of the dreams I'd been pretending not to know I had was to become a champion fighter like Sensei Benny. I had been successful in all kinds of martial arts competitions, but I had not at that stage fought full contact in a kickboxing ring. In my twenties, my dreams of competitive fighting had ended when I suffered a nasty injury in training. I was doing a high double-leg takedown on a heavier male training partner which meant I had him balanced in the air over my shoulder, before toppling him down to the floor. In the process, I zigged while he zagged, whiplashing my neck as we moved dynamically in opposite directions. Basically, the nice gentleman I was holding up high with my shoulders shifted his full body weight sideways onto my neck, which herniated two discs in my cervical spine. The problem with bulging discs is the pressure they place on the nerves. You have no idea how much you use your neck until it hurts to move it even a little. The neck is forced to constantly support the head, so the pain that comes with this type of injury is intense and persistent.

Now don't get me wrong, as a woman training with much larger men, I was used to getting hurt. But there is a big difference between getting hurt and being injured. Pain is something you learn to work through in training. Bruises, cuts and sore muscles are all fairly standard. You learn to keep the pain from showing on your face. You acknowledge it in passing, without giving it your full attention. It's like stubbing your toe and thinking to yourself 'Ow that hurt' while you keep walking, instead of hopping around on one leg, grabbing your foot and crying like it's been unexpectedly amputated. Things hurt, but you just get on with training.

This time I wasn't hurt. I was undeniably injured. It was the kind of injury that stops you in your tracks. When you know something is seriously wrong. Soon after it happened I ended up spread out on the floor and in excruciating pain. I was trying to tell myself it was just a muscle spasm that would be over soon. When I couldn't lift my head off the floor without an intense shooting pain travelling down my back, I knew I was unmistakably in trouble. I had to grab a handful of my own hair to pull my head up off the ground.

The pain didn't go away so eventually I consulted a sports surgeon, who told me I could no longer absorb contact without worsening the injury. If I carried on, I would need surgery to fuse the vertebrae in my neck together. Hello, Lady Frankenstein. Not a good look. He told me flat out that I had to immediately give up grappling (any kind of wrestling, either standing or on the ground) or I would end up in hospital. I'd been told by doctors before not to train in certain ways, but the pain in my neck meant this time I had to listen.

I made the difficult decision to let go of any grappling or wrestling sports I trained in, such as Brazilian Jiu Jitsu. I was especially saddened by having to give up my dream of competing in the emerging sport of mixed martial arts. I had been hoping to fight in Japan and was training to make that dream come true, but in order to do that I would need to be able to fight standing and on the ground. I tentatively tried training this way again, hoping things might improve, but each time I ended up in agony.

I was a huge fan of the Ultimate Fighting Championship (UFC) and wished that one day they would allow women to fight. I wanted that to be me. It was a dream that was replaced by my neck injury. Little did I know that the first women's UFC bout in history would later be held in my weight division. It was set at 135 pounds, which is near my 62-kilogram fighting weight, so there was a part of me that was gutted. It's amazing how one moment in your life can change its trajectory, the way injuring my neck that day had for me. The closest I would come to the octagon was training others who competed in the UFC.

Of all the injuries I've ever had, this was by far the most debilitating. I've had to sleep on my back for the last fifteen years because of it. I can't sit for long with my head on an angle or look sideways while I have a conversation. I'm full frontal most of the time to keep my neck straight and avoid looking as stiff as a robot for days. If I'm not careful, I pay a painful price.

Having to adjust my daily activities was one thing, but I also had to adjust the way I trained in the parts of martial arts I could still perform. I could do certain moves but had to stop doing others. I could spar in the boxing ring for practice, but had to make sure I didn't get hit in the head too much or too hard. Even a light blow on a bad angle would leave me feeling seriously sore and sorry.

The injury I'd sustained was affecting my quality of life so much that I was afraid to get hurt even worse. Now to those people who don't do a contact sport, this seems very sensible, right? Just stop doing it. But to those who have a love/hate relationship with a sport which both enamours and injures them, the idea of just quitting isn't really an option.

I know there are people who have been hurt way worse than me, who went back to doing exactly what they were doing before, and I eventually wanted to be one of them. My daily attempts to push the boundaries of what I could now do always ended the same way—with me in pain for days, unable to get comfortable while sitting still, let alone actually keep training.

Doing what I used to do, the way I used to do it, was now not possible for me. I had to learn to do things differently. It was either that, or give up completely. Martial arts were my passion. They made me happy in a special way that nothing else could. The feeling of sweat dripping off me in the middle of a training session, the excitement of learning a new move, the feeling of belonging when we line up together at the start of class. I loved it all so deeply that I knew it would be part of my life always.

◆

My new and different way of training eventually led to a different way of fighting. I developed a strategy that was in line with what Sensei Benny had been telling me all along—don't get hit. Sounds like good advice, yes? He told me fighters were sometimes too tough for their own good. They took shots in order to give them, and they received unnecessary damage to prove their toughness. He warned me this led to short fighting careers, as the body can only take so much punishment.

Sensei explained that in the ring, as in life, it is better to be a chess player than a checkers player. I did some quick research on their rules (too much Karate, not enough board games). What he meant was that it is better to have a strategy to win with the least amount of damage. You don't want to lose a playing piece in order to take one of your opponent's. It is better to be smart and win as quickly and efficiently as possible.

I started to think of ways to get around the problem I was facing—how could I fight full-contact in the ring without hurting my neck? I wanted to test myself at this level of fighting but I knew that I didn't want to be permanently injured. Most people would take this possibility as a reason to avoid competing, but I started to see it as a challenge. Could I be good enough to fight and win? How good would I have to be to compete without getting hit?

This was the art of defence in the ring that Sensei Benny opened up for me—to hit without being hit back. A total beginner can go in there and start swinging wildly at their opponent, receiving blows in return and trying never to take a backwards step. That's one style of fighting. But I came to see that it takes a whole other level of skill and consciousness to evade your opponent's counterstrikes. I knew if I wanted to fight, I would have to rise to this standard. In contrast to the tough guy mentality of many fighters, I would have to avoid being hit. I had to place the importance of good defence above all other skills. It wasn't good to *look* like a fighter, because if you did it meant you weren't necessarily a very good one. If your face was all broken up and scarred, it was a sign that your defence wasn't great and you got hit—a lot. I was keenly aware that a sport involving head trauma was an insane pursuit and I was quite fond of my mental faculties. Sensei was adamant to always avoid taking impact, both out of cautionary deference for the side effects of our dangerous sport but also as a mark of skill. This was the art in the martial.

Competing in kickboxing would be difficult enough as it involved dodging punches and kicks to the head. Thai boxing would be even more difficult as it also involved my opponent being able to hold and pull down on my neck. The idea of someone even touching my neck was scary enough, but someone grabbing my head and reefing it down so they could knee me in the face was worse. But if I wanted to test myself in full-contact competition, these were the sports I could compete in. By utilising kicks I could avoid the constant punches to the head that happen in boxing. If I used my footwork, I hoped to avoid anyone grabbing my neck.

My strategy for fighting became to control the distance between me and my opponent at all times. If she moved towards me to punch, I would also move to keep the distance at kicking range. If we were at punching range, I would quickly throw my combination of punches and move away on an angle to stop her hitting me back. I had to be focused and aware of everything that was happening at all times. I wanted to avoid injury, so I turned my cautiousness about getting hurt into fast defensive movement.

◆

I first had to put these defensive theories to the test successfully in controlled contact competitions, where there was only minor chance of doing further damage to my neck injury. Over time the challenge of competing had been wearing off because there was no real physical threat. I was winning in mostly theoretical combat only. I wasn't satisfied. I was restless.

My instructor came up with ways to make the martial arts tournaments more challenging, like telling me on a Saturday that I was to compete on the Sunday. With no preparation time, it would be a test of how well I could perform on any given day.

I was still successful, which in some ways made me complacent. I casually walked into one tournament with a coffee in my hand to the sounds of my division already starting. I put down my cappuccino, changed into my uniform and walked out onto the competition floor cold without a warm-up. The event was more difficult but I still came out on top and knew that the challenge was just not there anymore.

I loved teaching more than I was interested in winning further traditional competition trophies. I was excited to take my students to compete at the World Cup of Martial Arts and only competed myself at their request. My heart wasn't in it anymore when I knew there was little chance of any real threat I had to face as I competed. I won a gold medal that day, but my joy was more in watching my students test themselves. I knew that would be my last light contact competition and I had no choice but to move on towards something more dangerous.

I just couldn't shake the rumblings of wanting to test myself at a higher level, despite the risk involved with my neck injury. I had to play my cards right, though, and choose my events carefully. I was so interested in the efficiency of mixed martial arts competition that involved submission holds instead of just striking each other. Making an opponent tap out to signal they quit seemed so much more merciful and I liked the idea of being able to end the bout quickly if possible. Much of my training had been for real-life situations where the goal was to end things immediately. I decided to compete in Pankration, which didn't allow head punches but almost any other full-contact technique was permissible. In my first match, I was concerned about hurting my neck so I had a game plan to end it fast. In training I had set out in my mind some possible scenarios—'if she does this, then

I will do that'—type situations. My plan proved spot-on and I made my opponent submit with a guillotine choke thirteen seconds into the bout. I was hooked.

I competed a few more times in Pankration and each match ignited the desire to compete even more. Soon I felt that same need to up the ante and the opportunity came in the form of an opponent who was 25 kilos heavier than me. She was much bigger but wasn't a very experienced competitor, which evened things up somewhat. In my mind, I wanted to see how effective I'd be competing against a woman whose size made her a formidable opponent. The match ended in the first round when I caught her in an arm bar submission hold and forced her to concede defeat. Although the fight had been a challenge, it still wasn't enough. I knew there was only one way this competitive urge would be quenched. I had to fight full-contact kickboxing in the ring.

The time had unavoidably come to put myself to the test in a competitive full-contact fight where head strikes were allowed. I wanted to test my physical skills and I wanted to know how I would perform under the pressure of getting hurt, with a big crowd and the very real possibility of further injury. After all I had been through in my training, I wanted to see how I would fare emotionally. Would I be able to do all the things Sensei Benny had trained me to do? Did I have the true ability to use the mental edge? Deep down I wanted to see if I could be a champion fighter, but I was too scared to admit this out loud to anyone at first.

Fear is an unavoidable part of fighting. As much as I had confidence, I also knew every champion's journey involves finding the courage to climb through the ropes for the very first time.

Even as an experienced martial artist, I had to find a brave part within myself to do the same. My fear wasn't so much about my opponent, as it was about myself. Fear that I would make a mistake and end up having surgery on my neck. Fear that the emotional vulnerability I had experienced in training would for some reason re-emerge mid fight. Fear that all my hopes and dreams about being a fighter would be crushed and I'd find out I wasn't actually very good.

For someone so invested in her training, this was a huge risk for me. There was part of me that thought I should just let it go and stay safe. I pictured being old and looking back on my life. The fear of never knowing if I could have done it successfully troubled me. The regret of not having tried would be far more painful than any injury. So I made my final decision—it was time to fight.

◆

I had been trained for years in how to prepare for the highest levels of combat competition without ever being able to fully go all out. Now was my time. I examined all the training information that I had been schooled in by Sensei over the years and formulated my fight preparation plan. From the beginning, he had taught me to fight like a pro. Given the risk I was taking by literally sticking my neck out, I was going to train like this would be my one and only fight in the ring. I had scary visions of getting hit with the first punch and the discs in my neck crumbling. This was closely followed by me being carted off to hospital feeling like a fool for having even tried to go against the medical warning I'd been given. If I was going to compete,

I knew it was going to take all my wits and a big slice of luck. I was taking this seriously. Deadly seriously.

Sensei Benny had suggested that I shouldn't announce what I wanted to do to my students or the other instructors. Instead he said I should just quietly work towards it, with action being far more important than words. It wasn't about making a show of what I was seeking to accomplish, so I casually began visiting another gym where my focus was solely on my training and working towards my dream. There I could focus and sweat it out, without having my workouts interrupted

After a good amount of time I approached the gym's highly regarded Thai boxing head trainer about getting me a fight and he told me what weight division I should ideally fight within. I got straight to work trimming down and went back to him once I had made it to the correct weight on the scales. I was all eagerness and naivety, thinking this would be enough for him to get me a match-up. We talked about it, me with unbridled enthusiasm and him with relative ambivalence. Clearly this was just another day for him, but to me it was an important part in a process I had been dreaming about for many years.

Somewhere along the line I mentioned my neck. Now we had a problem. A big problem. I only said something because I thought he needed to know if he was going to be in my corner. That was a deal breaker for him, though. He said I shouldn't fight. He didn't want me to injure myself. Not realising how much it meant to me, he suggested I should just let it go. He was a good man who had trained many champions, so to him I wasn't an injury gamble worth taking. I understood his decision even though I was crushed.

Back to the drawing board. It was hard because Sensei Benny was oceans away in America, so I looked around at my training partners at the gym where I was teaching. I had wanted to keep my fighting aspirations separate to the place where I taught classes because I wanted it to be something I did for me, rather than lots of other people jumping on my bandwagon. I also knew it would damage my professional reputation if the worst-case scenario came true and my neck couldn't take any impact. It's frowned upon to make excuses about how you fought, so I knew there would be no get-out-of-jail-free card afterwards where I could say I had a pre-existing injury. If that ended up being why I lost, I wouldn't be able to tell anyone why.

I liked and trusted the guys I trained with at my gym so it was fun training there to compete. I was surrounded by champions of boxing, kickboxing and Thai boxing all training together, such as Andrew Berridge, Tomas Vysokai and Peter 'The Chief' Graham. I tried to dodge distractions, but people would see me working out and take that as their opportunity to finally talk to me about doing some private lessons. My iPod became my most crucial piece of training equipment. I had once been told by a very high ranking martial arts Shihan that you can either fight or teach, but trying to do both doesn't work. Now I started to get an insight into why he had said that. Fighting is a self-focused pursuit while teaching is all about giving of yourself.

My preparation was methodical, planning workouts and ticking items off my list as the weeks went by. I ran all of it by Sensei Benny to make sure my training was on point and in alignment with what he would have me do if I were physically with him. I'd been working very hard and told him about what I had been doing with a little bit of pride in my efforts. True to form, Sensei found a way to pull the rug out from under me. One thing I've learnt over the years with him is that just when I think I've got it, nope I haven't got it. As tough as that feels, it reminds me never to get too comfortable or self-congratulatory.

Sensei seemed approving of most of what I had been putting myself through in training, until I got to telling him about my abdominal conditioning. I thought I was pretty hardcore doing 200 sit-ups (oh, silly me), when he stopped me and said, 'No, I want you to do 500 sit-ups.'

'Sensei, you want me to do five hundred?'

'Yes. Do it three times a week,' he replied adamantly.

'Seriously?' It came out of my mouth before I had a chance to stop it.

'Do fifteen hundred sit-ups a week for at least six weeks to prepare to fight,' he said this as if it was no big deal at all.

'*Osu* Sensei. That's a *lot* of sit-ups,' I jokingly replied with a hint of disbelief in my voice at how high he had set this new bar. I wasn't shocked that he had told me to do more, but I couldn't believe he wanted me to do more than seven times what I had been doing.

'Nadine, I do one thousand every time,' Sensei Benny said to put me in my place, but with a hint of humour in his tone.

Whenever I think of a challenge as being hard, I always think of this conversation. What is hard to me is someone else's version of easy. It's all in your perspective. I try to imagine I have a tougher challenge than the one I'm facing, so that what I actually have to do seems easier to handle. As I trained to fight I used to scare myself half to death imagining I was training to fight Lucia Rijker, one of the most fearsome female fighters on the planet. I would picture having to climb into the ring and see her standing opposite me. Naturally, by fight time, I would look over at my less fearsome-looking opponent and feel an odd sense of relief. The mind games of competing were just as much with myself as those I was competing against, especially in the six to eight weeks of preparation.

Sensei Benny told me to always enjoy that journey towards competing, as the event itself is over very quickly. Those preceding lead-up weeks would always be a rollercoaster ride of emotions for me, a never-ending cycle of psyching myself up and trying to calm myself down. Never one to be overly relaxed about a serious situation, I always tried to put in my best effort and would have to wrangle my emotions afterwards if things didn't go well during training.

So much of the training just downright hurt, and the contact we made in the ring wasn't necessarily fun, but there was one particular drill that I dreaded. These were called 'bag sprints' and they were hell. Just thinking about them makes me feel a little sick. You had to explosively punch and kick the bag at absolute maximum intensity in prolonged bursts. The sprints were designed to resemble the full-speed full-power pressure of the ring.

Bag sprints are an anaerobic drill, meaning without air or going so fast you can't speak because you're gasping for breath (and quietly crying on the inside). You go all out for an interval of twenty seconds, then rest for ten seconds, and repeat for a total of four minutes. To get ready for a three-round fight, we would train by doing four rounds of four minutes, with a one-minute rest in between. Each week as the fight got closer, we would shorten the rest break. If it was a five-round fight, we would do six rounds of sprints, so that's going full intensity for nearly thirty minutes straight. Needless to say I would do these with a bucket beside me as I often pushed myself so hard I would feel sick to my stomach. I was a strong finisher, safely within reach of a bin.

I hated doing these rounds multiple times each week, but they forced me to push myself. About halfway through, every single time, I felt like I couldn't possibly finish. It would begin with an urge to slow down or go lighter, you know, just to cheat a little bit. Then my muscles would start to roar in pain at me and I didn't know how I could possibly get through it all. Actually, I wondered why anyone with even a modicum of sanity would put themselves through this. That mental noise became an expected event that I learnt to quickly diffuse over time. It became more of an 'Oh, here comes the part where I want to make excuses to myself' rather than something I actually paid a great deal of mental attention to anymore. I couldn't afford to. If I couldn't push myself to my absolute limit in the gym, then I wouldn't be able to do it on fight night. I'd seen plenty of other fighters not give their all in training and then watched them ease up too soon in the ring. I didn't want to be one of them.

There's a great fighter's saying, 'Train hard, fight easy,' which means work hard in the gym and competing feels a whole lot better. If you slack off in training, it will show on the night. It all comes from what you're prepared to do and how motivated you are in your own psyche. This was the battle that had to be won before I ever faced an opponent. When I walked out to centre ring and looked into my opponent's eyes, I wanted her to see how hard I had worked to earn the right to stand in front of her. Sure, the effects of hard training are physically evident, but I would have the confidence of so many weeks of sacrifice and exhaustive effort pinned to my chest like invisible medals. There would be no last-minute doubt in me as if I had shown up for a school exam without having studied enough. I wanted to walk out with my shoulders squared and my head up, knowing I had done every last piece of work to get there. That kind of confidence you can't fake, you've got to earn it.

Being well prepared is one of the best ways to calm nerves before competing. I did all I could to prepare in my training, but I also created routines that settled my nerves. Before the day of the event rolled around (and the anxiety set in), part of getting myself mentally ready involved writing a list of everything that would go in my bag on the night. I had nervous nightmares about hearing my fight called and going to get my mouth-guard but realising it was sitting forgotten at home. Then, on the morning of fight day, when the worst part of it all was the waiting until that night, I would relax myself by packing my bag from the list. Knowing I had everything organised made me feel like I had myself together and was ready. Then I would check the list again later in the day as a final preparation or maybe it was more something to keep my mind occupied. Either way, it made me feel like I was ready to go and the nerves would subside until they kicked in forcefully at the venue. They'd get most intense in the dressing room and during the walk out from there to the ring. It's a wild feeling, knowing you're stepping out into the arena but on the walk back to the dressing room your fate will have been decided—either heartbreak or elation. Knowing I'd done everything I could allowed me to *make peace with the outcome*.

There is no shame in being defeated by someone who is simply better than you. If you give your all, then you can be proud of that forever. I was determined to never walk out of the ring dis-appointed because I had given up on myself. Sure, I wanted to win, but more than that I didn't want to have to live with the difficult feelings I had watched others go through of having let themselves down. I had made peace with what I was risking both physically and emotionally, and I knew exactly how much this all meant to me. Whatever was destined to happen would happen, but I was determined to do everything in my power to reach my dream. Why not me?

Why not you? Be brave enough to dream, then dream even bigger. Amazing things have to happen to someone, so why not believe it will be you?

15

Face Your Fears

My first full-contact ring fight was under Thai boxing rules, which was the most dangerous option for my neck injury. I had been preparing for four months, with opponent after opponent pulling out of the match with me. Three days before the event, I got a call offering me a fight with a woman who had recently competed in Thailand. She sounded scary, but I desperately wanted to seize the opportunity. I said yes and proceeded to lose 3 kilos in two days to make the required weight of 62 kilos. Going to the weigh-ins on the back of my friend's motorbike, I was so hungry and woozy that I thought I might fall off.

I nervously weighed in wearing only my underwear in a room full of agitated fighters and thought how strange this whole business was. I was so relieved to finally be able to eat and drink again after making the competition weight. My friend Tomas Vysokai, who would also be fighting on the same night, and I went out for a meal together after the weigh-ins. We ate so much that we put the lost weight straight back on. Tomas was an experienced champion fighter, so I hoped maybe if I could eat as much as him, maybe I could fight as well as him, too. Worth a try.

The night of the fight arrived quickly and the familiar nerves of competing started washing over me. Before a fight, I get serious and focused. I don't want to talk much and I tune into a specific rhythm inside myself. It feels like a drumming inside my head. An incessant rolling beat that speeds up and slows down depending on where my thoughts travel. The drum gets louder when my hair gets braided (so my ponytail doesn't come out and hair doesn't get in my eyes), when I walk into the venue, when the doctor clears me to fight, when I get dressed in my fight clothes.

As I start to warm up, the beat quickens in my mind and I breathe more deeply to keep my nerves in check. I feel my heart start to pound and I remind myself that nerves don't make me afraid, they make me fast. I anxiously go to the bathroom, repeatedly. I ground myself as I shadowbox and visualise my opponent. I feel what I will do and how I will react. I have already seen myself win this fight a hundred times in my mind. I picture having my hand raised in victory after the fight. I see it before it happens. I feel how it will feel. I know it to be true. I make it my reality.

In the dressing room as I'm warming up I have very specific music playing through my headphones that allows me to create the mental and emotional state I know will stand me in good stead. Fight music connects me to the feelings I *choose* to feel before a bout. I pick some songs because they make me feel strong, like 'Bleed It Out' by Linkin Park, others because they make me feel energised, like 'Champion' by Kanye West, and some just because they're fun and make me feel alive, such as 'Let It Rock' by Kevin Rudolph and Lil Wayne. As the songs play I feel chills of excitement over my skin.

Sensei Benny taught me to listen to rhythm in music when I trained and then to follow my natural body rhythm. I knew if I felt connected to my body then I would avoid tensing up. If I locked up emotionally then I would do the same physically. Sensei had taught me that the way I felt created a physiological reaction in my body. I was sceptical at first but when he asked me where in my body I felt fear, frustration or even happiness, I knew I could clearly point those areas out. I knew if I needed my body to perform at fight time, then it was important I used my mind to get it into the correct state beforehand.

In my mind's eye, I visualise a large volume control dial on a stereo. I use it to choose the volume level for different thoughts and feelings. I acknowledge the feelings that are unhelpful to focus on in the dressing room before a fight, like fear of getting hurt. If you pretend you're not scared, then you give it power over you. The things we try to hide inevitably come out stronger. So I register those uncomfortable truths and then picture turning the volume down on them. Then I turn the volume up on deliberately helpful feelings like being confident and strong. I imagine cranking the volume right up on those so they are the messages playing loudest in my head as fight time draws near.

◆

As the clock winds down before my first fight, I understand exactly why it has been so important to spend years learning to change my thinking. When you're faced with great stress and potential fear, you have to work hard to keep your mental volume at the right level. I have to make sure I don't think too much about my potential for injury, because I have already made my decision to compete. Worrying about it at this point won't serve me, it will only make me fearful. I have to focus my mind on how much I want to achieve this goal and trust myself that I have what it will take.

By chance I find myself in the very unusual position of having to warm up in the same big dressing room as my opponent. This doesn't usually happen but the other dressing room is over-crowded so my opponent is now in here with me. As soon as I see her, I do my best to beat her mentally before we even step into the ring. I stay super focused and hit the warm-up pads extra hard, knowing that it might make her mentally attach to some nervousness or maybe even a little fear. In my own mind, I see her tattoos and her experienced trainer and know I am in for a fight. I have to back myself. If I don't, nobody else will believe in me. I have to back myself that I can avoid getting hurt and that I can win this fight.

> Back yourself with more belief than anyone else could muster.

All you can smell in the dressing room is scared sweat, adrenaline from nerves, strong Thai liniment and athletic tape being used to wrap fighters' hands. It is an intensely charged environment where everyone is on edge—fighters, trainers and officials alike. It's like the excitement of being backstage at a concert except half of the people might be going to the hospital afterwards. You're trying to focus as fighters come back into the room after their bouts, either victoriously celebrating or devastated from their loss.

The pressure is on as your bout number looms next on the card. This is when fighters sometimes jump out bathroom windows and walk home with no shoes on to avoid having to actually go through with it. I have seen it happen. They do mysteriously vanish from time to time.

I made my way through my warm-up, following the routine I have performed time and time again in the gym. Preparing my body for massive exertion, readying it to take heavy impact, strengthening my mind for the challenge ahead. The point of no return is when I get laced into my fight gloves.

Velcro is used to close our training gloves, but for a fight we use lace up gloves. I force my hand into the tight leather, which is even more taut with each closing lace. The tension peaks when my trainer tapes over the laces so they can't be taken off until after the fight. I no longer have the use of my hands and everything has to be done for me—having a drink of water, adjusting my clothes and putting in my mouthguard to protect my teeth. Then comes the Vaseline. It gets smeared all over my face to reduce the risk of my skin being cut open when I get hit. It feels like washing your face in bacon fat.

Every part of the preparation is now done and snapped shut. It is almost time.

This is the ritual. These are the steps fighters go through like a rite of passage and now I am one of them.

My heart pounds in my chest as they tell me my fight is up. It feels like being locked and loaded like a bullet in a gun. You reach a point where the only way out is forward, exploding down the barrel in a blazing burst of kinetic energy.

Now is the time to control my emotions under pressure the way Sensei Benny taught me. In these last few minutes before I walk out of the dressing room and all hell breaks loose, I know that all I can control is my thinking. I breathe deeply and give a sharp yell to break the physical feeling of nervousness. I tell myself who I know *I Am*—someone who is well trained for this, someone who wants to be here, a person who would regret it forever if she didn't face this fear.

They tell me my fight is about to be called. I only have one minute until they announce me and I walk out to see what my fate holds. I think of my fight music and bounce up and down, letting my body feel excited and happy that the time has finally come. All I need now is to get my feet to carry the rest of me out to the ring. Hmm, that's when I discover I can't feel my legs. Adrenaline is a powerful chemical that has given me a whole new body sensation under this stress. I try to laugh it off, but it has me a little worried.

Fighting seems like a good idea until you see your opponent on fight day and realise that you will be getting into a fist fight with them. This is not a game and there is always a small chance that one of you could get killed. That is how seriously I take fighting. Having known that local fighters had climbed into the ring and died, there isn't a whole lot of room for being blasé. My fear is healthy and realistic, but I can't let it control me under pressure.

Now when I need them most Sensei Benny's words of wisdom echo through my mind, louder now with every pound of my heart inside my chest. He taught me that to overcome fear, all it takes is *ten seconds of courage*. It is a relief to know I don't have to be brave for the entire fight. I only have to find a little burst of courage to start. Enough to walk out to the ring. Just ten seconds' worth. I know it will take ten seconds to get the courage to walk out in front of the crowd, when there might be an urge to bail out on doing this crazy thing. Then another shot of ten seconds with the courage to look my opponent right in the eye at the stare-down. Plus ten more seconds when the fight starts. I can repeat the courage formula as necessary throughout the fight when things go wrong, when I feel pain or have a flash of self-doubt.

I remind myself of Sensei Benny asking me in Thailand 'Why not you?' and I know that this is my time to believe my dreams will come true. The reality is that I have been in the ring with world champions. I train every day with champion fighters of all varieties. I am about to face a woman who is not yet a champion and nor am I, but I want to let myself believe that is where I am headed.

◆

My fight music starts playing and I hear my name announced. It's time. I wait for a few extra seconds until I know I am ready to go. I choose which thoughts will be my last before I start moving out of the dressing room. I tell myself, *This is my time. It is my day. I am well prepared and strong. I will give every-thing I have. I will show how much I love my training. I will show what I am capable of. I will make Sensei Benny proud by fighting my best—win, lose or draw.*

The music is getting louder as the adrenaline surges through my body. Here it comes. Here I come. I move towards the door and pause there for a few final seconds, absolutely charging with fight-or-flight chemicals in my blood stream. I take some deep breaths and throw some shadowboxed punches towards the wall, trying to shed some of the nerves before the spotlight hits me. I let out a shout and feel a rush of excitement come over me. It's like standing at the top of a huge slide, knowing that once you push off, there is no turning back. Down the chute. Here we go . . .

The crowd cheers loudly as I emerge from the dressing room. Well, my big group of friends cheer super loudly with the rest of the crowd probably just politely clapping. The noise they make warms me like stepping into the sunshine on a winter's day. I will fight alone, but my people are with me.

I climb through the ropes and my body is flying like I've had about fifty coffees. It is a huge rush and I know why people get addicted to fighting. Then, as my opponent is announced, I see her walking confidently to the ring. I feel the reality of the situation crash hard into me again. I will be fighting her soon, full contact, and I will be the only one keeping myself safe. I commit to making *this* what happens in the ring I am now standing in. I'm ready and excitedly waiting.

After the introductions, my opponent and I stare at each other across the divide. When the referee calls us to centre ring for final instructions, we do the face-off looking at each other from less than a metre away. Now I see beyond the tattoos and Thai shorts to the actual woman standing in front of me. She looks nervous and I'm surprised to see that instead of her face being covered in Vaseline like mine, she is wearing make-up. I feel both confused by this and concerned that she is going to get hurt. Then I have to quickly remember to only worry about myself. Looking after her isn't my job. I have to let her be strong.

My heart pounds, my muscles tighten and again I let out a loud shout to relieve the pressure building inside me. It's a physical way of expressing the stress, and it quickly resets me into a place of strength. It reminds me that I'm a warrior, that I can be fierce if I choose to be, but mostly it just energises me. The last thing I do before putting my hands up and showing I'm ready to fight is to wipe my feet on the mat one by one. No, not because my feet are dirty. It's a way of literally grounding myself. A last-minute reminder to be in my body, not up in my head. The time for thinking is done and now I must be fully present—sharp, ready and pin-point laser focused.

Hearing the bell ring to start my first fight is both exhilarating and terrifying. This is it. This is the moment of truth for me. It is time to find out if I am good enough, if I can take the hits and not give in. I want to know the categorical truth about who I am and what I'm made of. Once and for all. The end, by Nadine. This is who I am. I'm relieved that I have the opportunity to test myself. I don't want to fail and have to feel all the hard-to-handle negative emotions that will come with finding out I may not be as good, brave or tough under pressure as I hope I am. I want to know so badly that I'm prepared to risk my sense of self and my safety to find out.

I fire first and make sure she feels my power in the initial exchange. Then it happens. *Crack!* I feel that first punch in the face thrown with all her power. The boxing gloves we fight in are much smaller than the gloves we train in, so I can feel my opponent's knuckles hit me and hit me hard. That first full-contact punch received in every fight is the same. It is a shock that snaps me sharply into the reality that I am in a fist fight with someone who is trying to hurt me. This isn't a controlled friendly sparring session in the gym. This is real. And it hurts a lot . . .

The fear of getting injured momentarily shoots through me, as does the reminder that I can't take too many punches like that and keep my neck safe. I know that my fear doesn't make me weak. My fear makes me strong. It makes me quick. It makes me better. When an animal is scared, it often becomes more dangerous. I know this is also true of me. I am going to fight my heart out because the secret others don't know is that I am afraid of permanently damaging my neck. Sensei Benny told me that most people fight out of fear or anger. I know that I am not truly fighting out of anger, and I am prepared to make peace with my fear. I am not sure what I am more scared of—losing the bout and with it my dream of being a fighter, or of being injured so badly I would need surgery.

Now, at this point, you're probably wondering why I wasn't just at home sitting safely with a good book. There is a point in every fight where I wonder the same thing. This was something I just *had* to do. I couldn't bear the idea of getting old and regretting never having tried. These are the times when you decide who you will be in your life. Will you sit back and stay safe, never having risked defeat, or will you put yourself out there knowing that you may fail? That night, I just kept repeating the same words in my head . . . 'Trust yourself, trust yourself.'

I fight so fast and hard that first round that the whole thing is a blur. I go after her before she can go after me. About ten seconds into it, I slip and end up on my butt. Rather than get caught up in feeling embarrassed, I jump up and internally laugh at myself to reset my thinking. That time has already passed, so no point getting stuck thinking about it. The next thing I do is make sure she ends up flat on her back and I look closely to see if she knows how to reset her composure the same way I've been trained to. I see a chink in her armour when doubt and distraction flash across her face. I know I have her. She won't make it out of the first round. I go after her and soon the referee jumps in to save her by delivering an eight count. As soon as he's done, I have my opponent against the ropes and I know that if I throw a big flurry of punches the ref will stop it. There is no need to do any permanent damage, so I finish with a body shot that sends her to the canvas. It looks painful, but I know from experience that she will be fine after a few minutes.

As my hand is raised in victory, I am so relieved I haven't been injured plus I've taken out the win. Most of all, I am happy because I've been able to face my fears. I've done the thing that I was afraid to do, and it feels amazing. I want to do it again.

> You control the volume and visuals playing in your mind, so make them as helpful to you as possible. Picture the best outcome and tell yourself why it will happen.

16
My Time

I continued competing in both Thai boxing and kickboxing and managed to win all my fights. I kept my promise to compete in the 'Jet Fighter' shorts my friend Nadine had given to me after my black belt grading. I faced different fears each time I went into the ring—being sick on fight day, my strategy not working and having to change my style mid-fight, and even competing while everyone booed me because I was fighting against the hometown girl. Every challenge or obstacle that was ahead of me I managed to overcome, but there was one that I hadn't yet stared down—a title fight where a belt was on the line.

Once I had proven to myself I could get through a fight and control my opponent enough to avoid injuring my neck, I knew I needed a bigger challenge. This was where the 'Why not me' factor kicked in big time. Fighting for a belt instead of a trophy would be a big step up, not only in pressure but also in endurance.

It meant fighting five rounds instead of the usual three. This scared me because I was always exhausted after a normal bout, so I wasn't sure how I would squeeze another couple of rounds out of myself. It would be worth it to find out if I could become a champion. I wanted to know just how good I was and how much fear I could face. This was the way to discover the truth about it. When my opportunity came, I jumped at the chance. I quickly accepted the fight offer and locked my sights on that goal.

I believe most people choose their goals by only committing to ones they feel confident they can attain. I weighed up what it would take to achieve my dream and decided that while it would no doubt be hard, I could do it. I was prepared to train six days a week for eight weeks to ready myself mentally and physically. I was committed. I set the marker in my mind of how hard it would be and while it pushed my limits, it was also within the bounds of what I saw as achievable.

So the hard work began. I pushed myself through the first few weeks, which are always tough as your body adjusts to the high workload. Then about four weeks before the fight, I was in the boxing ring, sparring with a champion fighter. I had my hands clasped behind my training partner's back when we fell into the ropes. My right-hand ring finger dislocated as it got caught on the top rope with both of our body weights descending on it. I snapped my finger back in and cried on the way home in the car—not from the pain but from what I thought was the end of my dream of fighting for that belt. I lay awake all night thinking about how much I wanted it and what I was willing to sacrifice to get it. Just coming this far had been difficult enough. I knew if I were to continue training, I would have to move the marker of what I thought of as being hard. It would be tough, but I felt

I could work around this injury. When I walked into the gym the next morning my friend Andrew was waiting to hold pads for me. He knew what had happened and knew I wouldn't let this injury make me give up my goal. We didn't talk about it much and instead just got on with training every skill that didn't require my right hand.

A few weeks later, I was sparring with two heavyweight world champions. Okay so yes, I may have a slight habit of biting off a lot to chew. The method to my madness was that if you face adversity in training, like being up against 100-kilo-plus men, then a match against a 62-kilogram woman wasn't scary anymore. Not to say training with the heavyweights was easy. Quite the opposite as one of them hit me with such momentum that I spun in a circle like a cartoon character. That was a new and interesting experience. Then the other one kicked me in the leg, accidentally partially tearing a ligament in my knee. There were more tears on the way home that day, thinking again that I wouldn't be able to compete for the belt with an unstable knee. I saw a surgeon who advised me that I might do damage if I competed, but he gave me enough confidence to think the fight was still possible.

I started to get worried about how injured I was and how I would train for the match. Doubt crept in but I chose to listen to the little voice in my mind that said if I believed in myself enough to climb through the ropes, then maybe I could win. I decided that this was a goal I was prepared to suffer for in mind and body if need be. I had a strong gut feeling within me that this was *my time*. This was something I had to do and that it couldn't be rescheduled until later. I didn't know why, but the sense of urgency was undeniable. I desperately wanted to know what would happen in my own story. I felt that this was my moment. It was now, with this particular opponent. I pushed the doubt aside and recommitted to working around my injuries.

I made it all the way to the day before the fight. In fact, I made it to the last minute, of the last round, of the last training session before the fight. I threw a kick, put my foot down and tore the ligaments in my ankle. I couldn't believe how unlucky I was. So now I had three sets of torn ligaments—my right hand, left knee and right ankle. Going into a fight injured is quite common, but this was getting totally ridiculous.

> The fears you're most afraid to face are usually the most important for you to confront. The more you hide them, the more they control you.

It would have been tempting to pull out and let this whole thing go because the odds were becoming heavily stacked against me. In addition to the three injuries, my opponent had competed in four times as many fights as me. To add insult to quite literal injury, she was also five inches taller. This woman had a reputation for being hard to put away. I was worried that I was too injured to compete against her or anyone else. I was concerned that the voice in my head saying, 'I can do this,' might be lying to me. I was determined to make my dream come true. The risk in dreaming it wholeheartedly, was that I might fail and end up crushed. It was a risk I had to take.

Part of the reason I felt this was the time to compete for a title despite being injured was that Sensei was visiting Australia. With him beside me I could take on any challenge, no matter how stressful. True to form, later that night Sensei Benny deliberately added some extra pressure. He told me that we would make history because I would be the first of his fighters that he would coach from the corner during a bout. The cornerman is the person who gives the fighter advice and looks after them during the fight. In America, Sensei had a professional team of cornermen who would look after his fighters, while he stayed back and let them have the limelight. I somehow didn't know this vital piece of information when I had asked him to corner for me. Call it naivety or just ignorance, but it never occurred to me not to ask him. When I sat him down to ask, he didn't explain the gravity of what I was actually asking him. Sensei just smiled at me and said he would do it. I didn't know until that night that I would have the honour of being the first or the added pressure this would bring. I was both touched by the gesture and scared by it. I was already stressed from my injuries and now I knew I had to give my all. With Sensei in my corner, how could anything go wrong?

◆

Just entering into the competition venue with Sensei Benny was an experience in itself. I was nervous and tense, but there was such a buzz when we walked in. Immediately people started to recognise Benny 'The Jet' and wanted to meet him. Humble and friendly as always he happily obliged, but I could feel him deliberately sticking close to me. Despite all of the people around him, he stayed focused on me. Sensei took me to get cleared to fight by the doctor and looked after me like the seasoned veteran that he is.

Next we went to get a feel for the ring itself. Where possible, I had always found it grounding to get up into the ring before an event began. I liked moving around in there before a big crowd was present. It helps to get a sense of the bounce in the floor and the amount of spring in the ropes. The less surprises the better. The deeper reason for me is so I can visualise key things that are going to happen, so when they do I am less skittish and more able to be calm. It's like spreading the nerves out—a half dose before and the other half during the event. I imagine the emotions of first climbing through the ropes, of seeing my opponent, of the fight being only seconds from starting. I think about the challenging feelings of walking back to my corner exhausted, and I decide then and there that I will give my all. I shadowbox in the ring a little, seeing in my mind what I will do and how I will react. Then, finally and most importantly, I always visualise my hand being raised in victory and that belt being wrapped around my waist. I experience the joyful feelings of that moment that will make all the impending pain worthwhile. In reminding myself what I hope the outcome will be, I know I have prepared myself for the hardship ahead. It makes me feel determined, focused and ready.

As we walked into the dressing room, all eyes were on us. The other trainers watched the way the world champion did things as Sensei Benny set up our warm-up area. When someone asked to make a video of Sensei taping my hands, he politely declined. This was a special time between us, where he wanted to talk quietly to me. Helping Sensei with the tape was my right-hand

man, Andy Minnet, my student for some fifteen years whose
corner I would one day also be in. My friend Andrew Berridge
was there, too, having spent the past eight weeks getting me
ready for this fight. I had so much respect for him and all he
had done for me along the way. Andrew was a Thai boxing
champion in his own right, as was my other cornerman Tomas
Vysokai. I had such good men supporting and standing alongside me, and they inspired me to push myself harder than ever.

The waiting. It always seems to take forever. The championship fights are at the end of the card, which means you have
to wait for hours while all the other matches to take place. That's
a lot of time for your mind to run wild. If you're not careful, your
adrenaline will dump repeatedly, leaving you feeling exhausted
before you even warm up. While I'm waiting I use all the mental
strategies I have been taught to practise keeping myself under
control. I begin to make my way through the ritual. I immerse
myself in it and am taken away to a special place inside my
mind. I know it well now.

I unpacked my bag and got dressed in my fight gear. The
drumming feeling quickened in that familiar rhythm inside my
head. As I started listening to my music, I bolstered the hopes
in my heart. I knew I was injured, but I believed I could do this.
I started to warm up, slowly at first and then building my energy.

I could feel the aches and pains start, but I had a plan to work
around them. For the first time in my fight career, I would apply
some numbing gel to my hand. Other fighters habitually rub this
cream into their shins and forearms in order to stop the pain of
blows. It is the type of gel that dentists use to numb your mouth
prior to injections. I knew people used it, but had never previously chosen to myself. The torn ligaments in my hand were

going to be painful, so I had been advised to try numbing them a little. I didn't want to have a cortisone injection, so this was the next best thing. It was acceptable and within the rules, so I applied the cream and hoped for the best. Finally I taped a specially made tiny plastic brace, about the size of a bent five-cent piece, inside my right ring finger. This was to stop my finger over-compressing and, because it was on the inside of my hand, it posed no threat to my opponent.

Sensei Benny held pads for me and made me move around in the dressing room. The pressure built while we were watched intensely by other fighters and trainers. As time was running out, I had my gloves taped on and checked. I felt all the familiar intense feelings but this time they were pulled tight across my mind like the skin of a drum. My fight was about to be called. The pressure had reached boiling point. Now was the time.

Sensei, my cornermen and I all formed a line at the dressing room door. Sensei Benny stood directly in front of me, solid as a rock. As the crowd turned to look at us, he shielded me from view and talked to me in a low tone. His calm energy kept me relaxed—well, as relaxed as you can be at a time like that. Before he turned towards the crowd, Sensei reminded me that it was my time. I believed it was true. All doubt was shut out of my mind as I brought forward all my strongest feelings at full volume. I took the last precious moments for myself and turned to face the rear of the dressing room. I bounced on my toes and shook my body out. Andrew was behind me, so we were now eye to eye. In contrast to Sensei Benny's calm, Andrew's energy was intense. He was a great fighter and I knew he understood the specific place I went to in my mind. Andrew started talking hard at me, firing me up—'Go out there and *show them who the fuck you are.*' His strong words lit me up. I wasn't sure if it was what he said or the blazing way he said it. I wanted to go and show everyone outside who I was on the inside. In that instant I felt so much bigger than my small stature and stronger than my injured body. I locked onto that feeling and turned around. I put my hands on Sensei Benny's shoulders as my walk-out music started to loudly play. He moved forward and I moved with him. Suddenly we were walking out to the ring.

I had a huge crowd of supporters there to watch me fight. My friends and students, along with my family. Many of them stood up on their seats and cheered as we made our way towards them. The sound was deafening as we walked right through the middle of them down the aisle to the ring. I could feel their energy beaming at me. I stayed in my own little world under the hood of my fight robe, not wanting to break the powerful feeling I had created within myself. This was what I wanted to feel when I walked into the ring. That certainty, that self-belief. I let out a shout and banged my gloves together.

That's when I felt it. The numbing gel had not worked at all. My hand hurt from just hitting my gloves together and a flash of trepidation ran through me. This was going to be painful. Instead of panicking, though, I deliberately thought about all the pain I had learned to endure in training. All the times I had wanted to quit, but managed to hang in there. All the sessions where I had cried and then still went back the next day. The way I had learned to acknowledge physical pain and then disconnect from reacting to it emotionally. Pain was just pain. I knew how to let it exist without needing to do anything about it. I accepted the feeling and knew I was still going to take this once-in-a-lifetime opportunity. This was it.

I listened to the words of my fight song blasting through the speakers over my head. I had always chosen fight songs that had meaning to me and created a certain feeling. On this night, I had perhaps not chosen the most modern cool song, but instead one that encapsulated the sentiment of what this fight meant to me. It was Pat Benatar's 'All Fired Up', an 80s classic that was a bit of a fight cliché back in the day. I didn't care if it wasn't the trendiest song because I wanted to hear it as I walked to the ring. I had been listening to it for months as I trained and it activated the body chemicals attached to confidence and believing in my dream.

The sentiments of the song matched what mattered to me about this fight. That this was my time and that Sensei Benny was in the country to share it with me. Although not perfect, the way everything had fallen into place made me feel like it was somehow pre-destined. I couldn't stomach fate giving me an opportunity that I let pass by. I had won many competitions over the years, but none meant anywhere near as much to me as this one. I thought about the mistakes I had made when I was younger and everything I had learned along the way. In my mind, if I could become a champion fighter, then I would be proving something to myself and my loved ones. Like it was an opportunity for redemption and a way to come full circle. Even though I was injured going into the fight, I had to trust that I could do it. My heart was on the line. I took the chorus of the song as saying that the only person who needed to believe right now was me.

I paused briefly at the bottom of the stairs to the ring. At these times when it was tempting to rush, I knew it was important not to. This was my one last moment of composure before I was under the bright lights. I took a deep breath and gave myself that feeling of certainty one last time, then I climbed through the ropes. I immediately did a ritualistic circle of the ring, looping all the way around. It was a marker to me to remember that this was *my* ring and my opponent was in it. That this was my night and my fight. We were about to share an experience, but I had to trust my ability to create the outcome in my favour. I had to trust I could stop her from hurting me. I approached everything with certainty and confidence. The time for doubt was long over. I chose to believe that when the going got tough, I would have the spirit to hang in there and come out on top.

◆

Sensei Benny took my black satin Reyes fight robe off my shoulders. It was a thoughtful gift that had been the idea of my friend and student Danielle Vos and it had 'CHAMPION' embroidered across the back in bright red lettering. I loved it and always felt about ten feet taller when I put it on to walk to the ring. It matched my black and red satin fight shorts perfectly, which also had my name written similarly across the front. I always hoped that people knew Champion was my real surname since birth, not some overzealous attempt to act like I was the best before the fight even started. I wore a matching crop top I got in Thailand which covered enough surface area to make sure I didn't have a mid-bout wardrobe malfunction. Finally I set the whole ensemble off with black anklets that covered all the tape that held my torn ankle in place. This was my version of high fashion. When it came to the ring, I loved a good matching outfit.

I shook my body out and looked over at my opponent Ashlee Pilgrim. She had a reputation for being hard as nails, but I wasn't scared of her. I was excited as I paced back and forth with my eyes locked on hers. I had waited a long time for this and I just wanted them to let me at her. When the referee called us to the centre, Sensei Benny was right behind me. He stood just over my right shoulder and looked at my opponent almost as intensely as I did. We both just wanted to see what she was made of as a person. What was her energy like up close? Was she nervous? Would she show fear or aggression? I looked deeply in her eyes to see if she knew who she was and if she was prepared to show me.

What I saw was a woman who had been here before and knew how to handle herself. She looked like a nice enough person, but she was clearly also ready for battle. I looked straight into her eyes and smiled at her. Not in a friendly way, but with a knowing. On the outside it might have been mistaken for cockiness, but the feeling behind it was that I was totally ready to go. I was just happy that we were both there and the night had finally arrived. I had spent months feeling like a giant rubber band was holding me back, always pulling at my shoulders while I strained against it. Now was finally the time when I got to let go and I couldn't wait.

We touched gloves to wish each other luck, then went back to our respective corners. I gave Sensei Benny what felt almost like a hug goodbye, then turned and let out a loud shout to fire myself up. I wiped my feet on the canvas one last time and started bouncing with my hands up in a ready position, waiting for the bell. I knew there were only a few seconds left before we would clash.

The bell sounded and I went at her like that rubber band I'd been straining against had just snapped. My strategy at the beginning of a bout was always to be first to fire. I quickly touched gloves with her and started by blasting a kick straight down the barrel to her face, followed by two punches and a leg kick. Then I circled and changed position so she couldn't hit me back. I wanted her to be caught off-guard from the first second of the fight, hoping she would be uncomfortable and start getting mentally captured.

I loved being a fast starter and it always got the crowd to be vocal from the outset which increased the energy in the room. Sensei drew huge crowds the world over, so he viewed competition not just from the perspective of the combatants but also the fans and promoters. He knew that a good fighter was interesting to watch and became a crowd favourite. He taught me to '*be worth looking at*'. He gave me permission not just to perform, but to perform at my unashamed best in spectacular fashion. I loved dynamic techniques like spinning back kicks and superman punches because they were flashy and fun. When I launched myself at my opponent, the audience always knew I was there to fight and put on a show. I was always there to win. This was exactly the feeling I wanted my opponent to understand about me from the bell.

It was a fast and furious fight that was tough, and seemed to only get tougher. It quickly became apparent to me that Ashlee's strategy was to clinch me and pull my head down into a knee. As the taller person, this was a smart move. I knew she was looking to knock me out, as I narrowly escaped her knee repeatedly rushing towards my face. As soon as I got close enough, Ashlee would grab my head and pull down hard. By the second round my neck was out of place and painfully stiffening up, which affected my ability to resist as she drove my head towards her knee.

The middle rounds were a blur of frenzied attack, movement and increasingly tired arms from all the clinching. I had hit my opponent with shots that I expected to knock her out, but she stayed standing. I half-wondered if she might be some type of zombie who just wouldn't go down no matter what I did. I started to feel worried about how much gas I had left in the tank.

As I sat down on the stool between rounds in a mini panic, I asked Sensei who was winning. He looked at me with mild disappointment and said, 'Does it matter?'

Instantly I saw how I had lost perspective about what I was doing. The reason I was doing this wasn't to win a bigger trophy than the other woman. I was here to share an experience and give my best, all because of this crazy lifelong love for martial arts. I had to be fully present and enjoy the experience, instead of worrying about the future. That was what mattered more than the final outcome.

When the bell sounded to start the second last round, I was tired and knew the chances of me knocking her out were getting slimmer. Andrew Berridge and I had game-planned in training that if my opponent was still standing at this point, I might need to change strategy. I would use my push kick to keep her away from me throughout the round, so she couldn't clinch. Andrew reminded me of this and as the round started, my plan began working. Ashlee quickly became frustrated and tried even harder to get close to me, which only served to increase the impact of the straight kicks I was throwing as she rushed in. This gave me a much-needed chance to rest my weary arms and dictate the pace of the round. I knew I had to save my best effort for the last round. Last one, best one.

Sometime during the latter part of the fight, my opponent charged towards me while I threw a big punch and immediately felt my right ring finger snap in half inside my glove. It was a spiral fracture. I had the perfect excuse to give up and get out of the ring if I wanted to. Nobody would have blamed me for pulling out with all those injuries. Despite the pain, I just couldn't back down. I had come too far and this meant too much to me. I didn't show what had happened on my face. Now I knew what all that training around pain was for—right this second when I was in agony but had learnt to hide it from my opponent. In my head, though, I was exasperatedly thinking, 'Oh come on, this has to happen too? Really?' As if it wasn't all hard enough in the lead-up to competing, now I had to try to finish the fight with a broken bone in my glove. My focus shifted at that point to seeing if I could get to the end and be standing for the final bell. If I could make it that far without giving up, I hoped that at least I could be proud of myself for not quitting.

The final round started just like the first round, with me flying full speed across the ring at Ashlee, showing energetically that this was mine. Even though I was exhausted, I wanted her to think that I wasn't. I had to fight like I was fresh. I gave everything I had until my arms were literally moving in slow motion. I had her pinned in the corner but when I told my body to go, it looked like I was slapping her with limp lettuce leaves. This was all down to heart now, instead of cardio fitness. My opponent charged at me repeatedly, knowing this was her chance to win. As much as I wanted to stay still, I knew I had to move constantly. I had trained for a hard final round and I fought on with wobbly legs. Ashlee charged at me with all her might but I leant back into the ropes and let her run right into a straight kick to the body. Her momentum doubled her over my leg. As she stormed forward again trying everything she could to take me out, I moved at the last second and sent her crashing into the ropes. We were equally desperate to finish strong and pushed each other until the last bell sounded.

When the referee stepped in to stop the bout, we gave each other a tremendous hug. This had been a true test for each of us. I now knew things about this woman's spirit and belief in herself that I could only see from my bird's eye view of competing with her.

We had fought to the bitter end and knowing the fight was over came as the sweetest relief. There was a searing pain in my hand. Unfortunately, when my opponent took out her mouthguard after the fight, her front teeth went with it. No wonder I had broken my finger. It was a brutal fight where we both sustained damage, but Ashlee had very much won my respect. Without her, there was no way I could have experienced the depths of my own fear or tapped into a little courage the way I did. I was so happy that I had found a way to believe in myself enough to even step into the ring that night.

The referee called us to centre ring to hear the judges' decision on the bout. I hoped I had done enough to win but you just never know how the judges are going to see things. I bounced from side to side while waiting for the decision. I held my breath as they announced that I had won. I raised my hands and as Sensei Benny wrapped the title belt around my waist, it was one of the sweetest moments of my entire life. Not because I had achieved my goal, but because of what it took to reach it. I had taken what I thought of as being a hard challenge and multiplied it exponentially. I had been so scared to face all my fears that night, but I had quietly found the courage to do it.

Sensei Benny raised my hand to present me as the winner to the crowd and I had my very own *Karate Kid* moment. I could see all the people I cared about standing on their chairs and cheering for me. I was overjoyed to not have been seriously injured. The best part came when Sensei Benny looked at me and smiled, pride beaming from his face. All those years of learning hard lessons from him came down to this time in the ring, where everything else faded away and I saw that he was happy with my effort. He knew what it took to deal with pain and stare down your own fear. Now I had the beginnings of the same.

I joyfully hugged each of my cornermen before we climbed out of the ring. I soaked up every last second of that victory. As I walked through the crowd, I was surrounded by people showing me their support, but none more so than when I reached my large group. I hugged my mum and Uncle Tony while my friends crowded around. All the people who meant the most to me in the world were there. It was such a beautiful feeling of being joined together by a shared experience.

As I turned away, my neck started to stiffen up to the point I could barely move it. The adrenaline was wearing off and that's when the pain begins. Happiness eased the hurt intermittently, though. As I walked through the dressing room door, standing with one of his fighters was the Northern Beaches Thai boxing trainer who had turned me down when I wanted to have my first fight. How funny that the same person who had declined helping me get in the ring was the very person I saw after winning my first title. I smiled at him and said, 'Remember me?' He laughed and congratulated both Sensei Benny and me warmly. It was all meant to be, exactly as it was.

◆

As the adrenaline continued to wear off in the dressing room, the pain kicked in hard. Sensei Benny and Andy Minnet tried to get my taped hand wraps off while working around my broken finger. While I'd been fairly stoic in the ring, I now screamed in pain. It was the kind of white lightning burning that makes you shudder and feel sick to your stomach. As I immersed my now very swollen hand in a bucket of ice, Sensei and I talked about my performance. I had been over the moon and wanting to celebrate, but in talking about the fight Sensei starting giving me an unexpected critique.

Always my teacher before being my friend, he let me know where I went wrong and how I could have finished the bout sooner. It had been a good fight, but it had also been gruelling. As hard as it had always been for his students to hear (or not hear), Sensei never gave excess credit where it wasn't deserved. He felt I was capable of so much more than I had shown. As harsh as it was, I knew that kind of honesty is hard to find. Everyone else would celebrate with me and say what a good job I'd done, but he would tell it from a different perspective. It was a right he had unquestionably earned but it hurt to hear. In that exhausted hour I was so deflated that I shed an exasperated tear and asked if he was even proud of me. I didn't get a satisfying response of his approval and I remembered that what mattered was that I was proud of myself. I had without doubt seen Sensei's pride all over his face in the ring, though, so I knew at heart he was happy with me. I was happy with me. I had a full belly deeply satisfied feeling that I had tried instead of playing it safe. A risky move, but the injuries I sustained were only short term.

Sensei took good care of me and made sure he re-aligned my neck before we left the dressing room. I felt a bit like I had been hit by a truck. It took me six weeks to get over all of the strains and injuries, but there was nothing serious to worry about. Revelling in the victorious feelings made dealing with any pain much easier. I was on a high that I earned through finding a way to believe in myself when my chances didn't look good. Sensei Benny and I had shared an experience in the ring that night that would forever change the way I imagined what was possible for me.

That night was my second last fight, even though I didn't know it at the time. I would win another title in my next bout in kickboxing. But all the while, I couldn't shake the feeling in my gut that I'd had during that first Thai boxing championship fight. Despite being repeatedly injured, my instincts were telling me that I had to seize the opportunity. All I understood was that I had to do it right then, even though it may have seemed a little crazy and illogical to others. The same gut feeling was there during my final fight; that this was my moment and I had to make the most of it. I didn't know them that my whole life was leading to a day of reckoning that I could never have seen coming. A day where I would know what it truly meant to feel afraid. Terrified, even. That day came sooner than I could ever have imagined and tested me to the absolute depths of my courage.

Go out there and show them who you are.

ALL IT TAKES IS 10 SECONDS OF COURAGE TO CHANGE YOUR LIFE

ROUND 5

THE CHAMPIONSHIP ROUND

The moment of truth: living out my
10 Seconds of Courage.

17

The One I Didn't See Coming

He is going to die. My brother John, my father's first-born son, has stage four lung cancer. As soon as I got the call saying he had collapsed, I had one of *those* feelings in my bones—a shudder and the scent of a frightful odour, where you know your world has forever shifted. When they did the scans and ran tests, they found the cancer had already exploded into his bones with a fatal blast and made its way into his brain. No warning, no long lead-up symptoms and concerns, just straight to the final page. I listen on the phone, trying to absorb rapid-fire information in one over-sized gulp like a mouthful of water that makes me feel I might drown. He has fallen, he is in hospital, he is ill, very ill, he has cancer, he has stage four cancer, his body is already ravaged, he will need immediate treatment, he will not survive this, he will die, he will die, he will die. Soon.

I love my family, but they have always been a people divided. A series of ruptures and detachments that long pre-dated me has drawn a disjointed map of territories and allegiances I have had to learn to traverse. My half-brother John, while much loved, was rarely seen when I was a small kid. Given that he was decades older than me, I had a lot of growing up to do before I could have an adult relationship with him. Even when I had grown up, we had a sporadic relationship that involved a hoped-for closeness on both our parts that was never quite fulfilled. Before his illness, John unexpectedly invited me to his sixtieth birthday drinks. I said yes with an equal dose of trepidation and happiness. The last time I'd seen him in person was at my dad's funeral, more than a decade ago. John had opened the door for us to reconnect, and I was scared but eager. He looked like Dad, so I was afraid of that first time I'd see him again. I was worried it would be like looking at shadows of my father. Losing Dad still hurt so much, even though it had been many years. But the fear of reconnecting was outweighed by the fear of distance. As I walked into the party and finally saw John again it made me burst into tears. He did look like Dad and was no longer the young man I remembered. Accepting his invitation was the right thing to do and I was grateful he wanted to be closer to me. I had hopes of hearing stories about my dad, about who he had been and his relationship with John. I wanted to know more about the life of my brother who I had always known from so far away.

Now, only a year after we reconnected, he is going to die. They can't tell me how long he will survive, but I try to swallow the lump (more like the boulder) in my throat that tells me it won't be long. I feel regret already, that there isn't more time. I vow to make the time he has left count. Fear washes over me because I have seen what cancer can do. The day I said goodbye to my dear Nan, I held her hand and watched it take her right in front of me. I was afraid of seeing it come to claim John, too. I told myself to be brave and stay in this fight until the final bell. I willed myself into it and tried to conquer the urge to run away. I couldn't live with myself if I let my fear of what was to come put John in a protective box, to be pushed far from my breaking heart. If it were to break, then I would let it. There had already been too much distance between us to make the same mistake now.

We spent time together over the coming months, dinners where we laughed and ate oysters or visits where we drank coffee with conversation. I made audio recordings of John's voice and some videos of us talking. He played me his favourite music and told me stories. I was getting up the courage to ask him the list of questions I'd been compiling. Every time I went to visit him, it was like I broke apart inside before I even arrived. This pain was tapping into the bedrock running underneath me and sending all types of long dormant gases blasting to the surface. I was constantly under invisible pressure and destabilised, not sure how to handle these old family feelings interspersed with the new emotions of such a serious illness. The more John visibly declined, the greater the internal pressure became. It was like a giant clock ticking, constantly clanging in my head. What did I need to say before it was too late? What did I want to ask him that I would never again have the chance to? *Tick, clang. Tock, clang.*

I shared joyfully all the good news I could muster of things he had missed out on in my life. I wanted him to know who I was before he passed and I hoped he wanted the same. The sadness I felt was often overwhelming. I wanted to get closer, but in doing so I was falling apart. Yet I didn't know what else to do, so afraid I was of missing my one chance. I pushed forward, trying to balance more on my shoulders and hoping none of it would fall. Rapid fissures began to appear within me and they transferred to the relationships in my life. Being around people became harder the more I slipped into the darkness falling over my own heart. It's hard to make small talk when your inner voice is howling in disconsolateness. I tried to keep myself in the fight and face the impending knock-out of John's death head-on. I questioned if I was strong enough. I had never wanted to think of myself as a coward, but this grief was making me tremble.

I kept going back to see him, not as much as I would have initially liked, but I battled on. The visits deeply affected both of us because they were so loaded with old meaning. This was the case one day as I walked into John's living room and sat in place beside him on the couch. Unbeknownst to me he had decided today would be the day he would be my big brother. He spoke in a way that he had obviously put a great deal of thought into. He knew I had questions and he wanted to answer them. He wanted to talk about Dad and show me photos I had never seen. John wanted to have the special connection I had also been craving. I burst into tears, both because of my sadness that he was leaving, but also because I was so touched that he wanted to do this with me. It was a beautiful gesture and I was moved that I hadn't been the one to instigate it. He knew me better than I thought he did. That was the last good day.

John declined rapidly as the tumours in his brain took an ever-increasing toll on his faculties. He made less sense, he slept more and he quickly became frail. My fear grew exponentially, but I was comforted by the big brother day we had shared. As

I watched him slipping away, I kept going back to that day in my mind. I would visit him and replay it once he wasn't capable of being wholly present. My heart was breaking in slow motion and there was nothing I could do but try to have the courage to let it happen.

The day finally came to say goodbye. He was no longer conscious and his breathing had taken on the unmistakable death rattle. I used every ounce of fighting spirit I had to say my piece and hug him goodbye as he lay in his bed. I was glad he was at home for the final day. I told him stories, made him promises and thanked him for giving me the gifts we had shared over the past months. John passed away as comfortably medicated as possible in his sleep. I was grateful for the chance to say goodbye, but I had also been destroyed by it. I started to quietly implode. Within days my whole world would be shattered and would not fit together the same way again.

The cracks had blown open and I couldn't piece them back together. When I tried to re-group I couldn't make myself take on quite the same shape I'd had before. I had changed and I couldn't change back. I had been in a meaningful solid relationship for many years, but when John died the pressure just became too much. My partner Caroline and I separated only days after John passed away. We had taken a short trip away and everything had blown open. At the same time, we had both been facing separate life challenges that had created tectonic shifts between us. I will be forever grateful for her support and that we attended the funeral together, but the funeral itself presented challenges that sent me into a freefall.

After the service was over I knew I needed to be alone to try to stabilise my own inner world. I flew north to spend the remainder of the week by myself in Queensland, feeling like I was holding the sides of an elevator shaft as I slid at high speed towards the bottom. Death and heartbreak together are a powerful combination that had left me absolutely reeling. I tried to hold steady and remain calm, while my whole world was disintegrating around me.

I didn't find peace while I was away, but I did feel the speed of descent slow. I knew that when I was ready I had to go home. On the plane heading back to Sydney, I put my bag over my shoulder and felt a pain behind my collarbone towards the left side of my neck. I put my hand on the sore spot and felt a small lump the size of half a marble. It stopped me in my tracks, as that familiar cold shudder ran through me again. I told myself it was surely nothing and that I shouldn't worry about it. A fear crept into my mind that constantly gnawed away at me. Lumps, cancer . . . surely I wasn't sick, too? No, I couldn't be. I was already feeling weakened and emotional, so the last thing I needed was to worry about my health. Feeling afraid about that was too much. It made me want to flee and push those concerns as far out of my mind as possible. If all my experiences in training with fear had taught me anything, it was that the things you are afraid to face are usually the most important for you to confront. But life had taught me that at times this can feel almost impossible. I thought of John not finding out he had cancer until it was already at stage four and inoperable. I figured it was better to be safe than sorry. No matter how much I didn't want to deal with medical issues, I knew I would be worried about it in the back of my mind anyway. I picked up the phone and used my *ten seconds of courage* to make an appointment with my doctor.

♦

Dr McGrath had been my GP for more than fifteen years and I trusted her completely. I showed her the lump and expected it to be met with her usual cheery, reassuring manner. She was lovely as always but there was a tiny flicker of seriousness in her response that set off that shudder again. It wasn't bad, but it wasn't good either. She told me not to worry, but I had better go for an ultrasound. There was so much going on in my life and my inner world at that point that I was extremely tempted to push it out of my mind. I knew for a fact that the lump hadn't been there earlier in the year. I wasn't sure how to feel, but I assumed these were hoops I'd better jump through just in case.

The ultrasound technician gave the area a thorough going-over, chatting and joking with me as he did. I nervously asked him what he thought and he said it was probably just an infection that was showing in my lymph nodes. My system was likely just fighting something off. Right, an infection sounded good to me. It made sense given all of the stress I had been under. I had been feeling rundown and very stressed the past few months as John deteriorated. Plus I had been working long hours having only just started my dream job teaching martial arts and kickboxing at the new multi-million-dollar UFC Gym in Sydney. They had brought me in to be one of the founding coaches at the most state-of-the-art martial arts facility in the country. I had been giving my all to make sure that the opening had been a success. I'd made sure I was in fighting shape for it, but I suppose I was actually looking a bit skinny. I put it down to the excitement of being associated with the premier combat sports brand in the world, on top of having to deal with the stress of my brother's illness. I had been under strain for many months so it made sense that it was showing in my body.

The ultrasound results didn't yield much information so I was sent for a biopsy of the lump. Given the circumstances I had now officially decided it was just an infection. My understanding was that they were going to pop a small needle into it and find out what was going on. I tried to be positive and not think about it too much, so I went to the appointment alone. It was on a high floor of Sydney's Prince of Wales Private Hospital, where everything and everyone looked a bit serious. When they explained the procedure, it was more full-on than I had assumed. Ten needles in my neck later I resembled a bruised pin cushion and was starting to get worried. This was all more intense than I thought it would be for an infection. The urge to run became stronger. I had so many other things to deal with and this was the last thing I needed. I walked out of that appointment alternating between feeling thoroughly overwhelmed and totally numb.

I was told the results would be available in a week's time and given an appointment with a doctor I had never met. The waiting was further complicated by everything in my personal life feeling unmanageably difficult. I was trying to cope but wasn't sure if I was succeeding. I had moved temporarily into a serviced apartment, and I hadn't been sleeping very well. I was unusually tired to the extent that one afternoon I came back from teaching at the gym and had to go to bed. I had never been a napper, so it felt quite weird to be that wiped out I needed to fall asleep during the day. In the evenings, I was exhausted but restless. One night I woke up so drenched with sweat that my hair was wet. It had never happened before but I tried not to read anything into it and just put it down to being over-whelmed with stress. I started looking forward to the day when I could get my results and erase at least one worry from my busy, crowded mind.

The test results appointment was on the same floor of the hospital where I'd had the biopsy. Instead of going straight ahead out of the elevator, I had to turn down the left corridor this time. I was reading the name plates on the walls beside the doors looking for the correct doctor's suite number, when I finally found it. Under the doctor's name, it read 'Oncologist'. I was in shock. Why had nobody told me the doctor I was getting my results from was a cancer doctor? How does that massive red flag slip someone's mind? Isn't it something the patient needs a heads-up about? I wanted to sprint back to the elevator. Surely I was in the wrong place.

My heart sank as I checked the room number and saw it was the correct office. I took a deep breath to steel myself and walked through the door. Everything started to feel surreal as I sat in the waiting room. Despite the personal issues we were having, Caroline had insisted on going with me to get the results. I was so grateful I wasn't alone, as I now felt quite scared.

The doctor called my name and stood at his door, holding it open for us to enter. As I passed, we politely greeted each other, but something about his sympathetic smile set my internal chills off again. He introduced himself as we sat down and told me that he had my results. My thoughts started bobbing and weaving. Why was I in this cancer doctor's office? I'm young and healthy, so surely they've got the wrong girl. My own voice was racing in my head as the doctor was speaking to me. I don't think I even properly heard the first few minutes of him speaking. What

I could hear of what he was saying made me scared enough to interrupt him with a question.

'So they said it might be an infection. Are you telling me that now is time to let go of that idea?' I asked it with the urgency of someone bargaining for their life.

The doctor looked at me with a combination of authority and concern and said, 'You need to let that go now. It's not an infection. We believe you have cancer.'

His words hit me as heavily as a block of cement hitting the ground.

I burst into tears.

'Oh fuck.' It was all I could say as the air was sucked out of my lungs.

Me? I'm thirty-seven years old. I can't have cancer. I kept thinking about being an athlete, as if that gave me some healthy exclusion from serious illness. I shook my head and could barely hold the doctor's jumbled words in my mind. I was reeling uncontrollably as the doctor explained I would have to undergo surgery the next morning. I was finding it hard to understand what was happening. I felt grateful to have a supportive person there to ask questions on my behalf and write everything down. My thoughts felt like coming up from being underwater when you open your eyes but they're still half full of liquid. You can see, but everything is distorted. I was utterly rattled, but I also had an odd undercurrent of calm acceptance. I would need an operation to do a more conclusive biopsy on the lump in my neck and they would need to extract some bone marrow from my hip to see if the cancer had spread.

On some inner level I had known this was the truth from the moment I felt that lump. But there were already too many other painful things happening to let myself focus on it fully. If I had, it surely would have caused me to completely fall apart. Instead, I consciously chose not worry too much about it before the time officially came to worry. No point spending weeks freaking out that I had cancer, if it proved to only be an infection. Now was the time to totally freak out, but I didn't. I was absolutely floored, but I quickly started to become resigned to doing what needed to be done to win this fight, whatever that may be.

All I wanted to do after the appointment was look at the ocean. We drove to the water and it was decided I would move home immediately and that we would deal with our personal issues at a later time. Everything had stopped in that doctor's office and forever altered the path ahead. This was shatteringly hard on me and I can only imagine how cataclysmic it was for Caroline. There were things that needed to be said, but now the most pressing issue in the world had become whether I would live or die. Everything else instantly paled in comparison. The emotions were overwhelming. I was afraid of dying young. I was afraid that cancer would make me frail and skeletal, to the extent that I took a photo in my undies that night so I would remember what I used to look like. All I knew was that I didn't want to be someone with cancer. In those first few hours I was more afraid than I had ever been in my life because I didn't know what was going to happen. Everything I imagined was on some level a worst-case scenario.

The next morning we went to the hospital early and my fear had turned into a scared resistance. I didn't want to be there but tried to make it okay within myself. I did everything they told me to do and even managed a small silly dance in my pre-surgery hospital gown. I tried to laugh so the seriousness of the situation wouldn't consume me. I knew there were people in much more dire straits than I was, but I still didn't want to be forced to lie on a gurney to be wheeled into surgery. I was in a pre-theatre waiting room full of other nervous patients. It was like we were all about to face the firing squad. I felt as afraid as a small child and cried while Caroline comfortingly held my hand. I was in such a vulnerable place already before I'd even needed an operation. It all felt too much and I want to be anywhere but being prepped for surgery. I didn't want the doctors to cut into my neck but I knew they needed to so they could diagnose me properly. I wished they didn't have to do a lumbar puncture to check my bone marrow. I thought about all the battles I had faced before and knew that I had to face this one, too. There was no running away without major consequences. This was the way to find out what was actually happening in my body and how bad it was. I was panicky and nervous when I felt my gurney was being moved. The nurses reassured me and I was grateful for the early sedation they provided before wheeling me into the operating theatre. My last thought was that I hoped I would wake up again.

You may as well assume things will work out and save your challenging feelings for the appropriate time.

18

Pat The Dog, Eat The Cake

'Waiting to find out if I have cancer. I've been waiting a week,
but tomorrow is the day. Trying not to think. Staying positive,
but quietly fearing the worst.'

An entry from my journal on 23 July 2013.

All week while I waited for the results from surgery, I had nonsen-
sically hoped it was somehow a false alarm and I wouldn't turn
out to have cancer at all. Part of me was irrationally still clinging
to the idea that it was an infection. I wondered how such a close
call would change the way I lived my life, but I was scared that it
wasn't a false alarm and worried about how that would change
me. The final night preceding the results felt ominously like it
might mark the end of everything *before*. Before I had cancer,
before I was sick, before I'd be changed forever. Would it also
mark the beginning of the time *before the end*? My end.

Don't panic. Panic wasn't a good option at a time like this. I knew resisting would only make it all harder. What kind of cancer might I have, at what stage and would it be terminal? From leukaemia to thyroid cancer, my mind had been racing through the options at breakneck speed. Then I would force a state of calm over myself, like I had learned to do in the ring. I turned my thoughts towards what sincerely mattered in life. It had become so suddenly clear that I should have spent more time having fun with friends and loved ones. Simple. I felt pre-emptive wafts of regret seep into my mind about how I had spent my time. I began wishing I had lived as some type of gypsy with an awe-inspiringly exciting life. A joyful, constantly travelling lady who had spent her days seeing every beautiful sight of the world and engaging meaningfully with all of the wonderful new friends who crossed her path. Then I would gag a little as I realised how idealistic and flowery that sounded. My mind was all over the place but I just kept trying to hold myself steady inside. I repeated clear messages, as forcefully within my own thoughts as if I were coaching a fighter. I told myself that I would be okay no matter what the results said. Even if it was the worst, I would face it. I would be in my own corner.

As the day of reckoning arrived when I would get the surgery results, I found myself allaying other people's fears along with my own. Hearing my mum cry when I gave her cautious pieces of an update was one of the hardest parts. I reassured her and everyone around me that it was probably not going to be as bad as where the arrows were pointing. I didn't want to have to put anyone around me through the sadness of watching me be sick. Surely, after everything I had been through lately, life wouldn't deal me those painful cards . . .

I was sitting on my couch alone at home when I found out that I did actually have cancer.

That's how much I was hoping it wasn't true. I was trying to pretend it was a normal Wednesday. I had half-expected the doctor not to call at the designated time. It's uncommon to receive those kind of results over the phone, but there had been a problem the day before, when I went to the hospital for my scheduled Tuesday post-surgery appointment. When I met Doctor Brighton, my oncologist, he apologised that he unexpectedly hadn't yet received my biopsy results. There must have been a delay in the lab. He seemed relaxed as he explained he would call me the following day. I had inadvertently taken his calm and casual manner as a sign of hope that things would be fine.

'I'm sorry, Nadine, you have Hodgkin's lymphoma,' Dr Brighton said gently down the line.

A series of explosions went off in my mind like the lines of detonators in a building implosion. *Boom, boom, boom, boom, boom.* How could this happen to me? I didn't know what lymphoma was, but it sounded very serious and quite dire. I took a slow breath, but didn't cry. I felt a strange undulating mix of denial and acceptance. Dr Brighton and I agreed to meet and I hung up the phone. I shook my head trying to fathom that this was how my story would go and there wasn't a damn thing I could do about it. I had no choice in this and that felt very strange. Then the dreadful thought emerged of having to tell my loved ones, who were also waiting on my results. Oh God. That's when the tears came. I didn't want to fall apart, otherwise they would fall apart. I felt an overwhelming desire to move, to be outside, to do something, anything to not let this destroy me.

◆

Within days I was having a series of further tests and becoming part of the medical machine. I decided to try to find ways to laugh about it all. Music had always been the fastest way for me to access positive emotions in my training, so I took this handy skill with me into my cancer treatment. As I waited for my PET scan, I listened to the Imagine Dragons song 'Radioactive'. I couldn't help but giggle a little knowing that was literally what I was about to become, as they injected me with a tracer substance. I wasn't in control of what happened to my body now. Chemicals were being pumped into me during tests and I knew the chemicals to come during chemo were toxic. Yes, the treatment plan was ultimately my decision, but if I wanted to live I was going to pursue what was recommended. It was going to be brutal, so I knew I had to find joy in it wherever I could.

My first chemo was scheduled within a week, at the start of August. I made decisions about how I would approach it mentally and emotionally, just like I would for a fight. I created little positive symbols for myself that held meaning, like wearing a bright pink shirt to the first treatment. That was my happy shirt and while I was clearly not happy about having chemo, I was determined to approach it with all the positivity I could muster. On the way there in the car, we listened to 'Can't Hold Us', the Macklemore and Ryan Lewis hit that was a pump-up fight song for me. It was fun and gave me that same feeling as walking to the ring—*I can do this, I'm ready, let me at them, let's go.* I would listen to that song so many times over the coming months. It took on a different meaning over the next few years, but it has become my anthem.

That first time I watched the treatment chemicals push through the cannula into my veins I had no idea what to expect. I had been told that I would be given four separate chemo drugs through intravenous drip bags along with saline and that this process would take hours. I had imagined what it would be like to sit in that treatment room with other cancer patients. I thought all the people attached to drips would be like a posse who banded together and shared experience. In my case, what I found was a nervous reverence for the private reasons we found ourselves there together. It was kind of like prison, where it's not cool to ask someone what they are in for.

Caroline was my chemo support team and she was with me every step of the way. We added one more member in the form of a little Cancer Council teddy bear named Jose, who would sit with me during every treatment as my mascot. They both cheered me up and made me feel like I wasn't alone. I can only imagine how hard it must have been from the other side. I will be forever deeply grateful to Caroline for standing by my side at the scariest time in my life. It's a debt I can never repay.

As the hours wore on and I didn't feel anything, it dawned on me that I had assumed I would feel sick as soon as the drugs hit my system. Not true. Wouldn't you know it, though, smack-bang at the worst possible time, I got my period. What are the chances? During my first chemo I had painful cramps and as soon as it was over I made the unwelcome discovery. It was the most inconvenient timing and seemed like some kind of black humoured joke. Plus first-timer me got hugely freaked out when I went to the bathroom because nobody had warned me that the chemo would make me pee a bizarre fluorescent pinky orange colour. That was when it hit me hard that I had some very serious chemicals running through my system. It was 2.30 p.m. and I had an ominous feeling about what was to come. I kept picturing a photo I'd seen of the cyclist Lance Armstrong when he was very skinny after having chemo. I tried to counteract it with mental images of singer Delta Goodrem looking healthy and happy many years after having survived the same cancer I now had. I told myself to think about Delta, just think about Delta.

Sea sick. Waves and waves of nausea from 5 p.m. for the next five hours. The drugs they administered to stop me from vomiting were working, but that didn't mean I wasn't constantly feeling like throwing up. My new nickname was to become 'Slow Loris' because I was moving like a ninety-year-old. Never one to sit down for long or walk anywhere slowly, I was now keeping the pace of an invalid. The chemo after-effects had started with tingling lips and numb fingers and had progressed to my stomach turning constantly. I took every anti-nausea pill they had prescribed exactly on time, to avoid what I knew was trying to burst out of me. It was a surreal feeling that was desperately awful, but at the same time not quite as bad as I had pictured.

Then came round two. I didn't know it would be worse than the first time. Apparently that's quite common, but unfortunately nobody had mentioned it to me. This time I was lying on the bathroom floor wishing I could vomit, but the drugs just wouldn't let me. The tiles were cold but I couldn't move. I was heavy and exhausted beyond anything I had ever experienced. All I could do was lie there waiting for it to be over. I was in hell now and would have done anything to get out.

On my next visit to Dr Brighton to see how I was handling the chemo, I was shell-shocked from how sick I had been. I was afraid to think how I would get through the remaining six cycles of chemo without having to permanently reside on the bathroom tiles. I desperately asked if the anti-nausea drugs he had originally prescribed were the strongest he had. Dr Brighton told me there were stronger ones available and I could have sworn I heard a chorus of angels singing. He gave me a new prescription and I was relieved that the next chemotherapy was slightly more bearable.

Life became a two-week schedule of chemo blowing me away for a week, then trying to claw my way back towards feeling normal again the week after. Every fortnight the drugs would destroy my body and then I would have to find the mental resolve to get my feet to walk down that hospital hallway to do it all again. It was a mental battle before the physical one, every single time. I needed to use all of the tools Sensei Benny had ever taught me to win the fight with myself.

As the next cycle loomed closer, I would start to feel increasingly nervous. I had the mental sensation of my heels digging into the floor, like I was being dragged by the arms towards the chemo treatment room. I knew that if I didn't change my thinking by the time chemo day arrived, there was a chance I might give in to the urge to run away and hide from it. I had to treat this scary situation like I had when I psyched myself up to face fears in the past. I started walking down the hallway to the chemo room listening to music blasting through my headphones, always feeling like I was walking to the ring for a fight. I would bounce my shoulders and take big hard breaths, preparing myself in my mind the same way as in competition. I listened to Bastille's song 'Pompeii' because it reminded me to be optimistic about my circumstances. I knew there were so many things I could not control about this situation, but I could control the way I thought about it.

◆

Some people continue to go to work during their cancer treatment, but that wasn't the case for me. My job teaching people martial arts and kickboxing was very physical and the treatment made me very tired. Being sick shifted my priorities and making money seemed less important than it had before. I was lucky to have some deep kindness shown to me by some wonderful caring friends during that time, which culminated in a giant fundraiser hosted by UFC Gym Sydney. I was floored by the amount of support I received from friends, students, people I worked with and even strangers I'd never met who wanted to help. It was humbling and made me feel like people cared.

As much as I was grateful for the support I received, I had become trapped in a pattern of making sure everyone else felt okay about what was happening to me. Naturally, I didn't want anyone to worry so I automatically clicked into taking care of their feelings. People would say things like, 'If anyone can beat cancer, it is you,' and while it was well intended, it reminded me that I was expected to be strong. So much of me wanted to fall apart and inside I had started to, but I felt that I couldn't show it. People around me were scared by my getting cancer. If that could happen to someone as young, fit and healthy as me, then nobody was safe. My own fear was reflected in the reactions of everyone I knew. Privately I had splintered inside into compartments. Some parts held my gratitude but others contained some serious sadness and grief that I had to survive in my own mind by any means necessary. It was too much to put the full weight of it on someone else. Some people I cared for struggled to stay present and I couldn't blame them because I knew exactly what that felt like. I remembered how hard it was for me to go and see my brother John when he was very sick, so I never wanted others to have to feel that way about me. I just wanted to focus on living the life I had left and connecting to the part of me that was joyful to be alive.

I went looking for any small beam of happy light I could find in a day. Because I live near the beach, I spent a lot of time looking at the water and going for walks with friends when I felt up to it. I would see so many people walking their dogs and think how cute they were. I've always loved puppies, especially sausage dogs because I had my own when I was a kid. I remember the day when I was twelve that Dad took the whole family 'just to have a look' at some Dachshund puppies. He secretly bought my favourite dog for me and we named him Beau. On the way home, we had to make an emergency visit to the supermarket to buy everything the little furry guy needed. From that day on, seeing puppies makes me giddy with simple pleasure. But when I was ill, I became aware of how often I would see a cute puppy but wouldn't go over to pat it. Over the years I'd gotten into the habit of looking but not touching, but now it seemed crazy to rob myself of some good puppy patting action. Why wouldn't I squeeze every last drop of happiness I could out of each moment?

I had spent so many years needing to be serious and disciplined, that I knew more pleasure was on offer than I had been experiencing. Because of the rigorous demands of my training I would longingly look at cakes and baked goods in cafe display cases, but not order them for myself. I might have a small sweet treat on the weekend, but it seemed so indulgent to go to a coffee shop just to order a piece of cake instead of a meal. Not anymore. Life is too short to watch adorable puppies go by or habitually deprive yourself of tasty goodness. I was done sitting on the sidelines and watching other people have fun. I decided I wanted to enjoy the small happy parts of life more.

Pat the dog, eat the cake became my motto during the four months I was undergoing chemotherapy treatment. It became an in-joke to myself and those around me, any time a reminder was needed about living a fuller life. Saying it to myself took me out of the familiar old pattern of holding back. It was a prompt to have the courage to enjoy fun in my day and to live every day with the knowledge that there is no guarantee any of us will get as many days as we might hope.

I had become keenly aware that there is no other time than right now. We put so many things off to be done in the future, making the naive assumption that we actually have a future in which to do them. One of the chemo nurses asked me during treatment where I had always wanted to go. I responded that my bucket-list destination would be the Maldives, in an overwater bungalow. She asked why I had never gone. I had unconsciously scheduled it for the future, imagining it more as a honeymoon destination than a regular holiday. As I sat in that hospital room getting cancer treatment, I saw how normal but crazy that had been. Why reserve an experience until later when you could make it happen sooner? The planning immediately began for a trip to the Maldives as soon as my treatment was over. There is no time to waste in life, even if you are 100 per cent healthy. Now that I had seen behind the curtain of how quickly circumstances could change, I knew my perspective would also be forever changed. I felt wildly alive, with a side order of reckless, on a bed of wanting to feel safe.

This feeling of being intensely aware of how lucky I was to be alive was counterbalanced with a degree of sadness at my situation. It would erratically flip back and forth at random. I didn't want to feel sorry for myself because I knew I was probably going to one of the lucky ones who made it. Hodgkin's lymphoma has a high survival rate, even though I was already stage two with a huge mass in my chest by the time I was diagnosed. Sure, having cancer sucked, but it would have been narrow-minded of me to feel too hard done by. Every time I had a bad day at the hospital, I would force my eyes up from the floor and look around at all the other people facing their own struggles. I knew many were in battles far worse than mine, so I tried to count myself lucky. My brother John had been given no hope of survival, but I had, so I was determined not to waste it by being negative.

When things got terribly hard, I reminded myself to find the joy even during difficult times. Just like in training it at first always seemed impossible because I was focused on how hard things were and how much it all hurt. Then I would go looking for some small thing to be happy about. Instead of staying caught up in how I saw my circumstances, I would try to look at them the way someone else would from the outside. Perspective is everything. If you only look at a challenge from where you stand, you'll fail to see the whole clear picture. I knew I had to keep what was happening to me in a broader perspective. My toughest day in facing this challenge would be easy to someone else by comparison. When I was feeling low at the hospital, I went for a walk past the spinal unit. As much as having cancer was horrendous, I wondered if there were other people who might not see it that way. I didn't have to pretend I was happy about my medical treatment, but I knew there were likely patients in that very hospital who would trade places with me in a heartbeat.

Every time I got down during treatment, I actively went looking for a way to get back up. My hair was falling out on my pillow and anywhere else I looked. It bothered me. Now I could see why people shaved their heads at the first sign of trouble, rather than have it be a prolonged process. My hair was thinning on top, but I could still make a decent ponytail of it like an ageing guitar player. If I wore a hat, then I didn't look like I was balding. I was resistant to looking like a cancer patient because I didn't want to deal with the sympathetic looks from strangers that I knew I had unintentionally given out myself. For a good amount of time I got to be a normal person when I was in public and nobody knew what was happening in my personal life. Part of me wanted to hold on to that feeling for as long as I possibly could. Perhaps there was a measure of denial going on, where on some level I was still pretending that this wasn't really happening to me. I was determined not to give in to the worst parts of it. I bit down hard on anything that made me feel normal and alive. I was determined to have cancer treatment be part of my life, but not all of it.

Always work to keep your circumstances in perspective. Your problems rarely seem so bad when you put them in a broader context.

19

My Toughest Opponent (It's Not Who You Think)

Chemo breaks down more than your physical system, it also wears you down mentally and emotionally. As the months of treatment wore on unrelentingly, I kept patting dogs and eating cake. Naturally I started to puff up from all the sweet treats, which was the opposite of what I thought was going to happen during treatment. I didn't become a skeletal Lance Armstrong lookalike, but instead began to get a little chubby. Who gets cancer and gets fat? I didn't know bloating sometimes happened to patients, but it also made sense because I was now spending more time sitting down in a month than I previously would in a year. The chemicals they pumped into my body were having crazy side effects and this was just another less than ideal feature. My perception of myself physically wasn't as positive as it had previously been. This was only exacerbated by the fact my eyebrows were now falling out, along with much more of my hair. I had a rash on my stomach that had started as a secondary symptom, but became an itchy nightmare lasting many months. I had scars on my arms from sores that wouldn't heal because of my depleted immune system. Even the medical tape they used to secure the chemo IV drip to my arm had left permanent tape-patterned scars. My forearms looked like Christmas wrapping paper after the sticky tape had been ripped off.

The constantly changing physical symptoms made it hard to maintain a consistent psychological perspective. What was happening to my body would unsettle the stable ground I created in my mind. I would manage a positive attitude, but then partially wonder if I was in denial about what was happening to me. When I was down it was devastating, but when I was up I got concerned I wasn't appropriately grasping the gravity of my circumstances. I would feel good one day, knowing my treatment had a high success rate, but the next day it would hit me that I had cancer and I'd feel unsure if I was going to get out of this alive.

Searching for perspective, I asked my doctor point blank what the chances were that I was going to die. Dr Brighton calmly told me my chances of surviving were very good, but also made it clear that there were no guarantees. He explained that one of his patients the previous year was a young woman like myself, who had not responded to the same treatment and had passed away. They don't know why this happens, so it is the luck of the draw where fate decides the outcome. That hit home with me like a sledgehammer, but it was a truth I needed to hear in order to know how to feel. I wanted to believe I was going to pull through, but I also didn't want to kid myself about what was happening.

There were times when all I could do was stare down the barrel of the truth. Certain moments quickly went from bearable to devastatingly raw. Like the test they ran where I had to sit alone in a lead-lined room with a radioactive solution being pushed through my system. I wasn't allowed to move even a tiny bit, so there wasn't any way to pass the time by watching a movie or listening to music. Sitting in that room, all I could do was contemplate the harsh reality of my situation. There were no dogs to pat or bright-coloured shirts to wear to brighten my mood. There was only the cold isolation of a hospital room with tubes I didn't want attached to my body filling it with an unwelcome dangerous solution. I let myself feel how deeply afraid I was that maybe I wasn't going to live another year or make it to forty.

When they had diagnosed me originally, my thoughts flashed to the actor Andy Whitfield. I had read a magazine article the year before about his death from Non-Hodgkin's lymphoma. He was a very fit young man and the shocking senselessness of his death had bothered me for weeks. When I read about his passing, it just seemed so unfair because he was full of good life. Andy Whitfield came back into my mind as I sat immobilised in that radioactive hospital room. I quietly shed a tear for him and his young family, trying not to fall apart while I had to let the liquid just slide down my face. My mind flew from fearing I too would meet an early end, all the way to hoping I wouldn't. There was only one way to find out.

◆

After yet more tests, Dr Brighton finally gave me results that told me I was in remission. The treatment was working and my body was responding. So much of me had secretly been afraid that I would be one of the unlucky ones for whom chemo didn't work. I was so relieved and felt like I had slid safely in under the garage door just as it was closing. Phew.

Despite the progress I'd made, I still had to finish all the prescribed treatments. I was so happy I wasn't going to die, but I also felt ripped off that I still had to continue pumping my body full of these chemicals that were simultaneously healing and destroying it. The contradictory emotions made me uncertain about how I *should* feel, so I decided to just feel how I was— both ecstatic and devastated at the same time. I cycled through one side of this emotional equation taking the lead, then flipping to the other side, sometimes in a matter of minutes. I did my best to focus on optimism, but as my body got weaker from the treatment, my inner world became more fragile.

By the time the final chemo rolled around I was in an acutely vulnerable place, both in my body and my heart. I was seriously dreading the non-stop waves of nausea that I knew were coming for days. Everybody's experience with chemo is different, but I don't think it's easy for anyone. I felt like I was getting off fairly lightly in some ways, but it was still the worst illness I had ever been through. Anything I associated with chemo made my stomach turn when I thought of it—from medical tape to the jumper I wore, even the toasted sandwiches they served in the treatment room. Just imagining the subtle berry smell of the anti-nausea wafers I took to stop me vomiting made me feel sick and still does to this day.

On the day of the last IV treatment I just wasn't in a place where I felt capable of being weakened further, in mind or body. Some personal conflicts in my life were coming to a head and making me very emotional, which made chemotherapy seem impossible. I felt like I just couldn't go through with it this time. But I knew I had no real choice except to go to the hospital at the designated hour. So I put on my fight music and tried to toughen up mentally. I convinced myself that all those years of training meant I knew how to push through and get the job done, no matter how much it hurt.

As I walked down the hallway towards the chemo room, I had to push the tears down. They kept brimming back up in my eyes along with a lump in my throat. Now wasn't the time to fall apart because I feared I wouldn't be able to glue myself back together. I put my game face on and walked into the room, greeting the nurses and doing my best to stay strong. A painful side effect of the chemo was that one of the four drugs burnt on the way in. This had actually damaged some of my veins and made them collapse. As they tried to get a blood vessel for the final treatment, the cannula for the IV just wasn't hitting the target. Much larger than a regular needle, it's very painful to push through the skin each time. I was already feeling so fragile that each attempt brought me closer to my composure crumbling. I'd always had good veins and now they couldn't even find one. I felt like my body had been destroyed and my mental strength was about to go with it. One last attempt to push that cannula in was all it took.

'Stop!' I yelled to the nurse. 'You have to stop,' I said and with that I stood up and pushed my way towards the door.

'I can't do it,' the words themselves were almost sickening me as they came out of my mouth. I knew giving up went against everything I believed in, but I could not sit there one second longer. This was my breaking point. This was finally the challenge I couldn't face or overcome. I broke mentally. As I rushed out of the room, tears surged forward and flooded down my face. I sobbed as I fled to the end of the hospital hallway and crumpled in a ball on the floor. I cried out all the sadness I had been grappling with, the defeated childlike weeping of someone who couldn't take any more. I sat there crying for what felt like a year. My favourite nurse came over to briefly talk to me but it was no use. I was done. I quit.

I bargained feverishly with myself about the odds of my cancer returning if I didn't finish treatment. Maybe if I completed seven out of the eight chemo cycles then that would be enough? What if it came back, and I had been foolish enough to not have the final one? Then a wave of despair at how broken I felt would wash me out to sea again. I could not do it. I had tried to be strong for so long but today I was not. All I could be was sad and defeated.

I stared at the ground with tears streaming down my face for the longest time. There was nothing anyone could say to me. I just wanted to be left alone and never have to move from this spot on the floor. I didn't care who walked past and saw me, all my pride was gone along with my will to continue. I was destroyed and completely immobilised. I started thinking about how unfair it was and who I had been before this. No opponent I'd faced was anywhere near as tough as this. It wasn't even the cancer itself that was beating me. My toughest opponent was my own mind.

At this critical point my thoughts started wandering, recalling how all my training had carried me this far through treatment. I tried to imagine maybe I could do it if Sensei Benny were there to inspire me. He wasn't, though. The more I thought about him, I started to hear his voice in my mind. It echoed quietly, saying, 'Change your thinking.' I didn't feel like I had the strength to change it. I was planning how to get out of any more chemo when I heard his voice say, 'This won't hurt less if you close your eyes.'

I knew either way, if I had the treatment or not, the consequences were going to hurt. There was no way to extricate myself from this situation except if I gave up on myself. How could I live with that? Was I prepared to take the risk of not having the final treatment and endanger whatever life I had left?

I knew I couldn't stay on this hallway floor forever either. I was trapped and desperate for a way out of this predicament. That's when I heard it. Sensei's voice whispering to me over and over, 'All it takes is ten seconds of courage.'

I knew I wasn't brave enough to face the sickness of the last chemo, but maybe I could muster enough courage to get up and walk back into the room. As much as I wanted to live on that patch of carpet forever, I knew eventually I would be forced to move. I cried some more, because I just didn't *want* to have to be strong. I was facing a choice that I knew would dictate who I was going to be from this time on. Was I going to become someone broken by their illness, or would I find a way to dig deep when I had nothing left?

More tears came as I hugged my knees to my chest. I just didn't feel solid enough emotionally to tackle the unfair road that lay ahead. Finally, I took a deep breath and felt a surge of anger at my situation. I used it as the driving force to make myself stand up. I fought the urge to run away again. I looked down the hallway and felt that 'down the chute' feeling right before I used to walk out of the dressing room to the ring. I knew it would take ten seconds to walk back to that hospital room and face my fear. Every impulse screamed to turn right and sprint towards the exit. I took a deep breath, turned left and made my feet start walking.

The second I sat back in the chemo chair, I started negotiating again. This time it was on a scale that made me feel a little crazy. I agreed to let them call a special doctor to attempt to re-insert the cannula. I wanted to bolt for the door so badly before they arrived. I knew it was going to take another ten-second burst to hold my own body down in that chair against every desire I had to escape. I made a deal with myself that the doctor had just ten seconds to try to get a vein again. After that maybe I could decide if I would let them start sending the drugs through the IV system. I was psychologically bargaining with myself literally ten seconds at a time, just trying to take one step forward without retreating. I was trying to trick myself into walking the plank without looking down.

It took everything I had and more than a few tears to give in and let them push the first chemical through. I just had to submit, but it wasn't a fragile submission. It was the adult part of me putting her arm around the terrified little three-year-old kid inside, telling her we could do this and everything was going to be alright. As I watched the solution surge through the clear IV tube, I consciously told myself I could rest now. I had put myself back together again, tiny piece by piece, starting with finding a way to stand up off the floor. In my weakest moment, I had found the smallest burst of courage. I knew it wouldn't help to let my thoughts linger too long on how I had broken down. I had to focus on the fact that I wanted to live.

◆

After the chemo cycles were complete I had a month off from treatment for my body to recover enough strength to start radiation. The radiation treatment was to begin in early December and continue until after New Year's Day. I had to go to the hospital each morning and be strapped down as a huge machine sent radiation through me. I wasn't allowed to move at all and I definitely didn't want stray radiation firing around my body. I got into the habit of meditating to stay still and pass the time. I would run through a practice Sensei Benny had taught me that I called my 'daily five'. I used it to calm myself and stay positive. It starts with saying *thank you* for the day, then asking for *courage*, followed by *forgiving* yourself and others, then asking for *clear sight* and finishing with having *good intentions*. It was so important to choose how to feel for the day and what to think about. Then for the rest of the time I was being radiated, I would make a gratitude list in my mind.

It felt a little strange to feel happy when something so awful was happening, but I knew I had a choice in where my thoughts took me as I lay there. I knew I had to stay sturdy mentally to get my body through this process. These rituals made the radiation much more bearable by giving me something to focus on. I needed it day after day when my heart would sink as I entered the hospital and saw depressing sickness sights. It wasn't fun walking through doors marked with biohazard and radiation warning signs or getting taped down hard to a table while nurses scurried out of the room for their own safety. I worked hard to keep my head in the right place to avoid another meltdown.

After I had finished my last radiation session the nurses took me out into the waiting room and I rang the brass bell that symbolised treatment being over. I did it. I made it to the end. I cried as that bell rang out and it felt just like the final bell of a brutal fight. I was thoroughly exhausted, relieved and grateful to have made it to the end.

During this latter part of the treatment Sensei Benny came to Australia, as he does every year, to teach a series of seminars. When he saw what the treatment had done to my body, he didn't show even the tiniest glint of shock. I was surprised that in all our conversations he didn't once ask me how my treatment was going. He didn't even ask me if I was going to die. I was a little hurt by it, but I knew he was focusing on something else. In the end, he only asked me one question—'What will you *do* with this?'

I didn't have an answer, but his question niggled at me constantly. I wondered what could I do with the experience I had been through and what life would be like after I recovered. That's when I registered he had stealthily changed my thinking without me even knowing it. He had asked me six simple words that re-directed my thoughts in a specific direction. Sensei didn't want me to get stuck where I was mentally, but instead to look forward and imagine life after the cancer. He challenged me like only a world champion can. He expected me to make something of myself from having been through such a difficult experience. Sensei had always said that if I were to go through pain, I had better make sure it was worthwhile. Suffering for suffering's sake is pointless, but suffering that you use to grow is valuable. Those words echoed in my mind, especially in the darkest times.

The lowest ebb for me came after my treatment was completed. I didn't know at the time this is commonplace. You go into survival mode when the treatment is happening, which makes you keenly aware how lucky you are to be alive, but many come out the other side into much darker waters. I almost drowned in mine. The consequences and sadness of everything that had come before caught up with me after. I spent many sleepless nights crying and feeling devastated. It seemed like the fight was over, but it wasn't for me. It's hard to explain the contradictory emotions that were haunting me. I felt tormented that I wasn't happy and a poster child for blissful cancer recovery. I expected to/was meant to feel overjoyed to be alive, but I had never felt less so.

I wish I could share an inspiring story about how well I dealt with cancer's immediate aftermath, but that just wouldn't be true. The year after treatment was the hardest for me. I wasn't sure if I became depressed as a result of the illness or because I had been grieving and in pain going into having cancer. The sadness had massively multiplied and was waiting for me when it was over. Things became so gravely difficult that I found myself sitting on a cliff trying to think of reasons to keep going. It pains me to say it, but that is how low I went. There was a time where the whole world seemed midnight dark to me and like there were no answers to the problems I faced. I had to accept that sometimes there just isn't a way to feel better. Yet.

Throughout the most challenging periods I knew *this*—I just had to hold on tight and ride it out to see what was on the other side. It felt like I was gripping tightly for dear life to the handlebars of a motorbike as it hurtled full speed over rocky terrain. It was horrible to stay where I was and even worse to let go. I felt like the only two choices I had were both painful. I could not change where I had been or the way my life was now. I had been dealt some bad cards and some I had dealt myself. All I could do was cry the tears that needed to be shed and do my best to heal what I could. I knew I had to find a way to ask for help with the things that I couldn't handle. After keeping so much of my pain to myself during treatment I didn't know how to get back to speaking the whole truth of how I felt. I was wandering around lost inside myself.

As I fell apart, so did my relationship with Caroline and sadly we had to part ways. That painful story is not mine alone, so its place does not rest here on these pages. I will always hold dear how we laughed in the best of times, but in the worst of times she bravely sat with me while I crumbled. That took a kind of loving courage that, in my broken state, I could only watch with awe.

The demons I was wrestling threatened to pull me under, as I tried to come to terms with who I had become and how everything had changed. I was no longer the person mentally or physically that I had been before cancer. I felt so damaged by all I had been through that I didn't even recognise myself anymore in those early days. All the tangible things that had previously made me who I was had been stripped away. I had spiralled down lower than ever before and it had scared me.

Once again I found myself standing at that old familiar crossroads—to fight or not to fight? To let it break me or to get up and try again. We all face our own choices like this on some level, but I had never faced a choice where I felt so devoid of my coping mechanisms. I had always previously been able to mount an offence from within to push myself to achieve. Before I had been sick, the lower I felt, the harder I tried. It had always worked for me in the past and had been the fuel I had burnt to change my life for the better. Not this time.

My best coping strategy I'd utilised in life was to train. Now I couldn't physically exercise to make myself feel strong again, either inside or out. I was still deeply fatigued from the treatment and the doctors couldn't say if this feeling would ever go away. It was an invisible torment. I have heard this type of fatigue described as 'life draining exhaustion' and now I knew why. It made every small thing in my day that I had previously taken for granted into a struggle requiring focused effort. I felt like my body weighed two hundred kilos of cement blocks. I would catch myself repeatedly saying, 'I'm tired,' but that didn't come close to doing it any justice. I was exhausted all day, every day, as if I had been up all night. On top of this if I tried to exercise it made me feel completely shattered.

The fatigue was stopping me from getting back on track in every way that I desperately needed. It meant that I couldn't work much which had always been a way for me to feel valuable and successful in the world. My relationships with the people I cared about suffered as I mentally imploded. I had never felt more alone, even though there were people trying to love me. I didn't think there was any way to find a path back to myself. I felt like I was alive, but the old me was dead. My face looked different when I looked in the mirror, like I was an empty fraction of the shiny person I once was.

◆

'What will you do with this?' Sensei's words ran through my mind again and again. I was struggling to just survive the fall-out, let alone do anything useful with it. I waited. I held on and kept waiting for the feeling to pass. If I couldn't change it, I knew I had to respond to it in a better way, even if that was slow progress. I searched my mind for any tool or feeling that I could harness for the positive. Then it hit me—I gave myself a year to live. I took that pre-treatment feeling of wondering if I only had twelve months or so left alive and decided to use it again in a different positive way. I knew beyond any doubt that life had no guarantees anymore, so what if I did only have one year left? Someone with limited time left would live harder and try to make the best use of their days even if they weren't feeling great. Maybe I could use that feeling to live a bigger life. It could be a good thing to feel that way for a while, because it didn't come with all the pressure of making a whole new life with the challenges I now faced.

> What would you do if you only had one year to live?

I started chasing down anything intense and life-nourishing as if I were starving. Everything had changed, so I needed to change. It became a daily priority to seek out positive experiences. It felt crazy to have some good things happening, but to feel so low at the same time. I was constantly fighting an inner battle that people couldn't see. If some light appeared in the sky on the horizon, I would set my compass and trek in that direction as hard as my tired legs would carry me. I knew that in order to move away from the darkness, I had to go wherever I could feel the sun shining.

I found some solid illuminated ground by living alone properly for the first time in my life. I had more solitary time than I was used to and it was so important to spend it sorting myself out. I needed a place, my own place, to retreat to and find some stability within myself. I needed the hours and days of being solitary just to process the time-delayed shock of what I had experienced. I was more delicate in both body and mind than I had ever been, but that in itself was rapidly changing me. All my emotions sat closer to the surface, which meant I didn't have the luxury of keeping them under the radar like I unintentionally had when I was sick. I felt so raw that I was surely transparent to the eye. I walked around feeling like I had no skin. Once fairly composed, I was now visibly emotional in ways that I didn't always feel comfortable with. Words would leave my mouth before I had even considered them, flying forward from places inside me that were still on the mend. It was excruciating and freeing at the same time. My life had been torn apart and I didn't know exactly how I would put it back together. All I knew was that I had to try. If I had known what was to come in the next year, I would have been shocked.

You have a *choice* about who you will be from this moment on.

20

My New Friend TED

A stunningly beautiful picture suddenly flashes up on my phone screen of a grand empty theatre, lusciously soaked in red light illuminating the wide imposing stage in the centre. I stare at it in confusion, before wondering if it is perhaps the Opera House stage lit in a dramatic way I had never seen before. I am equal parts captivated by its majestic elegance and baffled by why my friend and student Jess Miller has sent the image to me. Today is my thirty-ninth birthday and I am sitting quietly by the water collecting my thoughts when this odd message arrives and it's taking me a few minutes to decipher it. Then my stomach drops and the reason behind it hits me with shock and trepidation . . . I'm in.

The photo was of the Opera House stage, alright. One day soon I would be standing on it, in front of thousands of people. This was Jess's way of telling me I had been chosen as a speaker for TEDx Sydney 2015, the largest TEDx event in the world outside the main global TED event in North America. TED started in 1984 as a conference of 'ideas worth spreading'. It has since become a global phenomenon where thought-leaders share groundbreaking advances with the world, alongside the interesting stories of regular people. This was a big deal. To me it was massive, especially given it would be my first attempt at public speaking. Yep, at the Opera House. By myself, on that massive stage. Fear ran through me in conjunction with a bolt of excitement. I reminded myself of Sensei Benny's definition of self-confidence—knowing you can do something even though you've never done it before.

Only weeks before, Jess had asked if I had ever thought about doing a TEDx talk. I had loved the TED talks by Brené Brown and Elizabeth Gilbert, but had never realistically considered the possibility of actually doing something like that myself. Sure, it had crossed my mind that it would be an incredible opportunity, but I had never gone as far as legitimately considering doing it. As in, for real doing it. On a big stage even, with people watching. I realised I was holding my breath.

Jess had been training with me for five years and was a dedicated student. She had stuck by me throughout my cancer ordeal and remained solid as I tried to get my vulnerable self back on track. She was involved in the organisational aspects of TEDx and wanted to nominate me as a speaker. I said it would be an amazing thing to do, but I didn't honestly think it was going to happen. I knew I was still so raw from cancer that I figured maybe the timing might be better in the years to come. Jess wanted to put me forward for the current speaker intake and eventually I said yes believing there was only a slim chance they would choose me.

Two weeks before my birthday I went through a phone interview about speaking at TEDx. We spoke for an hour about what my speech could potentially cover. The TEDx people asked if I would consider doing a martial arts demonstration and I said I would think about it. I was having a difficult day emotionally and had to put my best foot forward while speaking to them. As I hung up the phone, I thought I would never hear from them again. I wasn't my old bright, cheerful self and wished this process had happened a few years earlier. It just wasn't the best time in my life, as I was still trying to find some solid ground with my recovery. I felt disappointed, but also relieved that I probably wouldn't have to do a speech when I was still quite fragile in many ways.

◆

The Opera House picture was still on my phone screen as I messaged Jess, asking her to be clear on what this crazy image meant. It was my birthday, after all, so maybe I was misinterpreting her meaning. It had only been a year since my final cancer treatment and my mind was still quite foggy at times. I was used to things requiring a second viewing. Jess replied that I had been officially chosen as a speaker for TEDx Sydney. I didn't know whether to jump for joy or throw my phone into the nearby ocean and pretend I had never received the message. Maybe Nemo would like to give a speech instead? Perhaps if I started swimming now, I could make a new anonymous life for myself in New Zealand?

I was elated to be chosen for such an honour, but my thoughts immediately took a more fragile turn—all those people would be looking at me and now, more than any time in my life, I felt the least comfortable with my appearance. I was still getting used to having short hair, I was still shedding the extra weight from treatment without being able to exercise properly, and I was still wearing my heart outside my body emotionally. Was it crazy to agree to doing this speech? I thought back to my first title fight when everyone thought I was mad for doing it, but it turned out to be one of the best things I'd ever done. Experience told me to say yes, even though my fear pleaded with me to say no. That little sucker wanted me to quickly barricade a two-by-four across the door to my comfort zone. This battle with myself was so familiar and the only answer I could live with that didn't involve tackling regret was to have a bit of courage and say yes.

One idea worth sharing in a speech. What would you say? What matters enough to you that you'd use your one shot to share it with the world? Part of me was still thinking in life-and-death terms, so I framed it as what I would say if I knew I only had one year left. I rewound my brain to when I had been diagnosed and contemplated what mattered most. I started writing and what came out was a speech about the wild ride of what I had learnt in my training. I talked about all the wonderful things martial arts had given me and how they had ultimately helped me get through the toughest times. It was deeply personal but that was the only place I could come from. I had been stripped back to the rawest emotions and only the fundamental pillars remained standing in my life.

When the time came to read the initial speech draft aloud for the first time to the TEDx team, I was afraid of what they might say. Putting yourself out there on a deep personal level, especially when you're already vulnerable, is seriously daunting. This is why our comfort zones are so well furnished, with plush couches and bulletproof glass. Exposing your soft underbelly, when all your safety impulses tell you to bare your teeth, is counterintuitive and feels a little dangerous. The world is full of people who growl and puff up their muscles, or preen and only offer their good side. I've always been far more interested in those who roll over and show their weird little tummy to the world, getting an endearing pat rather than perfect praise. I knew the only way forward was to take a chance and live in the knowledge that I tried my best to speak from the heart, no matter what happened. If they laughed me out of the room, it would undoubtedly hurt. Though that would ultimately be better than if I had taken the safest speech route and been told I had written a cerebral structured piece that nobody would connect with emotionally. *Doing* is always better than wishing I had tried. Knowing that doesn't make the trying any easier or less scary, but it does make starting possible.

I read my draft speech to the TEDx team and none of the imagined critique eventuated. It didn't matter that I hadn't presented a high brow intellectual theory. Nobody scoffed or cringed uncomfortably at the honest nature of what I shared. In fact, they encouraged me to go deeper and to tell more stories. I felt relieved they no longer seemed focused on also getting me to do the martial arts demonstration.

After some time to digest, the team came back to me and suggested I should be the closing speaker on the day. I thought that surely they had hit their heads and weren't thinking clearly. They wanted *me* to be the final speaker at such an important event? *Me*, who was going to get up there and talk about my feelings following a day of erudite discussion? I knew some of the other speakers were notable public figures, such as the famed neurosurgeon Dr Charlie Teo and prominent barrister Julian Burnside QC. These were actual adults, who had things to say that others should listen to. Then there was me. I had previously thought of myself as a fairly confident person, but these were not confident times.

So the battle began, between what my heart wanted to say and whether my mind would let me say it. The desire to edit myself based on the imagined judgements of others blazed over my head like heavy fire at regular intervals. I believed in what I had written, but second-guessing thoughts about how personal the speech was crept in like spies infiltrating my camp in the night. I wanted to distance myself and put up higher defensive walls to fortify my base in case of heavy attack. I contemplated a secret escape route to avoid the war altogether. A forged passport and false identity were valid getaway options. If only I could get up on stage behind an armoured vest, then nobody would know how exposed to fire on the frontlines I genuinely felt.

For all the self-protective urges that careened through me, there was also a whisper floating through my mind that said— '*You can do this. Even if it doesn't go well, you can be proud of taking the chance to live a bigger life.*'

It was much quieter than the other message coming over my mental loudspeaker advising me to close all social media accounts and board a plane for Antarctica. I hear they don't often hold TEDx talks there. The more encouraging whisper came to me at a ten-to-one ratio, so while it was at a lower volume, I heard it more often in my mind. I made a choice to believe in it. A simple choice that the whisper might be true, just enough to keep me moving forward and preparing my speech. You know, just in case I decided to go ahead with it.

◆

Prepare my little heart out, I did. I knew that, like a fight, the best way to mitigate disaster was to practise hard. I went over my speech hundreds of times, despite having read that being over-rehearsed was the enemy. I had to do it this way for my own reasons. I knew myself well enough to feel sure that the only way to not blow it was to visualise succeeding. Every time I didn't want to examine my speech again, I just imagined freezing on stage with thousands of people looking at me. No, not an option, so off I went to give it another run through. On a deeper level, I was afraid my still foggy memory (or chemo brain, as it's called) would cause me to go blank mid-speech. To be honest, I was worried my mind would go pitch-black without warning.

This was a new phenomenon brought on by treatment that I had never before in my life experienced. If my memory had previously malfunctioned, it was in a way where I felt the word I had forgotten was on the tip of my tongue, soon to be remembered. With chemo brain, not only was the word not on the tip of my tongue, but it was like the dictionary had been snapped shut. Then it had been discarded on the library table after-hours while the janitor finished mopping and switched off the lights. Gone.

I knew the only way to counteract this possibility of going blank was to use visual cues, so I structured my speech around photo slides. They would serve to illustrate my point and help people see that I wasn't just talking about an idea—I had lived it. Secretly the slides were there so my chemo brain didn't become the closing speaker instead of me. If I was going to make this speech, then I was prepared to use whatever resources I could to do my best. Taking foggy memory into the speech with me would feel similar to my title fight with all the injuries. I hoped that, in the same way, if I had the grit to try, then I might just make it.

There was no room for self-sabotage or a casual 'let's just see what happens' approach. If I was going to do this, I was going to do it all the way. The more I focused my mind on my upcoming goal, the more I dug myself out of the darkness day by day. In writing about my experiences in training and the lessons I had learned, it was like I was teaching them to myself all over again. My heart started to fill up, being reminded of who I had been. It helped me discover the way to fight this new battle ahead of me. I had to give it everything, and make peace with the outcome.

One week before the speech, I knew I needed some quiet time to properly focus. I flew up to Queensland for a few days to clear my head. I wanted to lock myself in a hotel room and set my sights on preparing. I needed to be away from the buzz of the impending event and crowded noise of Sydney. Maybe if I did a few gazillion practices in front of the hotel bathroom mirror and then went for a sunset walk on the beach I would manage to avoid publicly humiliating myself? Seemed like a reasonable formula.

On the plane ride up the coast, I had been thinking about how lucky I was to be in this position and how far I had come since the first discussion with the TEDx team. I was relieved I didn't have to do the martial arts demonstration that they had originally requested. The pressure of just giving a speech was more than enough. As I let go of doing a demonstration, part of me got snagged on it as it went by. In my head I knew standing on that stage was going to take a bit of bravery, but right down in the pit of my stomach a lingering unspoken truth was rumbling—I didn't want to do the demonstration because I didn't think I was physically capable of it anymore. Cancer had made me fragile and less trusting of my body. I had many days where I was too weak to even open a bottle of water by myself. I was afraid that if I tried to do a demonstration, I'd be physically incapable and I might fail. That scared me more than anything.

Yet, I was tired of uncertainty derailing me and making me feel small. So when that familiar helpful whisper came to me again, I knew what I had to do. If I wholeheartedly believed in living with the kind of courage I wanted to give my speech about, then how could I live with myself if I avoided doing something important because I was afraid? I had already paid the price of lacking courage in other situations, so I knew better than to allow fear to win.

As I drove north from Cairns after leaving the airport, I couldn't stop thinking about doing the demonstration. I had an urgent need to pull over and call Jess. An idea had come charging into my mind with a truth that I either had to face head-on, or fold and run from forever. I wanted to attempt to do a martial arts wooden board break at the end of my speech. When I spoke to Jess, I had to talk extra fast to make sure I got all the words out before my fear made me stop. Jess asked if I thought I could do it. I replied that I wasn't sure, but that was the whole point. I hoped I could, but it had been years since I had tried to break a piece of wood with my hand. I hadn't done it since before I had cancer. Board breaking was a test of self-belief at the best of times, but it was now a symbol of acceptance for me. If the only reason I wasn't willing to try was because I was afraid of failing, then that was the very embodiment of the message in my speech.

It was all about changing your thinking around who you are and what you're capable of, then finding the courage to pursue it.

Jess loved the riskiness of the idea and agreed I should do it. I appreciated her enthusiasm, but I knew she had faith in me because she was unaware of how deeply the cancer treatment had affected me physically. As I then explained the idea over the phone to Edwina, the TEDx curator, my self-doubt was exposed. I honestly didn't know if I could do it, but I was willing to fail in public if need be. I believe there is honour in trying and I thought that if I did fail, that would be just as valuable. Sometimes all you can do is try, even if you're unsure you'll succeed. We have all failed at times. If you never risk, then you'll find safety in less chance of failure. Unfortunately, the price you pay is that you'll be guaranteed a less full life. Safe is comfortable but it's also limiting.

In my new post-cancer life, I was done with playing it safe. I was ready to fail spectacularly with a huge crowd looking on. I reconciled the idea of taking one for the team, for all the little guys who give their best but things don't work out. It had happened to me before and I would be damned if I was going to live the rest of my life limited by the fear of failing. I never again wanted to make a choice where the truth underneath was that it was a decision made because I was scared of a negative outcome. I couldn't live with myself if I took the easy way out and just gave a speech minus the demonstration. Now that this idea had been spoken out loud, I knew I had to face my fear.

◆

I am trapped in this tiny Sydney hotel room while the pressure mounts. It's like being in one of those movies where water is filling up a submarine compartment and the person is down to their last few gulps of air near the ceiling before going under for good. Today is the day—TEDx time. I have to leave the hotel where I'm getting ready in one hour to go to the Opera House. My call time is an hour and a half away, then I will be speaking another two hours after that. I open the hotel room curtains to attempt to alleviate this closed-in feeling, but all I can see outside is a wall. Mild claustrophobia ensues.

I've sat down to eat, knowing my body will likely not let me as the stage time draws closer. Pressure squeezes the need for food out of my body, which is rare because I usually always feel hungry. The larger the nerves, the smaller my bladder gets. Now is without doubt the time when I have to closely manage myself and complete the list of prelude tasks that are best scheduled early. Meal—check. Get dressed—check. Get undressed again because I'm overheating—check. Turn on air-conditioning and try to relax—double check.

The images from my speech slide by as I begin one more practice run in the bathroom. Being well prepared is the kryptonite to my nerves. I can funnel the pressure into an activity that quenches it for the time being. Like they're competing in the Olympics, I run my jitters through one more speech. I remind myself that I know what I am doing and am committed to it. Soon I will find out the answer to the question I have been fearing for months—can I do this speech with thousands of people watching? Then I will meet the final heavy answer to the more personal question—can I still break a board even after cancer has weakened me/am I still who I used to be or only a shell of my former self?

Such an old familiar feeling to be wondering about the outcome of an impending big event. It's as if it were Christmas Eve and

I'm not sure if I will get a shiny new toy tomorrow or another neglected Barbie. Before a fight I would often take a minute in front of a mirror earlier in the day to look myself in the eye and think about how I would feel later that night. How would I feel when I finally looked in the mirror again after it was all over? Would it be with joy or sadness? Would I have the visual markers of battle on my face, or would it be injury free? It was a dauntingly exciting feeling of not knowing what was about to happen. Now I felt exactly the same way as I stood in the hotel room. Would I see myself later in victory or crushing defeat?

I find it almost impossible to make conversation in the car as we head towards the venue. I have always been like this when the pressure is on. My personality fades inwards as I pull myself towards my centre. I begin the ritual by listening to music on my headphones and trying to focus as I watch the scenery roll past. The drive is short and as soon as I arrive I say rushed shallow-breathed goodbyes. My mum looks more nervous than me. I head straight for the stage door. It's like a final farewell before battle. A last hug without knowing what state I will be in later, held a little longer than usual, then swiftly broken as I steel myself to leave the safety of the familiar.

There is so much on the line for me today that I know it will make me or break me. I am about to take a massive personal risk that only a few people in the world know about, all of whom will be in that room as I do it. They have been nervous for me, questioning if this is genuinely the right time or decision. Even at the TEDx rehearsal, the curatorial team tried to get me to physically break the board to be certain I could do it successfully. I declined. The whole point was that I honestly didn't know if I could do it. I didn't want to fake that feeling. This was my real life and I wholeheartedly believed in what I was going to say and try to do in my speech. It was all about facing fear and finding courage for me. I'm not saying I'm a particularly courageous person, but I knew there was no way I could get through today without it.

As I arrive at the stage door I'm greeted by my long-time student Paul Nind, who bounds up to me like an eager puppy excited to play. He will be on stage with me today, because I have asked him to hold the wooden board as I try to break it. Paul was rock solid and always there for me when I was sick, so this is a way for me to repay him by sharing a special experience together. Stress makes me smile at him in a slightly strained way and he knows this is not play-time. The pressure is on—for me, this is fight time.

◆

Before I would compete there are some key points of stress where my adrenaline dumps into my bloodstream as the nerves kick in. Entering the venue is one of those times. It all becomes real in an instant. This is the location where the battle will take place. It will happen soon. I will either walk back out this door in a few hours in triumph or deflation. The most iconic white building in the middle of Sydney would be my arena today. Paul will be in my corner. We walk together through the underside of the Opera House towards the green room where the other speakers wait.

Like a dressing room at the fights, I can smell the nervous sweat and tingling anxiety as we are greeted by the TEDx crew. Fear is palpable. I aim a friendly smile at one of the other speakers I had been looking forward to meeting, but it isn't even seen despite her looking right at me. She is so caught up in her own mind that my greeting doesn't even register. I understand and let her be. Then I hear that she is to speak next and I see the fear in her eyes as the nerves put her in a vice grip. I have witnessed fear bring people spectacularly to life or suck the vitality right out of them directly in front of me. Even the most seasoned among us seems to be feeling the weight in the room. We exchange short conversations and duck and weave around each other with shifting concentration. None of the speakers want to engage with anyone for too long.

The smiling face of Jess comes into the green room and I am excited to see her. Giving her a big hug, I have the expectant excitement of a junior employee about to give a big presentation for the CEO. I want to do a good job for Jess, to honour her faith in me. I'm keenly aware how important it is for me to come through for her. She had chosen a risky proposition in first-time public speaker me. I want to knock the ball out of the park on her behalf, or at the very least try to avoid freezing then passing out on stage. Jess and Paul are all abuzz with excitement as we take a photo of the three of us to commemorate this special moment. The joy before the testing time.

Paul and I are taken to a private dressing room to wait out the hour before going on stage. To me it feels slightly akin to being led to the pre-execution cell on death row. The ever-smaller rooms getting closer with each narrowing corridor. These modest hallways would lead me to the cramped quarters of backstage and then through a curtain to one of the biggest rooms I have ever been in. A room where thousands are facing me and I am the only one staring back at them. I have been worried that the

awe of such a powerful moment, when the bright stage lights
first hit me and I can see the audience, will overwhelm me to the
point I might hesitate at the very start of my speech. I am scared
I will be overwhelmed with emotion about how lucky I am to
be there (both on stage and just alive itself) and then start to cry.
I am fairly together but my raw emotion is never far below the
surface these days. I remind myself that we aren't there yet, so
I have to keep my mind focused on the present time. No use
running ahead and releasing the nervous onstage chemicals into
my body too soon. It is crucial that I manage my emotions and
peak at exactly the right time.

> Good preparation is kryptonite for your
> nerves.

Performing under pressure has never been an exam you cram
for at the last minute. It's all about reaching that sweet spot of
being ready at precisely the right moment. TEDx had been the
same for me over the three months of preparation, right down
to this final hour before I spoke. It was all about pacing myself
in getting my speech written, edited and then practised, but also
pacing my emotional state so that I would be mentally baked
just right on stage. *Bing*, I'm ready.

The door of our final Opera House dressing room clicks closed
and I start sailing on the calm ocean at the eye of the storm. I'm
relieved we have a sanctuary from the nerves and noise of the
green room. It is just Paul and me now in a room that has seen

many a freaked-out pre-performance creature over the years. I do one final run through, standing in the middle of the room as Paul tries to relax on a couch. He knows me well enough to be sensitive about when to speak up and when to just let me be. This is a new level of intense experience, though, because when I was competing he wasn't quite so front and centre to watch me manage my nerves. Paul is under his own pressure today and I want to make sure he negotiates it well. I have spent years encouraging him to stand tall and proud, to trust himself when it mattered most. Now I am trusting him to stand firm when I need him and not wilt under pressure. It will take two people to break this board—one to hold it and one to hit it. I can't do it alone and I need him to be on his game. I have been there for him as a Sensei for more than a decade and now is his chance to be there for me, with me, on that stage. I am glad we are going to be doing this together.

Eventually the dressing room door opens and they tell us it is time to go. The final speech time is soon and we have to move down to the backstage area. My adrenaline rushes again as the familiar 'down the chute' feeling before a fight hits me—no pulling out, no exit strategy, no direction but forward. I smile at Paul and say, 'Here we go,' and walk towards the door. I don't check to make sure he's following closely or to see if he's got the board with him. I know I can trust him.

My blood quickens as I put my headphones in and start the music on my specially made TEDx playlist. I have sat through the nerves and waited until this exact point to start to pump up. Beginning the irreversible walk down the hallway, I forcefully clap my hands together and feel electricity explode through my skin. I know this feeling so well and I welcome the strength it brings. In my mind, I turn the volume down on the feelings that are allowed to travel no further than the dressing room—they will not help me now. Then I turn the volume up on the specific thought message that I have chosen to be in my mind. *This is my time. I can do this. I will do my best. I have practised and earned the right to be here. I want to be here right now. I am lucky to be alive. No matter what happens, there is honour in having the courage to try.*

As we reach the backstage area the crew is working feverishly in a crowded dark area. I take a quick sneak peek around the stage curtain and my stomach turns. There are thousands of people here. My microphone quickly gets taped to my skin and I can smell my own nervous sweat. Paul kindly acts like a bodyguard, keeping people from breaking my focus and making sure I have the space I need. He runs interference between the crew and I, organising camera angles with them and monitoring the schedule. Ever the faithful student, he signals how many minutes we have to go before it's time. I move further down a tiny corridor away from everyone and go into my own inner world. My music creates waves of good feelings within me as I start to half-dance-half-shadowbox backstage. Moving this way reminds me who I am and where I've been. I let go of the vulnerable cancer patient and bring forward the fighter within me. They will both be on stage today, but when I walk out there I need to access my most confident self. She is brave enough to get my feet to move from the safety behind this wall, where only a few people can see me, out towards that intimidating crowd.

Paul tells me they've said I'm about to go on and I move to the side of the stage. I peer around the giant velvet curtain and see properly for the first time the size of the room, the faces of the audience, the imposingly wide stage and the blindingly bright lights. They are all breathtaking. I see the round red TEDx carpet in the centre of the stage that each of the speakers must stand on. It hits me that this is genuinely happening and for a split second I want to panic. The tension of waiting always becomes so painful that it makes the actual doing seem like a relief. As I stare around the curtain towards the stage, I remind myself I can change my thinking. I decide that the red carpet out there isn't scary but instead looks like fun. I rapidly change gears and refuse to let this incredible experience pass me by just because I was too nervous to let my feet touch the ground. I know what it is like to have a whole event be over before I even knew what happened. Just like in the ring when I would wipe my feet on the mat before I competed, I decide that I would ground myself on that rug. This is too good to miss by feeling overwhelmed. Instead, I will have a great time. It seems like the simplest of decisions. I just hope it sticks. I don't want to mess this up with the stiffness of deer in the headlights anxiety. I'd much prefer to have the looseness of fun. There are far worse things in the world than this. Life is so short, and this means so much to me that I am determined to make it enjoyable. I fill my heart with joy, grin at Paul and walk out on the stage with a genuine smile. My highest hopes were less than what greets me when I place my feet on that centre stage carpet.

◆

As I step onto the red TEDx rug, I look up at the thousands of faces in front of me and feel . . . unexpectedly relaxed and happy. In all the times I have visualised this scenario, it has never occurred to me that I might feel like it is normal for me to be standing up here. Or that I will enjoy myself. I've imagined the nerves, the pressure to not forget my speech, the overwhelming emotions of facing my fears and the intimidation of such a large crowd. All I feel is welcomed by the positive energy in the room. I know these people want me to succeed. I start to sense an anticipation about what on earth I'm going to talk about. I think I've thrown them a little by being so casually dressed. The TEDx team suggested I wear my regular authentic clothes and it's made me feel extra comfortable.

The next thing I know I am waving at the audience and warmly saying, 'Hi everybody,' as if we are old friends who get together like this all the time. I point to the giant picture of myself as a little ten-year-old kid on the screen behind me and smilingly say, 'That's me.' The gesture symbolises I am ready to drop the armour and 'turn myself inside out,' as Sensei Benny would say. I want to speak from the heart about this idea that means so much to me and share with these thousands of people whatever outcome the wooden-board-breaking gods have in store for me.

As I make my way through my speech, I surprisingly find myself laughing with the audience. They are sitting so close to me I could reach down and high-five them. The crew had told me in advance that the seats came so near to the stage that you could hear the audience breathing. It is true and I can see every expression on their faces. We are in this together and I like it that way. I joke with them and feel like they are on my side. I am discovering something brand new about myself right before their eyes, something I could never have known without them. I had no idea public speaking would be fun. As I pass the halfway mark and the audience keep responding positively, I try to avoid getting overexcited. My mind is silently emitting little bursts of inner gleeful squealing: *Oh wow, I'm not sinking here. I'm remembering the words and enjoying this. It seems to be going well. Oh boy, oh boy, oh boy, weeeeeeeeeeeeeeeeeee.* I am having a good time, but I know the hardest part is yet to come.

The time is drawing very near. The board break. My moment of truth. It's looming on the horizon at the end of my speech like a storm brewing that I have no choice but to sail straight through. I feel emboldened by unexpectedly discovering I'm not painfully dreadful at speaking and it spurs me on towards finding out this final truth. If cancer has changed me forever, then damn it, I want to know. If I honestly can't do something like break a board anymore, then I am ready to find out. I have navigated so many challenging feelings by this stage, but I don't want to give in and let them shake me. I want to make a new life for myself, one where I don't let what has happened to me dictate what I feel I am capable of in the future. If I can't break the board, then I will accept it—but I can't accept living in the fear of not knowing who I am anymore. I want to believe I am brave, even though I feel afraid. Facing this fear is the only way to find out the truth.

As all six-foot-plus of Paul Nind walks out on the stage towards me with the thick wooden board in his hands, I'm now not quite sure how to feel. My mind is a swirling combination of all I have been through, mixed with what we are about to do. Paul sets himself up in the holding position and as I move the board I am looking directly at his face. It is filled with meaning and intensity. I can feel how much he believes in me and wants me to be able to do this. I know that even if I can't break it, he of all people will still respect me for having tried.

I hope the audience feels the same way. I look out across the sea of people and ask them to share this experience with me. I know I will need all the help I can get, so I ask them to aim some of their courage at me by raising their hands. Now, up until this point I haven't thought much further than that. As arms start to rise, it occurs to me that I'd vaguely assumed there would be a few hands raised followed by some awkward peer pressure type joining in. What I'm not expecting is for every hand in the Opera House to shoot straight up, all at exactly the same time. I am so overwhelmed by their support that my reaction looks like someone has thrown a glass of water in my face. I half-laugh but then turn away as tears fill up my eyes. I never imagined such a dynamic response and it makes me emotional. This risk is happening and it is very, very real for me. No guarantees of success, just like in regular life.

I try to regain my composure as I touch the heel of my hand to the centre of the board. As I pull my hand back, I wind my body up and then return my palm slowly to the target. I begin to visualise breaking straight through it. I own the outcome before it happens. Sensei Benny once said to me, 'If you're not claiming victory, you're claiming defeat,' so I make it a conscious choice to imagine the wood breaking. I picture holding it in two separate pieces ten seconds from now. I start to breathe more deeply. I focus the adrenaline in my body so that it works for me, instead of against what I need to do. I tune out the crowd, even though they are almost silent with anticipation. I separate from the insane vibration of their collective anxiety as thousands of bodies tense simultaneously in suspense. I zoom in so that even Paul is no longer there. It is only me and my self-belief versus a hard piece of pine board. If my thoughts make me hesitate or doubt myself at the most crucial point, then the wood will not break. In the event of that happening, I have given myself the option of having two more tries. If it doesn't smash, I will stay calm, re-set myself and try again. I fear the level of self-doubt and emotion that will rise up in me if my first attempt doesn't work. Before cancer, it wouldn't have bothered me to have a second go. Now only I know my true level of fear around what this break means to me. It's about believing that maybe I can still be the person I used to be, not necessarily in my physical capacity, but just within myself. Cancer broke my heart in many ways and attempting to break this board is about healing some of those wounds. Deciding who I am going to be in the future is up to me and I won't let it be dictated by what has happened to me. I know all I can control is my thinking.

I try to swallow the lump in my throat as my heart pounds in my chest.

Have the courage to face your fears.

21

Last One, Best One

I take my final preparatory wind-up at the board, focusing on the exact centre. Everything is quietening inside me now. Clarity rises with each breath. My internal energy has built to a crescendo, but I must time its release perfectly. If I try to break the board before I'm settled and ready, I won't get the desired result. I will go when my gut tells me to go.

Now. I have to do it now. I explosively launch my palm towards the thick pine board, as an unexpected shout leaves my lips. With a crisp loud crack, it smashes cleanly in half. The crowd erupts into a loud roar. I hit the board so hard I knock half of it right out of Paul's hands and we both look down at the broken piece for a second. Then a broad proud smile sweeps across his face towards me. We turn and face the audience, who have jumped to their feet cheering wildly, giving us a standing ovation. Many are wiping away tears and as Paul puts his arm around me I feel my own tears start streaming down my face.

I am astonishingly relieved. I am still me. My illness has not broken me and I feel in a sense reborn into a second life. I can barely contain my happiness that the conscious choice to face my fears has paid off. I gush with a good-natured desire for everyone to know that they can overcome their fear, too. Every person in the room shared this experience and I can feel how much they had invested in it with me. I look up into the crowd for my loved ones and raise my hand in victory. All the old familiar feelings from winning in the ring flood back unexpectedly. I cry even harder because I thought that after the cancer I would never get to feel this way again. Now I just get to experience it in a different way. The revelation rolls over me in waves of joyful relief and remembered jubilance.

As I rise up after being knocked down, my hopes come alive that I can rebuild myself into a person worth being. Maybe we all can, if we choose to. That decision might seem impossible when you're lying on the canvas. If you just make a ten-second run at standing back up, then you still have a chance that you might get back on your feet. Things sure look different up there from how they do when you're flat on your back. I know during the previous year I had felt like giving up and sliding down onto the floor in a broken heap. But that's when it's most important to listen out for that little voice inside you, no matter how quiet, that tells you to get up. Each time I hear it, I know I have to chase after it hard before it gets away. I have to find whatever fight there is left in me and use it. The part of me that doesn't want to quit. When you feel like you have lost almost everything, then maybe it's worth taking a chance. Just taking the risk to try even if you fail. If you don't attempt to get up, nothing can change. Having been down made me want to try on a grand scale to take a home-run swing instead of a safe bunt.

As I stood being my most vulnerable, tear-soaked self before thousands of faces, I knew that I had just taken one of the biggest risks of my life. This was not because failing to break the board would have damaged my reputation as a martial artist or led to an awkward, failed speech. It was a risk where I had put my heart on the line for all to see and share my fear. My hopes and dreams for my future self were also out on public display. The rawness of it snapped me awake in a way I had not been in the past few years. The more the tears came, the more I felt my inner circuitry being instantly rewired. My mind was clearing and I felt connected again. I felt like I had returned from the near dead. I felt like I had won.

◆

I practically floated as we walked off stage. Paul and I beamed at each other and had a tight hug. I was so proud of him and happy we had shared that intense event. We were led through the back-stage area and as we walked through a room filled with crew and volunteers, they all unexpectedly started cheering. I felt so touched by how warmly we were received. People began patting me on the back and hugging me with tears in their eyes.

Minutes later, as I did some media interviews, I looked down and saw a thick splinter sticking out of my wrist. The adrenaline was starting to wear off now and I discovered I had a two-inch thin cut on the inside of my right elbow that was lightly bleeding. Just then I understood how afraid I had honestly been and how hard I had hit that board. In the past I would break a board with a small wrist movement of about four inches, with complete relaxed confidence it would break. Seeing that cut on my arm, I knew my palm strike had travelled about twenty inches and almost hit Paul. I was surprised by it and decided the mark on my arm would serve as a reminder of my uncertainty at the outcome. Now I had done it, it was tempting to feel like I knew I could do it all along, but the truth would always be that I was filled with fear and doubt. I never wanted to forget that.

The board represented so many loaded emotions and a deeper meaning for me about how I wanted to live the rest of my life. I didn't want what I had been through or my fears to hold me back anymore. I wanted to take bigger chances, be less concerned about failing and spend the rest of my days in a new braver way. Getting up on that stage was a practical way to live that out. I had hoped the audience would relate to that feeling and connect with it strongly, but I was blown away that it had struck such a deep chord with them. I wasn't expecting to see it on their faces as it was happening nor was I ready for their reactions afterwards.

As we were taken out into the public Opera House foyer area, it took an hour to get across the room as so many people stopped me to talk. Person after person told me they had held their hands up for me when I tried to break the board. The sea of hands hadn't just been in the main auditorium either. Someone showed me a photo of one of the other separate theatres in the Opera House, where people had been watching my speech live on giant screens. Every single person in that room had their hands up, too. I couldn't believe everyone was responding so enthusiastically. It made me feel like so many of us share the same fight within ourselves.

The next day, as my phone filled up with positive messages, I received a call from a woman named Nanette Moulton. She explained in her voicemail message that she was from a company called Saxton. Something in her sweet but authoritative tone made me feel like I should have known the company name already. Nanette had acquired my number from the director of TEDx Sydney, Remo Giuffré. As I called her back, I had no idea what she wanted to talk to me about. She was lovely on the phone and told me how much she had enjoyed my speech. When I told her it had been my first time public speaking, she said that made it even better. Nanette asked me if I would like to give a speech again. I expressed my surprise at how much fun I'd had the first time and said I'd be excited to give it another go. After explaining she was the head of Saxton Speaker's Bureau (which I later found out is the leading speaking agency in Australia), Nanette asked if I would like to speak professionally. It had not occurred to me that this was even an option, but I quickly said I would love to. I didn't fully understand what I was agreeing to, but I knew it sounded like a challenge that I was willing to try.

At the end of the call Nanette gently said, 'What you did at TEDx will change your life. Brace yourself and hold on for the ride.' I was surprised by this and didn't know whether to believe her. I had no idea what I might need to brace myself for exactly. Her words were delivered with such genuine care that it sounded like she was letting me in on a warm secret. I was cautious but I let myself dream she might be right. When Nanette said, 'You've already been through enough. You've helped a lot of people. Now it's time for someone to help you,'

I felt myself exhale a little. I wasn't used to that but I welcomed help to build a new life for myself, one that contained unexpected possibilities and opportunities. Nanette seemed to know something was coming for me that I knew nothing about, but I was intrigued to find out what it was.

◆

One year on from TEDx and my life has changed dramatically, just like Nanette promised. I have become a professional keynote speaker and absolutely love what I do. I regularly travel, speaking about courage, leadership and resilience. I had no way of knowing the standing ovation I received at the Opera House would be the first of many. It still amazes me every time. Whenever I give a speech, I am filled with gratitude and wonder. This is true whether it's for big companies like Facebook and Telstra, a community group like the girls' boxing club at the local PCYC or a charity like the Cancer Council.

Imagine what wondrous unexpected adventures lie ahead in your future.

As I get ready before each speaking engagement, I listen to the same music playlist I used before TEDx and connect to those same feelings. I hear the first few lines of Kanye West's 'Amazing' and I smile to myself at how incredibly unexpected these life changes have been. I am so lucky to be able to do what I do now, especially on such a large scale. I still teach martial arts, but now I also get to talk about what it has given me to hundreds or thousands of people at once. Sharing a positive message of hope and courage feels like a good mark to leave on the world. I was so lucky to find a good teacher and I see how many people out there are hungry for that type of knowledge. It makes me happily humbled to share my experiences with them. They don't have to be a martial artist to relate to it, but I hope they can use some of the lessons I learnt along the way. If I only had a year to live (but hopefully/thankfully I will have much longer), I would choose to spend it this way, in a worthwhile pursuit where I get to make people smile.

Before I step on stage to speak, I still sentimentally like to listen to 'Can't Hold Us'. Recently my old buddy Mark and I were lucky enough to watch Macklemore perform that song live. As the crowd jumped up and down, I shook my head in wonder. I could never have imagined the fortuitous direction things were going to take, and that makes it even sweeter.

As I open each speech, I tell the audience my goal is to have each one of them leave a little more courageous than when they walked in. What they don't necessarily know is that in speaking to them I am reminding myself of that lesson. Walking onstage prompts me to be brave, keep taking a chance on putting myself out there and to live life with more intensity. Then I give the audience a chance to do exactly that. My favourite part of the speech comes at the end, where instead of me breaking a wooden board, I challenge someone in the audience to use their *ten seconds of courage* and volunteer to break it themselves.

After I show a brief video of me smashing the board at TEDx, I silently walk over behind the lectern and bring out a slightly thinner wooden board. Then without saying a word I step off the stage and walk down into the audience. Immediately a huge wave of nervousness erupts as they realise what is happening. Someone is going to live out the concept I've explained. The longest lasting impression is made by experiencing the feeling we have been talking about, rather than just thinking it. The collective jitters travel like a ripple as I move around the room. People often laugh awkwardly the closer I get to them. I am always fascinated to see who looks away or meets my gaze, whose shoulders tighten and who seems like they are about to run for the nearest exit or dive under their chair. It's a melting pot of the different ways we all deal with fear.

Once we are laughing as a group about being so on edge, I ask them, 'Can you sense that feeling right now?' When they say yes, and I respond by saying, 'That is the *ten seconds of courage* feeling. It's wanting to put your hand up and try something, but being scared to do it. It's the momentary hesitation you feel when you're unsure about the possible outcome. It's the queasiness in your stomach when you feel a challenge looming ahead of you. We've all had that nervous sensation before and it marks the crossroads of your decisions. To try or not to try. To go outside your comfort zone or miss out on a once-in-a-lifetime opportunity. To perhaps test yourself and find out what you're actually capable of. To allow yourself to reach your full potential.

When I ask for board breaking volunteers to put their hands up in the air, it is different every time. Sometimes no hands go up initially, and other times many arms shoot up. This occasionally causes someone to literally jump up out of their seat to stand out from the crowd. When I have chosen the brave person who will break the board, everyone gives a collective sigh of relief as I move back up onto the stage. Having shared this nerve-wracking selection experience, the audience are bonded together and extra supportive of the person who attempts the board.

I teach my volunteer how to do the break and focus their mind to a point where they believe wholeheartedly that they will succeed. There are no guarantees it will work, but I always have a back-up plan in place where we can break the board together if need be. It's not usually necessary, as I prime them into a high-performance mental state where they decide within themselves they can do it. My heart always pounds when I ask the audience to raise their hands up and aim their courage at the person putting their self-belief on the line. It draws everyone together as one united team behind the person facing the challenge, to the extent they tell me it feels like they are actually doing it themselves.

It's a beautiful moment to see a person experiencing their inner strength right in front of your eyes. I greatly respect their courage for nominating themselves. If I have learnt anything, it is that some of the best moments in life come from putting your hand up. It's just getting out of your own way in order to be able to live your fullest life. Every time I ask for volunteers, I see people who want to raise their hand but hesitate out of fear. If only they knew in advance that 99 per cent of the time, the board breaks. No, not because it's easy to break or in any way rigged to guarantee success. It breaks because I help that person to *know* they're capable of breaking it before they try. If you trust you can do something before you start, then your chances of success increase exponentially. Far more than physical strength, it requires self-belief. It may be shakily uncertain when their hand goes up, but their belief sure is solid by the time they sit back down. There's nothing wrong with allowing someone else to teach you how to access that part of yourself.

I love seeing the person's face when the board breaks. It's usually a mixture of surprise, relief and joy. The crowd always hold their breath before the attempt and erupt ecstatically afterwards. The brave volunteer is received as a hero when they carry their freshly broken board back into the audience. They didn't know when they woke up that day what opportunity life was going to throw at them. None of us ever do. Their achievement is real and they can carry that pride with them forever. Yet the price of admission they paid will always be that ten-second burst of courage to get their hand to go up in the first place. It costs them something, but worthwhile experiences invariably come at a price.

◆

The price I had paid during my TEDx board break was one of facing fear, but I was also settling a debt of gratitude. In speaking about the lessons Sensei Benny had taught me, I was respectfully bowing to him in my own special way. It was a heartfelt message of thanks after a difficult journey and hard-won battle. My fight continues daily as I duke it out with the ongoing aftereffects of treatment. Post-cancer fatigue regularly makes me feel like I've gone fifty rounds, but I will dutifully pay that price for being alive. I'm making peace with fears around my future health and the smaller things like the subtle ways my appearance has changed. Gradually I'm looking more like me again. I have an odd affection for the pirate scar that rests near my neck to remind me of where I've been and how lucky I am. I think of it almost like having had a knife held to my throat, but I made a lucky escape. That scar acts as a reminder of how close I could have come to dying.

I now live my days like someone who is just grateful to be here. I start every day by saying 'thank you' out loud and put lots of energy into talking about the good things in life. I write down the best moment from each day before I go to sleep at night. I put the effort into keeping my mindset focused on gratitude. I love creating situations to show my appreciation for how others have helped me along the way. My heart fills to the brim when these things come full circle. One of my favourites was being able to offer the chance to break a board to Nanette Moulton from Saxton's Speakers Bureau. It was a thanksgiving for the life-changing opportunity she had given me, when I needed it more than she could have known. She helped me create a new life and I wanted to provide a chance for her to thrillingly face her fears in front of an audience. Though a seasoned veteran, Nanette is a diminutive powerhouse who smashed through her board with excited glee. Many eyes filled with proud, respectful tears that day, my own included.

One of the proudest gratitude moments for me was putting my student and friend Paul Nind forward for his black belt test with Sensei Benny. As he held the board for me at TEDx, he wore a brown belt but we both knew his next grading was looming. That was also part of why I had him face the tension with me on stage that day. I wanted him to practise controlling his nerves under intense pressure. I was impressed by the way he handled himself at TEDx, but not as much as the way he conducted himself during his black belt grading. It was the pinnacle of the fourteen years I had been teaching him Ukidokan Karate. Sensei

Benny put him through a gruelling test that gave me flashbacks to my own grading almost two decades earlier. Paul went on an intense rollercoaster ride that would have made most people quit, but he always came back asking for more. That was the truest test of his will and his love for what we do. When Sensei Benny and I conducted the ceremony to award his rank, Paul became the thirty-third Ukidokan black belt in the world. It was the best gift I could have ever given him, but Paul has given so much more in return.

When you put gratitude out, I firmly believe it comes back to you in kind. Whenever I give a speech, I continue to give thanks to Sensei Benny in appreciation of how lucky I have been to have a true teacher in my life. Our connection has only grown stronger since he saw my TEDx talk. People always ask me what he thought of it. Sensei and I didn't actually speak about it for some time afterwards because knowing if he was happy with my effort finally didn't matter so much. Having said that, when we did eventually discuss how he felt about my speech I was touched by his words.

Sensei Benny said to me, 'The message was—trust in yourself to do it regardless of the outcome. I found myself smiling because I thought how true, how courageous. The smile and applause in my heart for you made me think wow, she really pulled through for herself. The realness of it is what makes it so powerful. You're not hiding the truth of it. People run from that and that night you chose to run at it instead. The point was if you tried and weren't successful, then just be glad you tried. The power is in the doing. Then you can at least be at peace with it and say, "I did it." I was very proud of the results. It was inspiring.'

Sensei waited until he visited Australia to speak these words to me in person. On the same trip to Sydney, he gave me the beautiful gift of a necklace in the shape of the Ukidokan symbol. This crest is a very meaningful and special emblem to me that somewhat resembles a coat of arms. This particular version of the design includes a unique blue stone which he placed there specifically for my healing. It was such a touching gesture and I wear the necklace daily as a reminder that I'm always progressing in my recovery.

A huge part in moving me to a better place in my mental restoration was that chance I'd taken on the Opera House stage. It was a clear indicator that the best way forward was to live at a more intense level and relentlessly pursue happiness despite the inherent risks. I am now keenly aware of the randomness of our lives and our inability to dictate their direction at times. I giggle at how much I used to think I could control things and all the rigorous effort I put into it. We can make all the plans we want, but that doesn't mean we will have the chance to fulfil them. That both terrifies and exhilarates me. There are so many unknowable things and I'm okay with that. Not many of us know what percentage of our lives are already over. We can add up how many days we've lived, but not how many we have left. This isn't necessarily a bad thing. It motivates me to live the rest of my life like there is no time to waste. The future is not up to me, so now I don't act like it is. I have direction, but I'm thrilled by the idea that we cannot know what lies ahead. Any unpleasant surprises can patiently wait their turn. I'm excitedly looking forward to unwrapping whatever gifts life has in my future as if I were a kid getting a new BMX bike on their birthday.

One unexpected life present joyfully came in the form of a beautiful partner. When my sea was raging amidst the darkest storm, Nicola signed on to help me navigate this new spontaneous adventure into uncharted waters. She sailed fearlessly through the turbulent ocean trenches of where I had been and set a fresh course towards the sun rising on the horizon. When I was below decks queasy with sea sickness, she kept the rudder steady until I could return to the helm. Without her, my ship may have been lost or shattered against the rocks onshore.

What makes me happiest today is that we sail in the same direction and take turns at being the Captain. Nic and I share a common outlook on the importance of having simple fun and the desire to live a full life together. My favourite pastime is to make her laugh. We play together like big kids by going skateboarding in summer or throwing a ball around for hours while we chat. She makes me feel like I won the grand prize in a lottery I didn't know I had entered.

I am lucky these days, but I know it's my responsibility to work hard making my own luck. You can't wait around to find a four-leaf clover or for a golden horseshoe to drop out of the sky onto your head. Sometimes you just have to fight your way into a better situation. When I was having a hard time prior to TEDx, I made my dear friend Kate a tearful promise that I would do everything I could in the next year to really live. I wasn't sure how I would make it through the coming twelve months. I decided to use that previous 'one year to live' strategy and wrote a bucket list of things I would do if my days were numbered. I figured if the chips were already down, now was surely the time to go all in to create a different outcome. What resulted was a series of adventures that put the wind back in my sails and reminded me that there's more fun to be had when you're not watching from a safe harbour.

I started ticking things off my list by accepting my student Paul's offer to kayak out and stand on Wedding Cake Island off Coogee Beach. I had been looking at that island for nearly twenty years and had always wanted to go out there. There was no other reason to do it than pure enjoyment and that's exactly what I felt as Paul's whole family and I paddled.

My chief accomplice in achieving many of these checklist activities became Nicola, and it was the foundation we built our relationship on. We both felt to some extent like we had spent too much time on the sidelines of our lives watching other people play. No more. The next thing I knew we were jumping off a cliff together into the ocean at Wattamolla. It was the kind of thing I would have previously cheered others on for trying, but now I had a serious case of the 'let's do it's. I was up for seeking out anything that looked like a good time—laughing under a waterfall, seeing Madonna up close in concert, playing roulette and firing machine guns in Las Vegas, or getting on a plane just to watch the UFC live in Los Angeles. I wanted to feel alive again and knew that it was up to me to create that reality.

How will you live the days you have left?
Make your own luck.

If you want your life to change for the better, then *you* have to change it. It's so tempting to focus on the difficult circumstances you've faced and make excuses. I know there are days when I get stuck in that thinking. I will also be damned if I allow myself to stay there for long. I have so much less care now about playing it safe. I want it all. I want to eat all the cakes and pat all the dogs. I want to live to the fullest with whatever time remains.

That means taking bigger swings at life and pushing myself out of placid comfort. After what I've been through I can never be who I was before, but now I don't want to be. I've changed forever and much of it's for the better. In many ways, I now take a more relaxed approach to things because I see them as somewhat impermanent. I don't hold on so tightly anymore. Instead of keeping my much-loved books in pristine condition, I now write in the margins and highlight them. I have a little dance when I hear a good song, no matter where I am or who is watching. I don't care if I look silly, so long as I'm smiling. Spending my money on laughing at comedy clubs has become a wise investment, just like having memorable experiences and making good people happy. Instead of being forever frugal, I splash out to treat myself and others with more kindness and have extra fun. The new me is hungry for life.

I now jump from the height.

I am quicker to speak what I love.

I say yes when I'm afraid.

That is why you're holding this book in your hands. Life can be over too quickly to let opportunity pass you by or miss out on doing the things that you've always wanted to do. I almost didn't even get the chance to write this book. I was so excited when Remo Giuffré, the licensee of TEDx Sydney sent an email to his publisher suggesting my story might make a good read. I had always wanted to write and was so excited that he had recommended me. It was a long-held dream that I had never taken the steps to make an actual reality. Remo had copied me on the email and included the YouTube video of my *ten seconds of courage* TEDx speech. I was crushed when I read the publisher's response, which complimented my talk but said they weren't sure there was a book in it. My heart immediately sank. I had a brief interlude of sadness and wishing that life would stop laying tyre spikes across my highway. I'd dared to dream about writing a book and now I sat there like I'd had the wind knocked out of me by a body shot. I didn't want to self-indulgently wallow in feeling like it was unfair. Then the strongest sensation came over me as I saw this chance slipping away through my fingers. *I will not let it go without a fight.*

I brazenly replied to the publisher, saying I felt it could be turned into a book and I would love the chance to tell them about it. I wrote with all the certainty and recklessness I had, in the hope of refusing to accept defeat. I could live with the outcome if I knew I'd tried to be a strong finisher and given it a final shot. I went after it in a blaze of brassiness that surprised even me. I later walked into their offices and turned myself inside out. If I was going to go for it, then I would lay my story bare. The next thing I knew I had a book deal. As I left the publisher's building, I marvelled at the unforeseeable wonders that were borne of my hardest challenges. If only I had known what joys lay ahead for me when I was in the hospital neck deep in my distress.

I need to say to you, my friend, please never give up on yourself. Life will knock each and every one of us down, but only *you* can decide if you will get back up. When you do rise, you must dictate who you will be upon finding your feet once again. It will likely require a conscious decision, teamed with a burst of courage. It's crucial to tap into even the smallest part we all have inside that is still willing to go to battle. When you do, I hope you fight harder than even you believe possible. It will take a brave display of guts, much sweat and maybe even a little blood. Yet if you fall again, there is honour and strength to be found in every attempt to stand. You must try and if it is your last, make it your best.

We are all fighting for something in our lives. Whatever your fight is, I hope you win.

Osu.

10-Second Thoughts

Round 1

Be your true self, even if other people don't get it.

♦

Girls really can do anything!

♦

If you don't choose to get up, staying down might become permanent.

Round 2

It's never too late to start fresh. Surround yourself with who you want to become.

◆

Leverage is better than force.

◆

What hurts now might lead to the best rewards later.

◆

The hours of hard work you do alone will pay off in the future (even if only because you're proud of them).

◆

How good are your 'worst day abilities'? Make it so you shine on the tough days, too.

◆

Fear doesn't make you weak. Courage is built on being scared.

◆

You can learn to control your emotions under pressure. If you give up, you rob yourself of any chance to succeed. *Just come back tomorrow.*

Round 3

How would you treat three-year-old you?

◆

Treat yourself with the respect you deserve.

◆

Don't waste precious time beating yourself up.

◆

Your truth is the truth whether you admit it
out loud or not (so you may as well face up
to it sooner rather than later).

◆

Change your thinking.

◆

Often the only thing you can control in a hard
situation is your reaction to it.

◆

Decide that you like being you and love yourself more than anyone else could ever love you.

◆

Laugh at your mistakes and find the joy even in the most painful times.

◆

Be Teflon—you can choose to let it all slide right off you.

◆

The general controls the troops. Use your mind as a powerful commander to get the best from yourself.

◆

It doesn't hurt less if you close your eyes. Pretending it's not happening doesn't change the fact that it is.

◆

Most of our fears are imagined and will probably never happen.

Round 4

Only you can win the battle within your mind.

◆

Practise being a strong finisher. When everyone else is fading, make it your habit to power through.

◆

Make your last one your best one.

◆

Why not you? Be brave enough to dream, then dream even bigger. Amazing things have to happen to someone, so why not believe it will be you?

◆

Back yourself with more belief than anyone else could muster.

◆

You control the volume and visuals playing in your mind, so make them as helpful to you as possible. Picture the best outcome and tell yourself why it will happen.

◆

The fears you're most afraid to face are usually the most important for you to confront. The more you hide them, the more they control you.

◆

Go out there and show them who you are.

Round 5

You may as well assume things will work out and save your challenging feelings for the appropriate time.

◆

Always work to keep your circumstances in perspective. Your problems rarely seem so bad when you put them in a broader context.

◆

What would you do if you only had one year to live?

◆

You have a *choice* about who you will be from
this moment on.

♦

Good preparation is kryptonite for
your nerves.

♦

Have the courage to face your fears.

♦

Imagine what wondrous unexpected
adventures lie ahead in your future.

♦

How will you live the days you have left?
Make your own luck.

Acknowledgements

Thank you to courage itself—for the necessary knock down when I had lost it, but also for helping me back up when I found some of it again. Writing this book as I re-built my life after cancer was a crazy mission of looking gently at the past to find the best way forward into the future. I am grateful for all the lessons I rediscovered as I wrote. They were a timely reminder that, I hope, will spark a burst of courage in others too.

A huge thank you to Jane Palfreyman at Allen & Unwin for believing in me. You showed me a whole new way to face my fears. My gratitude to Tom Gilliatt for taking the meeting that started it all. A huge thanks to Genevieve Buzo for your endless calm patience. Much respect and appreciation to Susin Chow and Julia Cain for their invaluable fine-toothed-comb editing skills.

The most heartfelt thanks to Sensei Benny for a lifetime of learning. My world is painted in the colours you helped me to see clearly. You of all people know how far we've come and the depth of my gratitude. Thank you for all the hard lessons and years of tireless diamond cutting. Above all, you taught me that unconditional love is not dependant on winning, but instead remains unchanged no matter how many times I fell. You turned my light back up and told me to do something worthwhile with what I had been given. This book is my humble attempt to express how much it all means to me. *Osu* Sensei.

To my entire Ukidokan family past and present. Thank you for all you taught me and let me share with you. The learning never stops for any of us. A special thanks to Sensei Paul for standing tall. Thank you to all my teachers, students and training partners over the decades. It's been an absolute honour.

To Doctor Brighton, Doctor Thompson, the medical staff at Prince of Wales Hospital and everyone who kept me alive to write this book. A heartfelt thanks to Caroline who fought the battle with me.

The indomitable Jess Miller—you changed the course of my life forever. Your belief in me at such a vulnerable time meant more to me than you will ever know. I hope only to return it in kind.

Remo Giuffre, Edwina Throsby, Jackie Dent and all the TEDx Sydney crew. Thank you for the life-changing opportunity and trusting me to risk rediscovering my truth in front of thousands of people.

A special thanks to Nanette Moulton and the fantastic team at Saxton Speakers Bureau. You have given me an incredible new life that I am so grateful for. Thank you for your endless kindness.

The wonderful author and my friend Joanne Fedler who encouraged me to make my literary dream a reality.

My dear friend Terra, the journal who talks back. The modulation who made me excited about writing over the past fifteen years. Consider this book a three-hundred-page email.

A deep thank you to all my friends for being in my corner. Thanks to Kate for my favourite yum cha sessions and to Mark for being a girl's best *cholo*. A big thank you to Prue, Dan & Renae, Yas & Anna, Turia Pitt, Gill Hicks, Vinh Giang, Kris Flegg, Liz & Brene, Lei Tai, JJ Halans and Simon Taylor Photography. Every other name that should be here is written in my heart.

My family—I love you. Mum, thanks for telling me girls could do anything. Not sure you intended for me to take it quite that literally. It's meant a lot every time you've told me you were proud.

Finally, to the lovely Nic—thank you for being your wonderful self and for the countless hours of discussion until all hours of the night. You have been a wise sounding board and my most trusted confidante. With many thanks for all the HMI help and the innumerable coffees. From the first official day of writing in Hobart on my 40th birthday, to the Valley then the Bay, I love you for making 'the year of the book' a truly special adventure that we took together.